$\mathcal{T}$IDAL PASSAGES

Flo (Manson) McKay in about 1945 on the hay mower at what's now Linnaea Farm, Gunflint Lake.

JEANETTE TAYLOR

TIDAL PASSAGES

A History of the Discovery Islands

Harbour Publishing

This book is dedicated to my mate Gerry Côté,
for listening with interest to the full-blown accounts
of each new tale and character I discover,
and for the fun of our rambles among the islands.

Harbour Publishing Co. Ltd.
P.O. Box 219, Madeira Park, BC, V0N 2H0
www.harbourpublishing.com

Edited by Susan Mayse.
Indexed by Hugh Morrison.
Map by John Lightfoot.
Cover design by Anna Comfort.
Text layout and design by Teresa Lynne.
Printed and bound in Canada.
Printed on chlorine-free, FSC certified paper made with 30% post-consumer fibre.
Hardcover ISBN: 978-1-55017-435-9. Paperback ISBN: 978-1-55017-460-1.

Harbour Publishing acknowledges financial support from the Government of Canada through the Book Publishing Industry Development Program and the Canada Council for the Arts, and from the Province of British Columbia through the BC Arts Council and the Book Publishing Tax Credit.

Canada Council
for the Arts

Conseil des Arts
du Canada

BRITISH COLUMBIA
ARTS COUNCIL
Supported by the Province of British Columbia

Library and Archives Canada Cataloguing in Publication (hardcover edition)
Taylor, Jeanette, 1953–
          Tidal passages : a history of the Discovery Islands / Jeanette Taylor.
Includes bibliographical references and index.
ISBN 978-1-55017-435-9

          1. Discovery Islands (B.C.)—History. I. Title.
FC3845.D57T39 2008   971.1'2   C2008-905067-3

Contents

THE DISCOVERY ISLANDS

Kakum Reserve
Jackson Bay
Read Bay/ Tekya
Robber's Nob
Tohnee Harbour
Port Neville
Jackson Bay Post Office
Blenkinsop Bay

Hardwicke Island
Chancellor Chan
**West Thurl
Island**

LEGEND

East Thurlow Island

1. *Fanny Bay*
2. *Bickley Bay*
3. *Hemming Bay*

**Sonora Island/Bute Inlet/
Stuart Island**

4. *Thurston Bay*
5. *Cameleon Harbour*
6. *Vancouver Bay*
7. *Asman Point*
8. Dent Island
9. *Big Bay*
10. Old Church House/
    Mushkin Reserve
11. Kellsey Point
12. Stuart Island Post Office

Cortes Island

13. Tork Reserve
14. *Squirrel Cove*
15. *Seaford Bay*
16. Mansons Landing
17. Paukeanam Reserve
18. *Cortes Bay*
19. *Stag Bay*

**West and East
Redonda Islands**

20. *Connis Bay*
21. *Redonda Bay*
22. Cassel Falls
23. *Tenedos Bay*

Location Map

**British
Columbia**

Campbell River

Vancover

Victoria

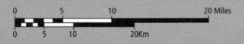

0   5   10   20 Miles

0   5   10   20Km

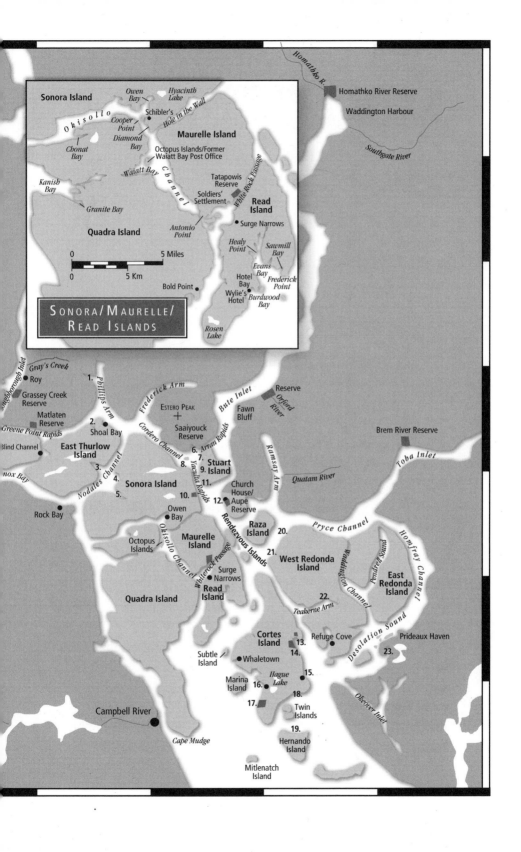

SONORA/MAURELLE/READ ISLANDS

Inset map:

Sonora Island
Owen Bay
Hyacinth Lake
Schibler's
Hole in the Wall
Okisollo Channel
Cooper Point
Diamond Bay
Maurelle Island
Chonat Bay
Octopus Islands/Former Waiatt Bay Post Office
Waiatt Bay
Tatapowis Reserve
Kanish Bay
Soldiers' Settlement
White Rock Passage
Read Island
Granite Bay
Quadra Island
Antonio Point
Surge Narrows
Healy Point
Sawmill Bay
Evans Bay
Frederick Point
Hotel Bay
Wylie's Hotel
Burdwood Bay
Bold Point
Rosen Lake

0 — 5 Miles
0 — 5 Km

Homathko R.
Homathko River Reserve
Waddington Harbour
Southgate River

Main map:

Snubborneh Inlet
Gray's Creek
Roy
Grassey Creek Reserve
Matlaten Reserve
Greene Point Rapids
Blind Channel
Knox Bay
Rock Bay

1.
Phillips Arm
Frederick Arm
ESTERO PEAK
Saaiyouck Reserve
2.
Shoal Bay
Cordero Channel
East Thurlow Island
3.
Nodales Channel
4.
Sonora Island
5.
10.
Owen Bay
Octopus Islands
Okisollo Channel
Maurelle Island
Whiterock Passage
Surge Narrows
Read Island
Quadra Island

Bute Inlet
Reserve
Orford River
Fawn Bluff
6. Arran Rapids
7.
8. Yaculta Rapids
Stuart Island
9.
11.
12.
Church House/ Aupe Reserve
Ramsay Arm
Quatam River

Brem River Reserve
Toba Inlet

Raza Island
20.
Pryce Channel
Homfray Channel
21.
West Redonda Island
Waddington Channel
Pendrell Sound
East Redonda Island
22.
Teakerne Arm
Desolation Sound
Prideaux Haven
23.
Okeover Inlet

Cortes Island
13.
Refuge Cove
14.
Subtle Island
Whaletown
Hague Lake
15.
Marina Island
16.
18.
17.
Twin Islands
19.
Hernando Island

Campbell River
Cape Mudge
Mitlenatch Island

Joe Casey (left) and Art Bellarby at Heydon Lake on the west side of Loughborough Inlet in 1919.
PHOTO COURTESY OF HENRY TWIDLE, MCR 4065.

Introduction

THE CROWDED ARCHIPELAGO OF THE DISCOVERY ISLANDS, bounded to the north by Johnstone Strait and to the south by the wide expanse of the Strait of Georgia, lies within a dynamic point of change. The soft coastal climate of Garry oak meadows that extends northward from California ends just south of the islands. Here the tides from north and south meet and race through the narrow passages that separate the islands. This is also the convergence point of two distinct aboriginal cultures, the Coast Salish and the Lekwiltok. Their languages have no common roots. The Salish have kinship with the people of southern BC, while the Lekwiltok are related to the Kwakwaka'wakw of north Vancouver Island.

The rich fishing grounds of the islands, oxygenated by the flush of fast-moving tides, are a danger to the unwary. The old people said the souls of drowned men and women haunt the rocky ledges of Seymour Narrows. And they warned of sea monsters in the Narrows and in Yuculta Rapids, the only north-south transit points through the islands.

This dramatic land and seascape, flanked on three sides by some of the highest mountains in the province, demands skill and courage of its people and in return infuses them with a rugged individuality. It has been a great privilege to collect and recount the stories of their lives.

The resulting book, and its forthcoming companion *Tidal Passages: Quadra Island*, started out as one manuscript that landed with a thump on Howard White's desk at Harbour Publishing. Its thirty years of research date back to my days on the curatorial staff of the Museum at Campbell River. It was hard for Howard to believe I'd exercised restraint, but I did.

A treasure trove of material about the islands still exists. Even with the manuscript out of my hands, the tales kept pouring in. "We've got some fantastic stories to tell you about gold in Bute Inlet," said Gisele and Danny Uzzell on one of their town trips, and friends on Read Island say I've passed over some terrific characters from the 1970s. All of these stories will have to wait for a future chronicle.

This book focusses on the early history of the First Nations and non-Native people, with a glancing look at recent decades. You'll meet many inspiring characters in these pages and a few rogues and scoundrels too. I've allowed them to speak for themselves as much as possible by drawing on the impressive collections of taped interviews, diaries, letters and newspaper accounts in the Museum at Campbell River Archives, Cortes Island Museum and the BC Archives. Teedie Kagume at the Powell River Museum was also very helpful.

Each island has its own distinct culture. Though eastern Read Island and western Cortes are geographically similar, they are otherwise entirely different. Read Island's era of Euro-Canadian settlement started with two back-to-back murders and dashed forward at a rapid clip, loaded with adventuresome eccentrics, intellectuals and religious zealots. Cortes had its share of eccentrics too, but they were of a more genteel strain that favoured dances on the Mansons wharf and the odd bit of neighbourhood rivalry. Bute Inlet has its own weather patterns, glaciers and mountain men and women. Okisollo's wicked tides and currents pose challenges, as does the isolation of the Thurlow Islands. Desolation Sound, Toba Inlet and the Redonda Islands bask in warmer waters and are a playground of yachters.

Many people have shared their memories and research with me. I extend my thanks to Jean Barman, Darren Blaney, Bill Blaney, Etta and Clarence Byers, Ronnie Buckley, Ross Campbell, Miray Campbell, Lillian Carroll, Sally (Taylor) Carter, Candy-Lea Chickite, Helen (Schibler) Clements, Sheila (McKay) Foort, Bill Foort, the late Pansy

(Schnarr) Eddington, Isabelle Edgett, Mae Ellingsen, Jim Foort, Sheila Foort, Kathy Francis, Harold and Maude Hayes, Mary Hayes, Alice (Shaw) Jackson, Bob Jamieson, Gary Keeling, Fern Kornelsen, the late Jimmy Lambert, Malcolm Lansall, Bob and Faye Logan, the late Rose (Manson) McKay, Margo McLoughlin, Pearl (Schnarr) Macklin, Frank Millerd, James Milne, Mike Moore of Misty Isles Charters, Ruth (Van der Est) Oppel, Sandra Parrish, George Quocksister, Win (Keeling) Roth, Dave Sayers, Larry Seeley, Thelma (Bendickson) Silkens, Commodore Jack Sullivan, the late Doreen Thompson, Ann Toelle, Adele Turner, Bob Turner, Gisele and Danny Uzzell, Silva Welsh, Charlene West, Dick Whittington, Tom Widdowson, and Rob and Laurie Wood. Though I didn't meet Gilean Douglas, Maud Emery and Edith (Hansen) Bendickson, I am indebted to them for their historical writings. Doris Andersen's excellent book *Evergreen Islands, The Islands of the Inside Passage: Quadra to Malcolm* set the stage for this book.

I'm also indebted to the people who have reviewed parts of the manuscript for clarity and interest: Marnie Andrews, Etta Byers, Gerry Côté, Etienne Côté, Elise Côté, Heather Kellerhals-Stewart, Mike Redican, Jocelyn Reekie, Kristen Scholfield-Sweet, Judith Williams and Annette Yourk. The Writers-in-Residence program at Haig-Brown Heritage House in Campbell River has been invaluable, providing an opportunity to hone my writing skills under the tutelage of Don McKay, David Carpenter, Myrna Kostash and Brian Brett.

Irene Ross, retired archivist with the Museum at Campbell River, combed the voluminous photo archives there, and my sister Leona Taylor uncovered countless nuggets in the *British Daily Colonist* and *Daily Colonist*. Leona was always at the ready to look up death, birth or marriage records and share my enthusiasm for history, as were Linda Hogarth, curator of the Museum at Campbell River, Sandra Parrish, archivist at the Museum at Campbell River, and Lynne Jordan of the Cortes Island Museum. Lastly I extend thanks and respect to my editor Susan Mayse and to Howard White, whose publishing house has done so much to make BC history accessible and fun.

A group of young Read Islanders. Back row (left to right): Bonnie Whittington, Paula Culbard, Cynthia Culbard, Kelly Landers, Bill Whittington, Forest Lambert. Middle row (left to right): Isabelle Hayes, unkown. Front row (left to right): unkown, Frank Tooker, Jack McMakin.

CHAPTER ONE

Read Island:
Skeletons in the Closet

O N A SUNNY FALL MORNING WE CLIMBED INTO MARNIE ANDREWS'S
battered Land Rover for a tour of Read. "It's the best car on the
island," she told us with a wry smile. Her claim was borne out
within minutes, when her Land Rover came nose to nose with a rusted-
out car decorated in sixties-style flowers. A middle-aged driver hopped
out for a visit. With her were two friends, a lanky young man and a
woman with a baby.

The visit ended and we got back into our vehicles, ready to edge
around each other on the narrow dirt track, but the psychedelic car
wouldn't start. We pushed it to a nearby hill to try a jump-start, but the car
rolled down without so much as a hint of a sputtered start. At the foot of
the hill, we assembled around the car again in puzzled meditation. The thing
looked like it had done time in a demolition derby. Most of the rear end
had long since rusted off and the hood was permanently lashed down.

The young man quietly took charge. Reaching inside what had once
been a trunk, he pulled out a plastic gas jug with an extra-long nozzle
and inserted it into the mysterious depths of what was left of the rear
end. He emptied the jug and then slid into the driver's seat, but the car
still wouldn't start. There was one more measure to try. Secured to the
gaping floorboards on the passenger's side was a spare battery with a set
of jumper cables that ran out the window and under the engine hood.
He switched the car over to the spare battery and ambled around to the
driver's seat again. This time the car responded beautifully.

As our two vehicles passed at the top of the hill, the other driver called to us to watch for a plastic bag containing a neighbour's mail, keys and some money. The bag fell through their floorboards, she told us, not far back along the trail. Sure enough, within minutes we found the bag.

The group in the derelict car had an unusual mission for the day. They were on a search for the bones of the young woman's dog, which fell prey to wolves some months prior. Our mission was no less eccentric. We were on a search for the bones of Edgar Wilmot Wylie, who was cemented into the cleft of a rock in Bird Cove in 1908. We scrambled over bluffs and through thickets for several hours, but Wylie's grave eluded us, though old-timers swear it's there, partially obscured by a fallen tree on Healy Point.

It would have suited Edgar Wylie perfectly to be as elusive in death as he was in life. He was one of the most notorious of dozens of eccentrics, rebels, bad guys and intellectuals who have made Read Island their home over the past century.

As in Edgar Wylie's day, most of the island's current residents live in a relatively narrow east-to-west band on the southern part of Read. While the island is about sixteen kilometres (ten miles) long, rocky bluffs and peaks take up the northern part.

Read is only a twenty-minute boat ride from the northern end of Quadra Island, but the lack of ferry service and the scarred blot of logged-over land in the centre of the island have limited growth. Seventy-five years ago, however, Read Island was in step with the other islands. Moorage, access to fishing and logging, a few inches of good soil and a water source dictated success for a settlement then, not roads and ferries.

The Native peoples' use of the island has declined over time as well. In 1885 there were about eight houses at the village of Tatapowis in Whiterock Passage,[1] a narrow channel that runs between Maurelle and Read islands. One family still lived there in the 1970s, but no one lives at Tatapowis today.

Other than fragments of stories about Whiterock Passage, there are no other records of Native people on Read Island. The deep clamshell middens (refuse piles) in sheltered places like Evans Bay and Burdwood

Bay, however, demonstrate that Native people lived here for thousands of years. It's likely these long-ago residents were the Mainland Comox, the northernmost of the Coash Salish. This loosely aligned group includes the Xwemalhkwu (formerly called Homalco) of Bute Inlet, the Klahoose—whose home village is on Cortes Island—and the Sliammon of Powell River.

The Mainland Comox lost thousands of people to smallpox epidemics and other diseases that swept up the coast in successive waves. The first known attack was a smallpox pandemic that spread from Mexico in about 1782.

When Spanish and British explorers sailed into these waters a decade later, they mistook Read, Quadra, Maurelle and Sonora for a single island, which they named Valdez Island. It was not until 1864 that further exploration and survey work showed Read was separate. (Charts continued to show the others as one island for another decade.) Captain Pender of the *Beaver* assigned most of the current place names to honour naval colleagues such as Captain William Viner Read.

When Captain Pender and his crew charted Read Island, the Mainland Comox were no longer in residence at Tatapowis. A group from the north—the Lekwiltok—seized control of the village in about 1830[2] and remained there for five decades. When they left, the Mainland Comox people returned to this important village site (see chapter 4).

A couple who lived as outcasts on a small island off Read's western shore—likely one of the Dunsterville Islets—are the earliest known residents of Read Island. If the romanticized account of Red Dougall and his Native wife Aumoc is accurate, the couple lived in the area in the last quarter of the nineteenth century. Lilly Joy Ward of Read Island heard the tale of these crossed lovers in 1906.

As Lilly explored a cluster of islands in Hoskyn Inlet, she came upon the crumbling remains of a cabin and grave. The grave was marked by a rotting board pierced with bullet holes. On it was carved the initial D, and nearby was a bracelet made from entwined strands of black and red hair holding a blue glass bead. She kept the trinket, and some months later a very old Native man told her the story of the grave.

Whiskey traders, he said, came to his village when he was a boy. A young woman named Aumoc, who was trapped in an unsuccessful and barren marriage, was traded to the men during a drunken spree. Aumoc formed a relationship with one of the men, a tall fellow named Red Dougall, who had flaming red hair and blue eyes. Red decided to stay in the area, and he and Aumoc built a cabin as a base for trapping and trading.

Red taught Aumoc to read and write, so when she had to stay home one winter to care for their new baby, they exchanged letters via passing traders. When Dougall returned at the end of the season, he wove strands of his hair together with Aumoc's to make a bracelet for their child. Every day, so the story goes, their love grew.

About a year later, Aumoc's first husband Seekla learned of her whereabouts. He sneaked up to the cabin one summer day and found Red Dougall alone, resting in the sun by the front door. Seekla shot Red without any warning, it later appeared, for his body lay slumped at the front door as if at rest.

Edgar Wylie's hotel, store and post office in northern Burdwood Bay were the focal point of the district. By the time of his death in 1908 he was a man of legends and intrigue.
PHOTO COURTESY OF THE SOPHIA HORAN COLLECTION, MCR 10,332.

Aumoc carved Red's initial upon his grave marker, where she left the little bracelet he made for their child. She packed up and returned to her home village, but soon learned her former husband was plotting to kill her red-haired child. Aumoc fled with the child in her canoe, which was later found adrift with her blanket still inside. From that time on, said the old man, his people shunned Aumoc's and Red's island. It was no place for the living, not even to dig clams in broad daylight.[3]

The sad tale of Red and Aumoc was already history when the first pieces of land were surveyed and purchased on Read Island in 1883. Alex Russell, a logger from one of the big lumber camps in Burrard Inlet (now Vancouver), bought two large properties totalling about 276 hectares (683 acres). One was on the west coast at Surge Narrows, and the other was on the east coast at Bird Cove.

It was probably work in one of Russell's logging camps that attracted the island's first permanent non-Native resident, who arrived in 1888.[4] Edgar Wilmot Wylie was an enigmatic figure right from the start. Stories of his nefarious activities have grown over time, placing him in the thick of the murderous Dalton Gang before his move to BC. The claim is an exaggeration, his descendants say, but archival records demonstrate Edgar Wylie was not averse to operating on the wrong side of the law.

In fact trouble with the law brought Wylie to BC in the first place. He had just been promoted from deputy sheriff to police chief in Valley City,[5] Dakota, when he made an abrupt departure in 1888, leaving his wife and children behind. As he later confessed, during a murder trial in which he was a key witness, he had to flee under a false name because of "trouble with a wheat firm." He and his childhood friend John Smith spent six weeks in Vancouver and then moved to Read Island, where Wylie lived under the abbreviated name Edgar Wilmot for a few years.[6] Read offered a useful combination of isolation and opportunity for an ambitious man. Several logging camps were at work on the island; William Blaney shipped 243,000 metres (eight hundred thousand feet) of timber in one boom alone in 1889.[7]

A remote, unsettled place like Read Island was ideal for a man on the run, but its lifestyle was lonely for a gregarious man. Wylie remained on the island with Smith for nearly two years before his family joined him. In 1890 he registered—under his son's name—for a pre-emption in the northern corner of Burdwood Bay. This cheap land deal, designed to encourage settlement, made land available at a dollar per 0.4 hectares (one acre) plus two dollars for 0.4 hectares in improvements. Hattie and at least two of their four children, Harley and Minnie, travelled up from Dakota with their friend Christopher Benson.[8] Hattie, who was a key partner in Edgar's enterprises, was the daughter of a prominent New York doctor.

It wasn't long before more old friends and family joined them, including the Wylies' grown daughter Stella Anderson,[9] who also claimed a pre-emption. The Wylies' first home, a two-room cabin on the southern boundary of their homestead, was on a bluff overlooking a small bay that became known as Hotel Bay. Behind it lay marshy land the Wylies drained for a hayfield and orchard; the place is now called the Block House Orchard.

Most of Wylie's fellow settlers focussed on clearing their properties to transform them into farms, but Wylie had a more pragmatic vision. He and Hattie spread their interests in a variety of directions, from farming and logging to blacksmithing. They also built a small hotel for boarders and ran a trading post in partnership with their friend Chris Benson. Their customers could buy or barter for basic supplies like flour, sugar, tea, coffee, flea powder, work boots, laces, suspenders and whiskey.

Wylie sold liquor for the first few years without the bother of a licence. Who was around to know or care that he stood loggers a much-needed drink now and then? He also overlooked the fact it was strictly illegal to sell alcohol to Native people, and received fines twice in the 1890s for this infraction. In both cases Native people died as a result of drinking too much at Wylie's Hotel.

When the Union Steamship Company started a freight and passenger service between Vancouver and the logging camps and settlements of the inner coast in 1892, it encouraged many new people to move to the island. The British Columbia Directory listing for Read that year mentioned "several pretty farms" on Read, and land records show Wylie's childhood friend John Smith pre-empted land next to him in Burdwood

Bay. About six others also pre-empted around Evans Bay and Burdwood Bay that year, including Arno Sutton, the Wylies' store clerk.

New residents were good for business at the Wylies' hotel and store. In 1893 Edgar Wylie became the postmaster for Read Island, and the Union Steamship boats made "in stream" stops, requiring him to row out to retrieve mail, freight and passengers.

By the mid-1890s Wylie was also running small logging camps and grubstaking others. He even tried his hand at mining in those busy years, with an iron ore claim on nearby Redonda Island. As his business interests grew, Wylie bought a steamboat called the *Hollybank* to tow logs and carry freight to logging camps and First Nations villages. Much of his property had a rocky, exposed shore, so he anchored the boat in the southern corner of Evans Bay, known as Steamboat Bay.

The Wylies expanded from their original log cabin home and hotel to a new frame structure in about 1894. As their house and orchard

A rare photo of Hattie and Edgar Wylie's hotel, by then a private residence, appeared in Lukin Johnston's 1929 book *Beyond the Rockies*. Wylie's Hotel, which had six guest rooms upstairs, stood on an open bluff facing Cortes Island and had a small dock to the north in Hotel Bay.
IMAGE COURTESY OF RON GREENE.

encompassed their only pocket of useable waterfront, they built their hotel on John and Laura Smith's place, on a bluff on the south shore of Hotel Bay.

Most of the Wylies' hotel guests were loggers who boarded with them between jobs, or people waiting for the uncertain arrival of the Union Steamship boat. A few years after the Wylie's Hotel (also known as the Burdwood Hotel) opened, they expanded it to include six rooms upstairs and a dining room, kitchen and bar-sitting room on the main floor. Eventually Wylie was able to collect enough signatures from his neighbours to obtain a liquor licence. A thick trap door was set into the barroom floor to give access to the liquor cellar.

The vagaries of the Union Steamship boat's arrival, affected by wind and weather, worked in the Wylies' favour. Loggers who came to the hotel to wait for the boat passed their time with card games and whiskey. Some didn't make it past the temptations at Wylies' for years at a stretch, spending their season's earnings there.

By 1894 the island's population was large enough to warrant twice-weekly Union Steamship service, and the provincial directory listed Read Island on its own for the first time. There were thirty-four names on the list. Their occupations were equally divided between logging and farming. Women were rarely named in directories at that time, but a number of Read Island women were on the list, and in a very rare move, some of these names appeared with occupations. Mrs. Estella Anderson (the Wylies' grown daughter) was a farmer, as were Laura Smith and Hattie Wylie. Also on the list was Mrs. Alex Evans.

A rise in population allowed for the opening of a school in 1894. At least five of the required minimum of ten pupils came from the Wylie and Smith families. Miss E.M. Carter taught the children in the sitting room of Wylie's Hotel. It's likely she also boarded there, along with the Wylies' friend Chris Benson.

Miss Carter must have regaled her friends and family with tales of her year on Read Island for the rest of her life. One month after the school opened, Chris Benson's body was found in his little skiff, adrift in the channel. At first his death appeared to be an accident, but rumours led Justice of the Peace Mike Manson of Cortes Island to inquire further. Mike paid islander William Belding $120 to woo Laura Smith under the guise of being her lover in order to extract a confession. It took nearly a month of visits before Laura opened up and told Belding her husband clubbed Chris Benson to death.

Laura and the children moved to Cortes Island during the year it took for the case to go to trial in Vancouver. Edgar Wylie was a key witness, as were Laura Smith and two of her children. Vancouver newspapers and others across the country reported their testimonies in detail.

Murder victim Chris Benson was described as a tall man of about forty-five with a quiet disposition. Just weeks before his death he registered for a pre-emption in Evans Bay, planning to make a home for his wife and two daughters, then in Tacoma, Washington. He had been a partner in Wylie's store for the first few years, and at the time of his death they were involved in another unspecified business, likely a logging partnership.

On the stand Laura admitted Benson had been her lover for about a year. When the children went to school and her husband was safely out of the way, Benson came to visit Laura. On October 9, 1894, she told the packed courtroom, John Smith came home unexpectedly and caught her in the arms of her lover. He clubbed Benson over the head with a shake-cutting mallet. When Benson fell to the bedroom floor, Smith hit him several more times and left him to slowly die.

Ten-year-old Myrtle, who was the first to arrive home from school that day, said she heard the dying man's groans from behind her parents' closed bedroom door. After dinner Laura sent the children to play out of view of the house while she and Smith carried Benson's lifeless body to his skiff. Then John towed the boat out to sea and released it into a stiff southeast gale. Early the next morning, as Myrtle corroborated, Hattie Wylie helped clean a pool of blood from her parents' bedroom floor; the bloodstained boards were produced in court. Hattie, said the child, also took away a pile of Laura Smith's blood-spattered clothes from beneath the bed.

John Smith, as he told his lawyer, was an impoverished settler whose logging activities failed that year. Somehow he managed to hire William

Bowser, one of the best lawyers in the province, who later became the premier of BC. An accusation was floated in the trial that Wylie paid Smith's court costs, but Wylie stoutly denied this when he took the stand. After this trial, however, it appears John Smith's land, on which the hotel stood, fell into Wylie's hands.

Smith's lawyer did not ask him to take the stand. Instead he presented his client's version of the story, backed by testimonies from Edgar Wylie and several of their friends. They claimed Smith went hunting with them on the day in question, when they killed and gutted a deer, accounting for the blood on Smith's clothes and the bedroom floor.

Wylie and his friends' theory was that Benson, who had been ill over the past year, took a fainting spell and keeled over in his boat, where he hit his head. Furthermore, witness John Furry said, Laura Smith was not a credible witness. "Her conversation is vulgar, and she will discuss the most obscene subjects with men." According to Furry, she said she'd go with any man who would take her. In her own defence, Laura told the courtroom she went with other men only because they brought much-needed food into her household.

William Bowser, reported Vancouver's *Weekly News Advertiser*, gave one of the most eloquent appeals ever addressed to a Vancouver jury. Chris Benson fouled Smith's connubial nest, said Bowser. To counter this the Crown lawyer gave a damming summary of the case. He urged the jury to consider the tarnished character of chief witness Edgar Wylie, a man forced to flee the US under questionable circumstances. He also reminded the court of Wylie's recent conviction for illegal liquor sales to Native people.

The all-male jury deliberated for about an hour and returned with a verdict of not guilty. The judge checked a "swelling torrent of applause" from the packed courthouse and told the jurors that he must support their decision though he didn't agree with their verdict. "You are acquitted, owing to a considerable extent, no doubt, because you had a bad woman for a wife," pronounced Judge Walkem. John Smith stepped down from the dock and shook hands with the foreman of the jury. At this the judge rose from his seat, said Victoria's *Daily Colonist*, and shouted, "Hear!

What in the world are you doing? Get out of here; get out of this building. You'll want to shake hands with me next."

After the trial Laura Smith took her youngest child and moved in with a logger at Port Neville to the north of Read Island. Her fifteen-year-old daughter Cora stayed with her father on Read Island for about a year until she married Horace Heay of Cortes Island, taking her younger brother with her. Eventually John Smith also moved to Cortes, but nothing further is known of young Myrtle Smith, who testified against her father.

The Wylie family also split up a few years after the all-too-public furor of John Smith's trial. Hattie and the younger children moved in with her relatives at Langley Prairie near Vancouver. One of Hattie's contemporaries said she left because the lifestyle on Read Island was "too wild," but Laura Smith's public declaration that Hattie was romantically involved with her husband John Smith may have complicated things. Whatever the case, with the Wylie and Smith children gone, the Read Island School closed.

For a few years the Wylies' grown daughter Estella ran her father's farm and hotel. In 1901 she married William Belding, the fellow who posed as Laura Smith's lover to extract a confession. Estella was another complex Wylie family member. While she listed herself in the British Columbia Directory as Mrs. Estella Anderson through the 1890s, she said she was a spinster on her marriage certificate and gave her parents' names as Edward and Hattie Anderson. After their marriage Estella became a housekeeper in the Kootenays, and Belding got a job in Vancouver. When Belding passed away in 1910, Estella remarried, once again saying she was a spinster, but this time giving her parents' real names.

The notoriety of the Smith-Benson murder case negatively affected population growth on Read Island for a few years. At least one family who contemplated a move to the island received warnings against it because of this and another murder just a year earlier. But things eventually balanced out again, and more settlers arrived on the east side of the island, instilling a new ethic based upon unconventional religions.

A Pious New Era for East Read Island

A steady increase in the number of logging camps in the area brought enough families to the east coast of Read Island to reopen the school in the late 1890s. Edgar Wylie's hotel and store remained the social and commercial hub. His nearest competitor in the hotel trade was the Ireland-Ward family at Bold Point on Quadra Island. When their liquor licence was revoked in 1902, Wylie's Hotel became the only legal place to buy a drink for many kilometres around. He regularly had up to eleven lodgers staying at his hotel on a semi-permanent basis. Next door to the hotel were a dance hall with a hardwood floor, a post office and a boarding house, all linked by a boardwalk along the rocky shore.

Wylie's reputation, tarnished by the Smith trial, didn't keep more friends and family from joining him on Read Island. When his daughter Estella left in 1901, Wylie hired Charles and Mary Longe to manage his complex books and take care of the cooking and housekeeping at the hotel. A 1903 *Daily Colonist* article said Read Island was blessed with "some enterprising settlers from Dakota." Five of them followed Wylie to the island and two more were on their way, including one of Wylie's brothers, a son-in-law and a brother-in-law.

Herb Aldrich, a brother-in-law and old friend, was married to a half-sister of Wylie's estranged wife. The Aldrich family, who looked after Wylie's farm starting in about 1905, moved into John and Laura Smith's cabin in Burdwood Bay, where they had to replace the missing bedroom floorboards removed for the Smith trial. Mary Aldrich, a skilled nurse and herbalist raised in a family of doctors, was a welcome addition to the community.

Wylie was still bootlegging, undeterred by the tragic effects of his previous alcohol offences. He hired his young nephew Wally Aldrich to deliver boxes of apples to the neighbouring reserves. All the boxes looked the same, but some were priced at two dollars and others at ten dollars. To the lad's surprise, the expensive ones were in greatest demand.[10]

In 1903 Wylie donated 0.4 hectare (one acre) of land for a six- by twelve-metre (twenty- by forty-foot) school built by the government. Fifteen children were enrolled, but in the fluctuating economy of a frontier community, attendance dropped below the required minimum, and the school was closed two years later. It was not opened again for several decades.

Log prices fluctuated through the first decade of the twentieth century, making Wylie's business a challenge. His biggest problem, however, was the need to provide credit to his customers, a risky practice in a place with a transient workforce. In addition, the combination of lonely working men, alcohol and gambling often led to fights at his bar. At this difficult juncture, Wylie's health began to fail. With his finances in disarray, it's hinted he lost both his homestead and hotel to gambling debts.

A howling southeast storm battered the rocky shores of Burdwood Bay the day Edgar Wilmot Wylie passed away on April 2, 1908. He left his beggared estate to his faithful housekeeper Mary Longe, who had separated from her husband by this time. She and Wylie's many friends followed his express wishes to place his coffin into the cleft of a rock at his favourite place at Healy Point in Bird Cove. Rocks were piled over the coffin and it was capped by cement, with his name spelled in small stones. The Brockman-Whittington family, who arrived on the island the year Wylie died, heard a rifle was tucked into his coffin. He was a man, so locals said, who had much to fear in the hereafter.

Wylie's will didn't mention his estranged wife Hattie and their children, which spared them the complications of his involved estate. Hattie had moved on with her life. Three weeks after Wylie's death, she remarried.

According to Wylie's probate papers, his estate was worth $1,487.85, but $1,200 of that was owed to him as credit at the hotel and store. Wylie in turn owed $2,590 in wages and trade debts, and it appears Wylie's land was no longer in his name. The worst blow for Mary, however, was yet to follow. She assumed the hotel's liquor licence would automatically transfer to her along with the hotel. It didn't, and when she applied in her own name, she was refused.[11] Despite all these disadvantages, Mary tried to continue with the hotel and store for a few years in concert with Frederick Percival, who became the postmaster. With so many debts, they were forced to close the hotel in about 1912.[12] It never reopened.

The mechanization of the logging industry in the first decade of the twentieth century made it expensive for operators, though they could now log much farther inland. Camps became larger and worked on location for years. The Fraser River Saw Mills Company—owned by Chicago, Winnipeg and New Westminster partners—had three mechanized camps on Read Island, at Whiterock Passage, Hoskyn Channel and Evans Bay.

Loggers and settlers could pick up their mail and supplies at Burdwood Bay, Cortes Island or Quadra Island. They could also buy things from itinerant salesmen who plied the coast by boat, selling everything from clothing and jewellery to sex. As an antidote to the latter temptation, the Columbia Coast Mission provided medical, intellectual and spiritual service by boat.

Lilly Joy Ward of Read Island wrote a regular column for the CCM's magazine, *The Log of the Columbia*. Her husband Bernard and his partner Matt Storey had a logging camp on the southwest end of the island, cutting a big stand of timber that stretched east to west from Hoskyn Inlet to Lake Bay. Bernard Ward was a competent, well-seasoned logger, raised on this part of the coast by veteran timber cruiser Moses Cross Ireland.[13] Bernard ran the steam donkey, and in an industry with a high accident rate, he was adept at stitching up wounds.

Lilly Joy and Bernard met in Seattle in 1902,[14] when Bernard left the country to evade a bootlegging charge at his stepfather's hotel at Bold Point on Quadra Island. He hoped all would be forgotten, but when he returned to the island in 1903 with Lilly Joy, he was promptly fined three hundred dollars, about half a year's salary at that time.

Lilly Joy and Bernard were an unconventional couple. Lilly was a heavyset woman about eight years Bernard's senior. He was in his midtwenties and she was thirty-four. Lilly was a devout Theosophist, following a relatively new spiritual practice that incorporated elements of various world religions and the occult. The leading force behind Theosophy, Helena Blavatsky, believed in vegetarianism, reincarnation, clairvoyance, telepathy and prophetic dreams. Theosophists were firmly opposed to the use of alcohol and considered marriage an unnecessary social contract, which perhaps explains why Lilly Joy and Bernard did not marry until some years later.

Lily's beliefs were quietly accepted in an out-of-the-way place like Read Island, though her views on temperance were a hard sell. Her good-natured, sometimes patronizing articles in *The Log* drew rebuttals from loggers like James Forest Hinchy, who died of alcoholism a few years later. "I was sorry to see that Sister Ward had to work so hard cooking for the loggers," Hinchy wrote in response to Lilly's complaints about running her husband's camp kitchen for two weeks. "When she gets next to those short horns she will have a snap. Just roll in a bale of hay, sister, and shake whiskey on it and you won't need to make a fire."[15] Her beliefs did, however, have a reforming influence on Bernard, the convicted bootlegger, who banned liquor from his camps.

Lilly Joy was a prolific writer, pumping out stories, articles, poems and letters from her logging-camp shack. "As I approached the foreman's cabin," wrote Reverend Antle on one of his first visits with Lilly, "I was not a little astonished to hear the click, click of a typewriter, and on entering was introduced to Mrs. Ward, whose busy fingers had been hammering out the interesting article which you read in last month's *Log*." Antle, who may not have been fully aware of Lilly's "immoral" religious and social beliefs, praised her virtues, ending with a wish for the refining influence of more such women on the coast.

Lilly also wrote letters to members of the Universal Sisterhood of America, providing solace to those in need. She painted landscapes, collected natural history specimens to exhibit at a fair and railed against the practice of shooting eagles—sanctioned by the government—and the pillage of logging. In her passionate poems and prose, she described the beauty of the seashore and forests and wondered if she was alone in her awe of nature. Her writing was sometimes tinged by the sadness she carried from the loss of her first husband and child in Arizona about a decade prior. "Though I am often sad, I never let anyone know it and always try to have a smile when anyone comes around," she wrote in a letter of condolence to a mother whose son died in Storey's and Ward's logging camp.

Storey and Ward moved their base camp in the spring of 1906,[16] towing their portable buildings from the west side of the island to the finger-like indentation of Lake Bay at the southeast tip of Read. From there they built a skid road up a stream to the shore of Read Lake, now called Rosen Lake.

Storey and Ward finished up on Read Island in 1907 and moved on. For some unaccountable reason, at this same time Lilly Joy and Bernard sanctified their union in Vancouver. Shortly thereafter she paid homage to Read Island with a poem in *The Log*:

Farewell, Reid Island, Farewell [17]
(first and last verses)

Accept from me, this tribute e'er we part,
My fir-crowned, rock-bound, sea-girt Isle!
Whom I bid farewell with saddened heart,
E'en though I leave thee with a smile.
Thy silent lake, thy rocks, and hills,
Where e'er my wandering feet have trod,
thy granite cliffs, and wind-swept hills,
Have brought me nearer Nature's God.

. . . .

Three long years I have been thy guest,
With lavish hands, thou gave of thy wealth,
Of all of thy jewels, the richest and best
Love, Contentment, Peace, and Perfect Health.
Thy loving kindness I'll never forget,
Though far from thy dear rugged shores I may dwell;
Oft will I miss thee, and, with a sigh of regret
Will long for the Isle that I now bid—Farewell!

From her new home on the mainland, Lilly Joy wrote her final piece for *The Log*, giving an account of her discovery of the body of one of their crew, who went missing shortly before they left Read Island. The loggers searched for days for young "Johnny Boy" Norwood. They checked nearby settlements and dragged Rosen Lake, where he was last seen. But, there was no sign of Johnny Boy until one evening at sunset when Lilly Joy went for a walk at Rosen Lake in response to "an uncontrollable impulse."

As she gazed into the water in the evening light, Lilly whispered a silent prayer for the missing boy and inched out onto a boomstick. As she did so a "chill, as of a cold wave of air," passed over her. Just beneath the surface of the water were a few little bubbles of light like a glowing circle. In the centre of it was Johnny's head. His hair gently waved in "a wreath of scintillating phosphorescence." She ran to the donkey engine and pulled the steam whistle to give the emergency signal.

Nothing further is known about Lilly Joy, except for the fleeting mention of her involvement in the formation of a literary group based in Heriot Bay on Quadra Island in 1908. She died[18] and was buried at Bold

Wiley and Dorathy (Brockman) Whittington and their children took over the homestead of her parents in Burdwood Bay after their untimely deaths. The Whittingtons lived in several locations on the island's east coast over the years, moving with their logging camps. Their grandson and grand-daughter continue to log woodlots on the island.
PHOTO COURTESY OF RONNIE BUCKLEY.

Point sometime before 1917, when Bernard married a young woman who deserted him several months later.[19]

Ida Brockman, another woman with an ache in her heart, moved from Oregon to Read Island in 1908. She was part of an extended family who settled on two large properties on the east coast. Ida and William Brockman brought their grown daughters, Nina, Ledocia and Dorathy. Dorathy came with her husband Wiley Whittington to live on her parents' property in the southern part of Burdwood Bay. It was a well-established homestead, having been worked by seven prior settlers over the previous sixteen years. By the time the Brockman-Whittingtons got the place, it had a bearing orchard, pasture and several houses. The last owners, Henry and Rose Tiber, built a remarkable boathouse on the beach that was an island landmark.[20]

Another branch of the family came to the island as well. William Brockman's brother Newt and his wife Lydia settled at the head of Evans Bay on Lot 20, the current site of the Coast Mountain Expeditions Lodge.

An established homestead was a blessing for Ida Brockman because her husband was a drinking man, driven by the obsessive wanderlust of

Wiley and Dorathy Whittington's daughter Bonnie (Brown) became a famous cougar hunter after a cougar killed her dog. She had ten kills to her credit when she was still just a girl.
PHOTO COURTESY RONNIE BUCKLEY.

After Ida Brockman died prematurely, her daughter Ledocia married Read Island postmaster Harold Mclelan. She left him to follow her dreams of glamour and excitement, and family story says her alcoholic father William shot himself because she had "gone wild." Her fourth husband, seen here with Ledocia, was a California senator.
PHOTO COURTESY OF RONNIE BUCKLEY.

prospecting. Ida, her daughters and her son-in-law Wiley Whittington took charge of the homestead, and a few years later Ida and William agreed to an informal separation. To his credit William sent money home when he could, but between hard work and a troubled marriage, Ida's health suffered. In 1915, at the age of forty-two, she died of a heart attack in a small boat en route to the Rock Bay Hospital, many kilometres to the west on Vancouver Island.

Ida's death precipitated many changes for the family. Within months of her passing, young Ledocia agreed to a hasty marriage in 1915 with an older islander. Harold Mclelan, the Read Island postmaster, had taken over the Smith-Wylie property at Burdwood Bay. The marriage quickly soured, and Ledocia, a beautiful and ambitious young woman, headed for the US in search of bright lights and fame. She married several times more, and one of her husbands was a California senator.

Things didn't go well for Ida's estranged husband William either. He returned to Read Island following Ida's death, but within a few years he took his own life in Seattle. He left his homestead to his daughter and son-in-law, the Whittingtons, who became long-time residents. Wiley and Dorathy raised three children on the island, Leta, Bonny and Bill.

Read was a haven for people seeking religious and personal freedom. By the 1920s so many different kinds of religions were represented that it was hard to find a suitable day for community celebrations. The Christian, Jehovah's Witness, Campbellite and Seventh Day Adventist families each recognized different days as sacred. Isabelle (Hayes) Edgett, who grew up on the island, says these varying religious, financial and racial circumstances taught island children tolerance and open-mindedness.

John and May Lambert, Seventh Day Adventists, were a leading family on the island. They heard about the possibility of farming at the head of Bute Inlet while living at Alexis Creek in the Chilcotin, so after a work stint near Seattle, they rowed upcoast in a dory in 1913. Bute Inlet proved too isolated,[21] so they pitched their tents at Frederick Point at the north entrance to Evans Bay to wait for a cheque from John's surveying job in the US. They never did get paid, but Read Island was their home for many years.

While the family lived in the Chilcotin, two of their children contracted TB. May Lambert struggled to keep their bedding and eating utensils isolated from those of the others in their rustic camp, but when a third child began to show signs of the disease, they moved across the bay into an abandoned building at Wylie's hotel site. The place was a shambles, but it was a vast improvement on living in tents, and a kind neighbour gave them a cow.

Better living quarters didn't stop the effects of TB. Ralph Lambert died in March 1917 at the age of twenty-three, followed by sixteen-year-old Lillian on October 17. Both were buried on Healy Point in Evans Bay, not far from Edgar Wylie's grave. Though there's no death certificate for the child, Tom Widdowson recalls the Lamberts lost a third child, Rose, to TB. "A beautiful child, who seemed healthy until she started coughing up white flecks." The rest of their children—Joy, Forrest, Violet and Jimmy—escaped the contagion.

The Landers family, also Seventh Day Adventists, followed the Lamberts to Evans Bay in 1918. For a time they lived at the old Dick Davis ranch, now Harper's Landing. While there, Mary Landers went

Read Island was a haven for people of non-traditional faiths by the 1920s. At one point so many different religions were represented, it was hard to find appropriate days for community celebrations. May (left), John and his brother Tom (bearded), Violet, James, Forrest and Joy Lambert were Seventh Day Adventists.
PHOTO COURTESY OF BILL WHITTINGTON COLLECTION, MCR 5694.

into early labour while her husband was away logging. She sent her oldest boy scrambling along the beach to get help from a neighbour, but the baby was premature and didn't survive. After this the Landers moved into Wylie's old hotel, where they stayed with the Lambert family for several years. The dance hall was the best preserved of the ruined buildings at Hotel Bay, as Sylva (Landers) Welsh recalls, with its polished wood floor. Later still the Landers moved to Sawmill Bay at the north entrance of Evans Bay. Their final move was to a property at the current Evans Bay dock, a place James Landers dubbed Done Movin.

Some of these families taught school to their own children. May Lambert (a former schoolteacher) used the Bible as the children's text book. She had a great interest in art and encouraged them to draw as she or John read their favorite Bible stories. Their daughter Violet amassed a sketchbook of scenes from the Bible and wild flowers she gathered on the mountain behind their home.

John Lambert revived the Read Island School (or South End school) when he persuaded his church to provide a teacher in 1921. Miss Martha Essler's salary was paid by the government. She had a class of nine, the oldest of whom was near her own age. The school inspector said the children were a backward lot, but they were "working earnestly." Violet Lambert was seventeen when she first attended the South End school and she continued until she was about twenty-one, finishing grade eight.

The Whittington kids joined the Landers and Lamberts at the South End school, held in the old Burdwood Hotel for a few years. Bill Whittington recalled exploring the dilapidated rooms of the hotel and climbing down through a trap door into the cellar beneath the saloon, where the kids played with the mass of corks that littered the floor.

It was hard to keep teachers in isolated rural schools. Martha Essler left at Christmas, eighteen months later, because she was required to complete her teaching degree. Ruth Verchere, who had an Academic A Certificate but no teaching experience, replaced her. Her nine pupils were all in different grades and at various stages in the curriculum. As she later told Katie Lambert, who wrote a history of Read Island schools, her first-class education didn't include any teacher training. She wasn't even sure what phonics were, so she caught a ride over to Cortes Island to confer with the teacher there. In her end-of-term report, Ruth said general conditions in the community were bad, but "if one is fond of wild and picturesque scenery, hiking and fishing Read Island is ideal."

Ruth, like Martha Essler, stayed for eighteen months. The next teacher thought Read was such a dreadful place that she didn't even stay long enough to open the school in September 1924. Eva Ambrose happened to be on the spot in the teacher's hiring hall when the job was reposted, so she took it, but she stayed only until Christmas because school-board secretary Carl Ekman interfered in her personal life.

Carl Ekman, though he had no children of his own, served on the school board. He and his wife also provided board for the teachers at their home on the west coast of the island. Ekman went across to meet the next teacher in his leaky rowboat at the Bold Point dock in 1926. Doris Davies wrote an article some years later about her experiences on Read Island. It was pouring rain when she arrived at the Bold Point dock

The Ekmans of Hjorth Bay lived on the west side of Read Island. Carl Ekman had no children but was secretary of the Read Island School Board and provided board for the teachers, who complained he meddled in their personal business.
PHOTO COURTESY OF DORIS DAVIES COLLECTION, MCR 12,187.

at 4:00 a.m., where the Bell family gave her a hearty breakfast. Carl helped her aboard his boat and stood to row, with short, jerky strokes. When Doris was settled, he passed her an old tobacco tin, telling her in his thick Swedish accent to bail.

When Doris came to the island to teach, the school had been moved from the hotel to an old logging camp cookshack pulled up on the beach in front of the Brockman-Whittington homestead at Burdwood Bay. The Eckmans' homestead was connected by a four-kilometre (2.5-mile) trail. Carl walked Doris to school on the first day, warning her about some of the more difficult pupils like Leta Whittington. Leta's mother confirmed this when she arrived with her daughter. "If you need to strap Leta I'll come over and hold her for you," she said. But these grim warnings came to naught. "Leta turned out to be a strong, well-developed girl of fifteen with a hobby of riding steers bareback," wrote Doris Davies. "And as I was rather a young 19-year-old we soon became fast friends."

There was no playground on the rocky school site, but the children made their own entertainment. One group of boys built and operated a log-hauling apparatus, complete with donkey and high-lead spar, and

The Lambert family started out in tents in Evans Bay and later lived in several locations around Evans and Burdwood bays. Their final home was near the south entrance to Burdwood Bay, where from 1924 to 1946 they had a post office and store serving the south end of the island.
PHOTO COURTESY OF SHEILA FOORT COLLECTION, MCR.

the kids found a flat spot on a rocky knoll just large enough for a game of softball.

About a year later the Lamberts bought or pre-empted a homestead south of Burdwood Bay, where John became a Justice of the Peace and postmaster in 1924. By then he and his oldest sons had their own steam donkey and logging operation. John Lambert ran the store and post office out of their home, while his sons and brother logged. The Union Steamship boats stopped at a float anchored at a small island inside the bay to drop mail and supplies.

One of the Lamberts' contemporaries described seeing John's brother, with his long white beard, pass along the road leading his ox cart as his nephews walked on either side. It was like a scene from the Bible, she recalled. The Lamberts ate meat—mainly venison—and fish when necessary, but tried to observe the vegetarian diet prescribed by their religion.

No one now recalls for sure what Wiley Whittington's religion was, though people agree it was an obscure sect, either Millerite, Campbellite or Two by Two. All agree, however, that he was a devout Christian who lived by the Bible's tenets. As a result, for example, the women in the family never cut their hair.

Wiley and Dorathy lived on her parents' homestead in southern Burdwood Bay for a few years and then went to California to look after ailing relatives. Around the time her father died, they returned to Read Island and took over his homestead, where they kept a cow, chickens, pigs and a large kitchen garden. When Wiley—joined later by his son— got into logging, the family lived at log various sites in Evans Bay. They started out working with oxen and horse teams and later developed their own custom-built arch for hauling. One of their early logging sites was at present-day Sawmill Bay. They also logged at the head of Evans Bay on the site of the modern Coast Mountain Expeditions Lodge.

The east coast of the island, with its protected beaches and somewhat warmer rain-shadow climate, was the first and largest community on Read Island, but there were a few settlers on the rugged west coast as well. No one would have guessed in the early decades of the twentieth century that someday Surge Narrows would become the island's hub. Like some other communities in the region, it was one particular family who made this happen, aided by the capricious nature of the coastal economy.

The Early Years at Surge Narrows

On June 25, 1893, Jack Myers (alias Ben Kennedy) sailed his nondescript sloop through the inner coast to sell "Gaelic whiskey" and champagne to Indian reserves and logging camps. He was heavily armed and stocked with over sixty cases of liquor that he and a partner had stolen from a Vancouver dealer. He anchored at Drew Harbour on Quadra Island and paddled a skiff to the reserve at Cape Mudge, where he engaged the services of a prostitute named Kitty Coleman. The resident missionary was alerted, and Myers was ousted, but Kitty and her husband followed Kennedy back to his sloop, where a rowdy party ensued.[22]

From Drew Harbour, Myers went to a logging camp in Whiterock Passage. Jack O'Conner, James Burns, Salem Hinkley, Angus Cameron and John O'Neill had just knocked off work for a few days of rest when Myers strolled into camp. He was a striking man, with his sharp-eyed look and a mop of dyed black hair shoved into a slouch hat. He wore a blue shirt and dark trousers tucked into tall boots, and in the fashion of the time, had a thick mustache and sideburns. Myers stood all hands to a drink, leading to the sale of numerous bottles of his special brew and a drunken night of cards. The next day a few of the men went hunting, taking Myers's dog with them, and that night the drinking resumed until all but Myers and Salem Hinkley had passed out.

About midnight Jack O'Conner roused himself from a drunken stupor in his cot and rejoined Myers and Hinkley. O'Conner was still so drunk he could hardly hold his hand steady to light his pipe. With the pipe lit, he waved a hand toward Myers's dog and pronounced it a useless mutt. Myers rose to his dog's defence. He put five dollars in his waistcoat pocket, placed the waistcoat beneath his dog and told O'Conner that if he could get that vest away from the animal, he could have the money. O'Conner swaggered over to the dog, opened his fly and peed on the dog's head. The dog ran for cover beneath a bunk, so Myers shot at the dog and it ran out the open cabin door.

"Don't shoot your dog! Any dog would run away," O'Conner called after Myers as he chased his dog. The two men had a heated exchange, and Myers returned to the cabin. This time his gun was trained on O'Conner. "If I had a gun I'd take even chances with you," said O'Conner. He made a grab toward a rifle above a nearby bunk, but as he did so, he knocked over a coal-oil lamp and pitched the room into darkness.

Salem Hinkley, the only other man present, said he heard O'Conner fall after the light went out. Then there was a report from a gun and a flash of light. When Hinkley got the lamp relit, O'Conner was on the floor with Myers crouched above him. "Call the boys," O'Conner shouted. Hinkley grabbed at the revolver in Myers's hands and begged him not to shoot. At this, Myers struck Hinkley in the stomach and knocked him out the cabin door. As Hinkley fell, he heard another shot. By the time he scrambled back inside, Myers had fled out a window, and O'Conner lay in a pool of blood.

At the second shot, some of the other drunken loggers dragged themselves from their beds. They carried O'Conner to a bunk, where they were assembled when Myers crawled through a window and demanded they testify that O'Conner shot himself. One of the loggers attempted to snatch Myers's rifle but failed. "I've killed four men before," bragged Myers, as he stood triumphantly over O'Conner. "You're a big man, and a good man," he said, "but you've struck a better one."

As the night wore on, Myers began to regret his actions. The men made plans to take O'Conner to a doctor in Comox, but the man's injuries were too serious for them to move him. "What money I have I would give to see that man back on his feet," said a now repentant Myers. When O'Conner finally died many hours later, Myers laid his rosary, a gift from his sister who was a nun, on the dead man's chest.

With O'Conner now dead, Salem Hinkley was able to slip away to get Cortes Island Justice of the Peace Michael Manson. As it was many hours before Manson got to the crime scene, he assumed Myers would be long gone, but as Manson sat with the loggers taking their evidence, Myers strode in. He had two Colt revolvers poked in his belt, a dirk knife tucked in a tall boot and a Winchester fully cocked and levelled at

Manson's head. Manson had many times before proved himself a smooth talker in tricky situations. To pacify Myers, Manson assured him that if he was innocent and everyone backed him up, there was nothing to fear. Following more threats and angry words, Myers finally went back to his sailboat, and Manson took O'Conner's body to Comox, where initial hearings took place.

A few days later a small posse that included Manson searched for Myers, but according to the press, the search was bungled. A second attempt was made with a larger posse that included police officers from Vancouver, and a five-hundred-dollar reward was posted. The men visited all the camps and settlers in the region until they hit on Myers's hiding place in a cabin in Ramsay Arm. The officers exchanged gunfire with Myers as they approached, but Myers dashed for the hills and eluded them for a few more days. It was his cooking fire that attracted the posse's attention. As the posse came toward him, Myers made as if to flee again but instead quietly surrendered. He was starving, said the newspapers, having eaten his little dog some days prior.[23]

The Myers murder case was covered in great detail across North America. When Myers arrived in Nanaimo, "the male population of the city, almost to a man," were at the wharf to inspect the criminal. Myers's case was tried in New Westminster, where he was sentenced to life in prison for manslaughter, but about a year later he was shot as he tried to escape a work gang.

Only a few settlers lived along the rocky shores of the west side of Read Island when Myers shot O'Conner in Whiterock Passage in 1893. A few Native families lived on the reserve across from the logging camp, and there were one or two non-Native homesteaders, including James Rea, who pre-empted land facing Sturt Island at the north end of Hoskyn Channel in 1891. Logger Charlie Newcombe had a homestead opposite Conville Bay on Quadra Island, and George Ashton pre-empted land in 1893 across from Tatapowis. They got their supplies at the steamship dock, hotel and store at Bold Point on Quadra Island after it opened in about 1901.

The best-known of these early homesteaders was a Welshman named John Jones. He came to Read Island in 1892 at the age of twenty-four to work in a logging camp in Whiterock Passage. His cousins, the Allen brothers, pre-empted land on Cortes that year, so he too decided to stay. His first pre-emption was in Evans Bay but he gave that up in 1894 for landlocked Lot 309. From then on he systematically pre-empted successive claims, each requiring daunting work to meet homestead requirements for clearing, fencing, ditching and other improvements. While many of his fellow settlers barely met the minimum pre-emption requirements after years of hard work, Jones amassed more than 240 hectares (six hundred acres) in fairly short order. District Lot 333 eventually became his homesite, where his old orchard still produces an abundant crop.

Radio salesman and serviceman Jim Spilsbury wrote about Jones in his book *Spilsbury's Coast*. Jones was a taciturn man who lived in miserly squalor, said Spilsbury. But Lukin Johnston of the *Province*, who wrote about the Discovery Islands in 1925, said there was no more solid citizen in the country than John Jones. Jones was a stoop-shouldered man, bent by his prodigious work schedule. He planted over a hundred fruit trees in a methodical grid near his house and grew enough produce, including onions and potatoes, to sell by the sackful to logging camps and other settlers. He also ran about eight head of cattle on his large property.

It's hard to imagine Jones taking time away from his gruelling schedule to woo and win the affections of a woman, but in 1908 he married Florence Moore in Vancouver. They likely met through their mutual family connections on Cortes Island. Stories handed down say Florence was a very pretty woman when they were first married, but the hard work and isolation of Jones's lifestyle wore her down. By the time of Spilsbury's visit in the 1930s, she had become a befuddled recluse.

John Jones became the postmaster for the west coast of Read Island in 1912. His place was a thirty-minute walk from where the mail was dropped off at Surge Narrows at a floating wharf in the south end of the bay. As the government road came out at the north end of the bay, settlers had to paddle across to retrieve supplies. This was a huge inconvenience for Jones, who had to be on hand to meet the Union Steamship boat. Its arrival time, affected by wind and tide, could be anywhere from 11:00 p.m.

to 4:00 a.m. twice weekly, so Jones had to wait in the wharf shed. He covered himself with gunnysacks and kept a coal-oil lantern at his feet to keep warm. The smell of the old man—a blend of coal oil, gunny sacks and sweat—was memorable. Once the mail arrived, Jones rowed the sacks and parcels to the end of the road and carted them home to be sorted in readiness for pickup. His neighbour Bob Tipton asked him why he didn't get a horse to haul the mail. "The horse eats while I sleep!" said the old penny-pincher. For this gruelling routine Jones received an annual stipend of $104.

George Stafford moved to property north of the present Surge Narrows dock in 1909. The bachelor was a famous storyteller among the islands. He peppered his tales with the expression "by-God," giving rise to his nickname of By-God Stafford. His young friend Bill Law of Quadra Island loved to recount By-God Stafford tales:

Bob Tipton of Surge Narrows store with By-God Stafford. Bill Law of Quadra Island loved to recount Stafford's tall tales and described him as "a thin, oily kind of fellow, not very tall." The handlogger had had two or three wives, recalled Law. "He'd get them up there as housekeepers."
PHOTO COURTESY OF D'ALTROY COLLECTION, MCR 5623.

There was this fellow known as By-God Stafford. He lived up at Read Island. One time I went in there and he was feeding milk to two or three pigs in a trough that he had dug out of a log. I asked him where he had got the milk and he said it was whale's milk. He said, "One morning I was wakened here early in the morning," he says, "and bellowing was going on and splashing water on the beach and echoing on the hills. I got up and looked out the window and there was a whale backing water out there in the bay, by-God, you know that? Do you know what was the matter with her, by-God, Billy? She'd lost a young one and had too much milk. So I rowed out there in a canoe and milked her, by-God, you know, and I filled the canoe right full and I had to go ashore and get the 18-foot row boat, by-God. They give a lot of milk, one of those whales, you know." He says, "She came every morning to be milked—dawn. I had milk all over the bay and drifting out in the channel and I thought it was such a waste I would get some pigs and raise some pigs. So I got me three or four pigs. I'm trying that, feeding them whale milk."

It was a lot of bologna. I saw him at Campbell River later, and I asked him how the pig farm was coming along. He said, "Not very good, by-God, you know, I'm not gaining a bit. There's a bear that comes and steals the little pigs, by-God, you know." I said, "Why don't you shoot the bear?" "He's the smartest bear in British Columbia, by-God, you can't shoot him or trap him." "Well," I said, "I guess the only thing to do is put some lanterns in the piggery." He said, "I've tried that too, by-God. He never used to come around, he never shows up unless I got to get my provisions, see. I laid for him with a rifle but he don't come around. He knows when I'm home. It's when I go away when he steals the pigs. I tried the lanterns in there and I thought I had him beat. By-God," he says, "it was all right for two or three weeks then one morning I heard a hell of a racket out there and squealing and grunting, you know. I grabbed the old .30-.30 and ran outside there and there was that bear going up the side of the mountain with a pig under one arm and the lantern in the other. He must have heard me pull the hammer back because he blew the light out and I missed him, by-God."[24]

Carl Theodore "Charlie" Rosen and his father John pre-empted property in about 1910 on the north shore of what came to be known as Rosen Lake. Not much is known about Charlie's father, who doesn't appear to have stayed long on the island.[25] Charlie served in the Swedish army before he immigrated to the US, where he crossed the country working for the railway. He was a powerfully built man, made for hard work. Some said he was the strongest man "in this part of the country," a claim backed by stories of him lifting a rail single-handed. When he quit the railway he changed his name from Anderson to Rosen (his mother's family name) to avoid the railway's blacklist of quitters.

Charlie handlogged his property with a partner in 1910, cutting 243,000 metres (eight hundred thousand feet) of timber. He and his father cleared about five hectares (thirteen acres) for a meadow and orchard and broke apart beaver dams to lower the level of the lake by about one metre (three feet). The Rosens lived in a little cabin while they built a drystone foundation for their dream house on a rocky promontory on the lakeshore. Behind it was their orchard in a swale that ran uphill from the lake. To one side of the orchard were a big root cellar lined with rock and an impressive barn made from massive hand-hewn timbers, built against a sidehill to give access to both storeys. Near the barn was a smokehouse built into a burnt-out snag.

Charlie Rosen, like old John Jones, had to transport everything in and out of his landlocked property along a rough dirt track. He kept a horse and built an ingenious stoneboat for hauling, with runners fashioned from a curved fir limb. When the stoneboat was empty, the big man rode at the back, perched atop a wooden crate.

His favourite horse, Lindy, named for the US aviator Colonel Charles Lindbergh, met an ironic end. Lindy leaped for an apple one day, missed and fell into the crotch of a tree where Charlie found him hanging. Rosen sorrowfully dug a pit beneath the dead horse and then cut the limb to let the horse drop into its grave, but not before he had removed all the useable meat to process in his ingenious cedar-stump smokehouse. He shed a tear every time he ate some of Lindy. "Did you hear what happened to Lindy?" Charlie is said to have asked a man who passed by where he was working on the road one day. He had tears in his eyes as he continued. "He hanged himself!" he said, waving a thick slice of smoked meat at the man. "Here is Lindy!"

The Reverend Alan Greene of the Columbia Coast Mission failed to appreciate the gravity of Rosen's grief when he wrote an article in *The Log*, repeating Rosen's praise for the tenderness of horse steaks. Charlie took offence to a report that made him sound like an uncultured man. He got his well-educated neighbour Benjamin Widdowson to compose a letter of rebuttal. Widdowson was happy to do so, for he too had eaten some of the ill-fated horse.

Benjamin Widdowson's son Tom wrote an article about old Charlie Rosen. He recalled Charlie laughing over the ambitious scale of his projects. "I thought I was going to live to be 500 years old," he told Tom.

In all his years at Rosen Lake, Charlie's dream of building a house didn't materialize, but was dashed by his childhood sweetheart's decision not to follow him to BC, some said. His sisters came to live at Rosen Lake for a time, wreaking havoc upon his bachelor housekeeping. The rest of the time he was on his own. If he was lonely, it didn't affect his sunny disposition. Rosen loved to swap tales over his famous cider or entertain islanders at swimming and skating parties at the lake. He was a light-footed dancer, for such a big man, and he loved to pull out his little gramophone to play Swedish tunes for his guests. The joy and vigour he poured into his homestead are still evident in his mature orchard, his pasture and the stone foundations of his various structures.

Another famous Discovery Islander lived on the west coast of Read toward the end of his life. "Lord Huey Horatius Nelson Baron Bacon, The Only Lord in America," was born in New Brunswick and baptized Huascar Bacon. Some said Lord Bacon was the outcast of a nobly born family, a well-educated man who loved to quote at length from Byron, Keats and Shakespeare. He separated from his wife before going to the Yukon gold rush and came to BC in 1908, where he made a name for himself as an inveterate drunk and a prospector. He had many eccentric beliefs, including the notion that he couldn't sleep outside under a full moon for fear of its effect upon him.

Bacon had mineral claims throughout the islands and in the lake system behind Campbell River. According to Reverend Greene of the Columbia Coast Mission, Lord Bacon had great hopes for his Read Island mines, the Soleyman and Freya. In his old age he asked the minister to write his will, leaving all his worldly wealth—which never materialized—to the building of an orphanage.

Just before Christmas in 1938, Lord Bacon admitted himself to the Campbell River hospital. He knew he needed medical care but didn't want to stay in the hospital overnight, so he slipped out and made a camp near Big Rock, just south of town. When the police found him sitting by a fire, he told them he'd just come back to see what happened to the rock he heaved at some blasphemous enemy, perhaps harkening back to a time when a rival miner shot his finger off in 1915. "Hermit Comes Back to Life," announced the *Comox Argus*. "He has gone back to his prospect at Read Island and silence closes over the record once more." As indeed it did. Lord Bacon died several years later in a provincial infirmary.[26]

Robert "Tippy" Tipton moved to the west coast of Read Island with his wife Nell in about 1918, after his war service. Tippy's father, a successful

Bob "Tippy" Tipton, whose father purchased land for him and his wife Nell after World War I, had no teeth. His hawk nose curved down to meet his upturned chin, leaving barely room to wedge in his eternal pipe.
PHOTO COURTESY OF D'ALTROY COLLECTION, MCR 7790.

cotton broker, purchased the ninety-six-hectare (238-acre) property at Surge Narrows for them. Robert and Nell cleared the logged-over land to transform it into a farm, with a modern prefab bungalow that still stands. It wasn't ideal farmland, but with a pension to support them, it was workable. When Vancouver journalist Lukin Johnston visited in 1925, the Tiptons had four cows, two horses, a flock of chickens and an orchard. They sold most of their produce on contract to the surrounding logging camps.

The Tiptons, who were childless, took in Nell's niece and nephews—Garry, Clarence and Win Keeling—when their mother died in 1924. The school on the east side of the island was open again, but it was too far for the Keeling kids to attend, so for the first few years the Tiptons hired their own teacher. To attract families with school-aged children to the west side of the island, Robert placed an ad in the *Province* in 1925:

PRE-EMPTIONS

~~~~~~

Acreage—I WILL LOCATE FREE OF
charge a few families with children of school
age on preemptions 100 miles up Coast. Box
1536 Province.

A crippling recession caused by rapid industrialization during World War I was just beginning to ease in the mid-1920s. A move to a place like Read Island, where it was possible to hunt and fish for much of their own food, had great appeal for families in straitened circumstances. The Tiptons received thirty-six replies from all over Western Canada. The writers poured out tales of recession-era poverty and hardship. The Tiptons must have chuckled over responses from people who wondered if there was nearby rail service or access to stores. A Vancouver father of six waxed poetic about how a sea view from his window would be ample compensation for less productive land. He was looking for a place "devoid of worries and responsibilities to be found in City life." Another man, A. Bottrell, sounded like a good fit except for his needy wife. He was a seasoned logger wanting a day job in a camp. "I would like to get

The Charles and Emily Redford family moved to Read Island in response to Bob Tipton's advertisement in search of families with school-aged children. Enough families arrived to open a school. The Redfords spent their first winter in a canvas-and-board shack on the beach.
PHOTO COURTESY OF DORIS ANDERSEN COLLECTION, MCR 18,332.

work so I could be home nights, as my wife is nervous and we have a little kiddie eight months old so I would not like to leave her alone in a strange place."

A few among Tipton's correspondents appeared to be good candidates. Among them were experienced farmers, caught in the city during the recession, and others toughing out adverse conditions on bleak farms in the BC Interior or Alberta. Vernon farmer Dan Patterson was eaten out by grasshoppers in three successive summers. He hoped for better things on the coast and was saving up the two hundred dollars needed to move his cattle, horses and machinery to Read Island.

In the end five or six families from the thirty-six respondents moved to the west coast of Read Island. Among them were Charles and Emily Redford and their two sons. It was a challenge for the Redfords to save the money they needed to make the move. "I am in receipt of your letter of recent date," he wrote to Bob Tipton, "in which you inform me that I am in danger of losing my pre-emption. I don't wish to prevent your children from getting an education, and if the fact that I am holding that lot is proving a hindrance to you getting a school, I am prepared to let go, but I should be extremely sorry to do so." To speed up the process, the Redfords moved into a three- by four-metre (ten- by fourteen-foot) shack built from boards, split shakes and canvas, where they lived for their first winter.

Major Fred Foort and his beautiful Lebanese wife Ameenie came to the island as a result of Tipton's ad. With them were Fred's brother, Stanley Foort, his wife Mabel and their children. The Foorts bought an established homestead to the southeast of the Tiptons, bringing five children to the island. Fred's and Ameenie's son Jim wrote about the experience in his memoirs. He thinks his father had a religious commune in mind when he moved the family to Read Island, though this didn't transpire.

Ameenie Foort, a well-educated woman from Lebanon, was not raised as a farmer but her innate love of gardening helped her adapt to island life far better than her English husband Major Foort. PHOTO COURTESY OF JIM FOORT COLLECTION, MCR 19,481.

Islanders thought Major Foort had a private family income, but in fact his circumstances were quite the reverse. He did come from a wealthy English background, but with the death of his father the family fortune dissipated. Fred had to send five dollars a month—ten percent of his modest monthly pension of fifty dollars—to help his mother.

By 1927 sixteen children were ready to attend the new North End school. John Jones donated the land, inland from Surge Narrows and southwest of a junction now known as the Maple Triangle, and the community pitched in to build a log schoolhouse. The Tiptons' horses and oxen hauled the logs, and Ameenie Foort and her children helped gather and tamp moss chinking between the logs as weatherproofing. The chinking did little to keep out the chill winter winds, as Jim Foort still recalls. The students coveted the seats nearest the wood stove.

The two Foort families stayed only a few years. Their dreams of a wilderness life were unrealistic given their temperaments and backgrounds. The only ones who could have made it work were Ameenie Foort and

Clarence Keeling haying at Surge Narrows, on his aunt and uncle Tipton's farm.
PHOTO COURTESY OF WIN (KEELING) ROFF.

the kids. Though she was raised in a large city in the Middle East and spoke at least three languages, Ameenie had an innate love of farming. "While everything was bleak to the adults," wrote Jim Foort, "not so for us little kids." They revelled in their adventures on land and sea, but Major Foort, with his eccentric religious and philosophical ideas, was better suited to urban living. Their Read Island experiment ended when Major Foort and his brother had a falling-out and Stanley returned to England. The Major and Ameenie Foort family stayed with the Tiptons for the remainder of the school year and then moved to Quadra Island.[27]

The Redfords stayed for many years on their property to the north of the Tiptons. Like the Foort kids, the Redfords thought their new life was a grand adventure. But when their father realized how hard it would be to support his family on Read Island, he went back to the prairies in 1928 and got a good job. Charles came back to Read to get his family in 1929 just as the stock market crashed. He decided to hunker down on Read Island and wait out the Depression, but wound up raising his children there until they were grown. It was a happy fate for the Redford brothers, who loved the coast. One of them became a boat builder at a young age, the other a fisherman.

The increase in population around Surge Narrows resulted in two stores opening. Nell and Robert Tipton became storekeepers by happenstance, as their niece Win (Keeling) Roff recalls. Their neighbours often borrowed staples from them, as happened one day when Constable Dawson paid them a visit in 1927. "Do they ever repay you?" asked Dawson. "Sometimes, but not always," replied the Tiptons. "Why don't you open a store?" he asked. The Tiptons were surprised by the suggestion and refused at first, until Dawson explained how easy it was. He promptly filled out a five-dollar licence, and they were in business. The Tiptons started out small, converting the unfinished bathroom in their house into a store. The business rapidly grew, so they moved it into a cabin on skids on the beach below the house. In about 1935 they replaced this with a large store on pilings that remains on-site.[28]

Their neighbour Sid Frost also opened a store at about the same time, using the bedroom of his house near the government wharf in the

The class of 1928 in the island's first school included, front row: Isabelle Hayes, Paula Culbard, Diana Culbard in front of Stanley Wilson, Joyce Wilson (dark dress) and June Wilson. Second row: Georgina Wilson (corkscrew curls), Frank Culbard and unknown. Back row: Bill Whittington, Maud Hayes (tallest), Donald Wilson behind her, possibly Mrs. Eckman, unknown, Bonnie Whittington and Minnie Harrogen Natches. PHOTO COURTESY OF BILL WHITTINGTON COLLECTION, MCR 5691.

south end of the bay. On their coastal cruises, Francis and Amy Barrow enjoyed their stops at Frost's store, where customers could get a few conveniences. For larger items and perishables they went to Tipton's.

Schooling determined where the population centres developed on Read Island, and children and families built communities. As Robert Tipton demonstrated, a school is the lifeblood of a community, a place to gather and a service that sustains a youthful population. Read Islanders of today argue the same point in their ongoing battle to maintain their school.

Living Off the Land and Sea

Read Island's population reached an all-time high during the late 1920s and 1930s. In 1911 eighty-two people lived on the island, according to the census. The provincial directories for 1923 and 1931 both estimated the population at 110 people. By this time the island had three stores, two schools, and twice-weekly steamboat service with mail, passenger and freight delivery from Vancouver at a choice of two docks.

The blended Hayes-Lilburn family came to the island in 1927 in response to Tipton's school ad. The Culbards followed them in April 1929. The children from both families enrolled at the South End school, however, as a good trail connected southwest Read Island to Burdwood Bay. They walked to school with their teacher, who boarded on a nearby homestead, and in winter their hours were shortened to 9:30 a.m. to 3:00 p.m. to allow them to walk in daylight.

The Hayes-Lilburn farm was fairly well established when they arrived, with a bearing orchard of apples, pears, quinces, plums and cherries and a large hayfield that Harold Hayes cut with a scythe. There were lots of berries to can: raspberries, strawberries, loganberries, gooseberries and blackberries. The farm proved a Depression-era haven, as Isabelle (Hayes) Edgett recalls in her memoirs:

> There was always something to pick and make into jam, jelly or just can. For our meat there were fish, clams, grouse, deer and some of the neighbours who had cattle would butcher and we'd buy some. These were all canned too. The eggs were put down in a large container with isinglass, I think it was called. This kept the eggs fresh. We didn't have electricity so no freezers. Green beans were put in a large crock, a layer of sliced beans, then a layer of salt and kept on till the crock was full. Mum had a plate on top with a heavy rock to hold them down. When we wanted beans for dinner they were taken out the night before, well rinsed and then left in fresh cold water and cooked the next day and they tasted like fresh.
>
> Every Monday was wash day. We had a large copper boiler and it was filled the night before so we had enough hot water. The washing machine was a wooden tub with a wooden dolly on the lid that was turned by pushing up and down on a wooden handle that turned a large wheel and then the dolly. My brother Art would work the machine and read his western books. We had a hand wringer and two large galvanized tubs for rinsing. My job was turning the wringer and Mum put the clothes into it. Bluing was put in the last rinse to make the clothes whiter. We had two long clothes lines on pulleys from the

front porch. Mum made sure we pegged the clothes properly and in the right order—dish cloths, tea towels, pillow slips and sheets on the first line. Face cloths, towels, undies and clothes and lastly work clothes on the other one. In winter or rain we gradually brought them in and they were hung on a rack let down on pulleys from the ceiling in the kitchen near the stove.

Tuesday was spent ironing—sad irons we used—and they were heated on the good old wood kitchen stove. We always got at it early before it got hot. While I went to school Mum had that chore on her own.

Jim Spilsbury travelled the coast during the Depression, selling and servicing radios. He made a memorable sale to John Jones. The old man still continued his demanding routine as a farmer and postmaster for Surge Narrows, now a lively little community of about seventy people. Jones picked up the sacks of mail, weighed down with parcels at Christmas, and trundled them along the wearisome trail back to his home. There the Tiptons, the Frosts and Sid Mace had to follow him to retrieve their mail and bring it back to their homes at the Surge.

John and Florence Jones lost their first home to fire after lightning struck it. For their new house they hollowed out a basement in a rock outcrop and clad the upper storeys in tin moulded to look like rusticated stone. The house still stands a few kilometres inland from Surge Narrows.
PHOTO BY JEANETTE TAYLOR.

When Jones learned he could find out the expected time of arrival of the Union Steamship by radio, he sent word with Bill Frost to order a radio from young Spilsbury. The old man's neighbours speculated over whether Jones would actually invest in such a luxury and stood by while Spilsbury showed John Jones his wares. Spilsbury offered him a simple little radio that would suffice, but to everyone's surprise, Jones insisted upon a huge eight-tube RCA Victor model "with all the bells and whistles," including a big console cabinet. Jones, it seemed, had gotten wind of his neighbours' gossip and wanted to prove them wrong. Spilsbury borrowed a horse to haul the new radio in a travois up to the Joneses' farm. Florence Jones stood by in silence while Spilsbury tested the radio, filling their rustic house with music. But Jones wasn't interested in the music stations. He instructed Spilsbury to mark the tuner to the frequency used by the Union Steamship Company and leave it at that.

When John Jones bought the radio with $220 in small coins, it confirmed the general rumour that Jones had amassed a fortune. If he had, it was not evident in his lifestyle. Spilsbury described their metal-clad house in his autobiography. The living room, with bedding on the floor in one corner, was attached to a kitchen. A third room contained Jones's postal scales and mailbags and feed sacks for his livestock. Though Florence had become almost completely senile, John kept her at home until about 1940 when he was urged to institutionalize her. A few years later old John Jones's neighbours had to take him to hospital as well, where he died in 1942.

The rumours of Jones's hidden wealth grew over the years. He was said to have between twenty-five and fifty thousand dollars hidden somewhere in the house or property, but the lads who searched his place found nothing.

Sid and Marie Mace lived south of Tipton's store in a quaint little house that overlooked the sea at the Surge. Sid was a bachelor until 1926, when his brother died just before his mail-order fiancée was due to arrive in Vancouver, so Sid took his place.

Picnics and dances held at island schools brought together the unlikely mix that made up Read's population. Charlie Rosen was sure to be there, for he loved to dance to John Landers's fiddle. (John's Seventh

Day Adventist wife was sure he'd go to hell for his love of fiddle music and dancing.) The Read Island Musical Mariners were a popular band. Art Hayes played the drums, Kelly Landers and Jim Edgett took turns on an accordion, and violinists might include Milton Lilja, Ralph Edgett and Hugo Johanson.

In summer there were picnics with foot races and ball games in an orchard and meadow at what's now the Maple Triangle or on Dick Davis's big hayfield, now Harper's Landing in northern Evans Bay. For skating parties, in years when Rosen Lake froze, islanders strapped sharpened files to their boots as skates. A visitor who saw the Hayes-Lilburn kids skating on these sent them real skates of various sizes when she returned home to England.

Some women found their housebound isolation a trial, but not Mary Lambert of Evans Bay. A *Comox Argus* reporter happened upon Mary seated on the porch of her comfortable little home on a fall day in 1932. The reporter was charmed by Mary's old-fashioned flower garden,

Tom Widdowson and Bill Whittington identified many of the people in this photo of the Ekman's silver wedding anniversary on August 24, 1944. "The photo was in poor shape, and some of the faces were obscured, but still we could positively identify most of the old timers there," wrote Tom Widdowson. "As Bill said, 'If we both agree, who is left to argue with us?'"
PHOTO COURTESY OF SHEILA FOORT COLLECTION, MCR.

loaded with marigolds, daisies, dahlias and a few gladiolas. The reporter asked about loneliness, and Mary said she'd never live in the city. "Why should we? We have everything to make us contented here and we are not so isolated as one should imagine, with a telephone line across the island, which comes in handy in case of illness."

This convenient telephone system, using cast-off hand-crank phones Art Lilburn salvaged from another community, was hooked up around the island. "Each family had a letter in Morse Code," recalls Isabelle (Hayes) Edgett, "so we rang shorts and longs." Everyone knew who was receiving calls, and at times so many people listened in that the line grew weak. For off-island calls, Read Islanders had to row across to Bold Point or Heriot Bay on Quadra Island or to Whaletown on Cortes.

The Lamberts seemed to be dogged by tragedy. In the fall of 1939 John Lambert took a small group across to Campbell River by boat to visit his daughter-in-law Winnie in hospital. With him was his infant grandchild Ron and several neighbours, including teenaged Maud Landers. Tom Widdowson, whose mother Katharine was on board, described her experience:

> The boat was a covered inboard speedboat with an uncovered engine. Off Cape Mudge, the old man slumped over the wheel, dead of a heart attack. Maud and my mother did not know he was dead. Maud held the baby with one hand and steered the boat with the other. My mother tried to hold the old man off the hot engine, which brought her close to a leaking exhaust manifold and she passed out (fortunately not falling on the engine herself.) Maud now thought she had two corpses on her hands. She got the boat turned around towards Heriot Bay. She could steer, but did not know how to stop it. She chose a sandy spot in Drew Harbour and ran it on the beach. Her boyfriend, Jack MacMeagan, who happened to be walking by, got on the boat and stopped it. My mother was out for six hours but finally came to.

The Lamberts' upper-crust neighbour Stephen K. Marshall, of eastern Read Island, hired carpenter Harold Hayes to build him a fine new house in 1938 in readiness for his sister, who he hoped would immigrate from England. It had four bedrooms upstairs, a big parlour, a den and a kitchen with a pass-through opening to the formal dining room. The

Stephen Marshall, an English gentleman with family money, had a fine house built on his farm on southeast Read Island in readiness for his sister's arrival. After she left the island, he used only the dining room and bathroom in the big house, preferring his cabin on the beach among his books.
PHOTO COURTESY OF MILTON LILJA COLLECTION, MCR 5609.

house also had the unspeakable luxury of a full bathroom, and Marshall had the house fully wired for electricity, though there was no power source to hook into.

Stephen was a bachelor, one of four or five British expatriates on the island who had family money. He enjoyed farming, and as Tom Widdowson recalls "he was a mean hand sharpening and using a scythe and a cross-cut bucking saw." Stephen had help from various farmhands, including Milton and Edith Lilja. Edith, who was English, knew how to prepare meals to Stephen's taste and lay the table with cutlery and linen. Milton tended the livestock, orchard and hayfield.

Stephen's sister arrived as hoped, but she wasn't impressed and returned to England after a short stay. Stephen promptly moved back into his little bachelor shack on the beach, where books lined the walls. Thereafter he used the big house only for his weekly bath and evening meals, beautifully laid out by Edith.

Stephen maintained a turbulent friendship with a difficult character from similar circumstances. Walter Maclean bought the old Edgar Wiley property, including the farm and the hotel, which he transformed into a comfortable home. He was a self-focussed man who lorded it over his neighbours, flaunting the comfort of his family income. Some said he was a remittance man, paid a generous sum to stay away from home in Britain. He made himself unpopular with island children when he barb-wired off the old trail that cut through his farm field, making their walk to the South End school much longer.

Worse still, he somehow won the affections of Leta Whittington. Tom Widdowson recalled hearing that when Maclean first came to Read Island, he thought it would be fun to seduce his religious neighbour's sixteen-year-old daughter, "only to find that she was rather more than he bargained for." Leta eventually turned her affections elsewhere and moved to Nanaimo, and in the late 1940s Maclean moved to Vancouver. "At first he drove a fancy car and lived high off the hog," recalls Tom Widdowson, "but later fell on hard times and went to work in the post office."

Read Island families supported themselves in various ways. Many logged, but some earned their keep by fishing. There were fish-buying stations scattered around the coast, including Surge Narrows, where Robert Tipton became a fish buyer during World War II. There was a strong wartime market for cod and dogfish livers, which were rendered into a vitamin supplement for the troops. Tipton paid sixty-three cents a pound for cod livers and twenty-three cents for dogfish livers.

Relatively few island men enlisted in World War II because they worked in services that were considered essential, including farming, logging and fishing. A Vancouver writer named John Cowper (signing himself JSC) wrote about Read Island. He had some property on an island in Hoskyn Inlet, so when he was refused for war service work in 1943, he moved to Read Island. "Circumstances within the last three months introduced this correspondent to an agreeable mode of life—independent, generous and alluring," wrote Cowper. "It's the life of the coastal rancher."

John Cowper stayed with a bachelor neighbour for a week before settling in at his homestead. The neighbour enjoyed his company and invited Cowper to stay for the winter as a paying guest at two dollars per week board. "You couldn't possibly board me for $2 per week," Cowper protested. In reply the man took him to the cooler at the back of his house where he had a fine buck hanging, along with rows of bottled vegetables, sacks of potatoes and carrots, and a line of smoked salmon. "We've got everything we need here for the winter," the neighbour told him. "I lived better during that week," wrote Cowper, "than ever I have done in the city."

The theme of Cowper's article was the incredible thrift of island ranchers. One settler's wife canned eight hundred quart sealers of fruit, vegetables, fish and meat. Another put up five hundred quart and half-gallon sealers. One family of three lived on thirteen dollars per month while another, with six in the family, lived on forty dollars per month. The property tax on Cowper's forty-hectare (hundred-acre) island in "the rapids"—where he had a cabin, orchard and hay meadow—was seven dollars per year.

Some families lived on pensions, wrote John Cowper, like Benjamin and Katharine Widdowson. Benjamin had an Oxford University degree in theology and chemistry, and Katharine was working on a degree in French and English literature when they were married. "He was a Church of England minister," recalls their son Tom, "with three parishes in England—but he didn't like being told what to do." In 1939 Benjamin's search for freedom brought the couple with their son Tom to Read Island to live on Katharine's small family income. They had a mentally handicapped daughter, Mary, while living on Read.

The Widdowsons were brilliant if eccentric. Benjamin translated the Bible for his own use and published his treatise, *An Outline of Lay Sanctity*. He taught their son Tom at home after the South End school closed in 1941. The school opened briefly in the late 1940s and then closed again for good. Tom went on to get his doctorate and taught at the University of Victoria and in California, New Zealand and Hong Kong.

Several more Seventh Day Adventist families followed the Lamberts to Read Island, including the Betts and two Japanese Canadian families, the Tanakas and the Ishiis. Forrest Lambert married Raiko Tanaka just months before the bombing of Pearl Harbour. Raiko (Tanaka) Lambert was allowed to remain with her husband—"though some thought that she would lead the Japanese Imperial Navy to bomb Read Island," recalls

Tom Widdowson. "The rest of the Tanaka family, probably because of their Seventh Day Adventist connections, were allowed to move to Alberta." The Ishiis were recent arrivals at Steamboat Bay and didn't have useful connections, recalls Tom, so when the government removed all Japanese Canadians from the coast as a war measure, they were interned in prison-like camps in the BC Interior.

Another scholar who moved to the island about a decade later was Mr. Albert Taylor, who liked to be addressed formally as Mr. Taylor. He had a master's degree in applied physics and specialized as an electrical engineer with a particular interest in radio electronics. His father also was a scientist, a professor of physics who was one of the inventors of radar. Mr. Taylor's family recall he worked only briefly in his profession, spending the remainder of his life dabbling in scientific research. He had a lifelong plan to write about his youthful travels in Europe, based upon his journals written in a variety of languages. He tried various back-to-the-land retreats in the US and eventually landed on Read Island, where he hoped the lifestyle would allow him time to write. But as it happened, his enjoyment of his country retreat was sufficient unto itself. Gardening and clam digging became his passions. Though he continued to carry out some experimentation and write for journals, a book never materialized.

Taylor's family think he hoped to establish a Decentralist community, based on Ralph Borsodi's book *This Ugly Civilization*, on Read Island. Taylor's daughter Sally Carter has her father's voluminous journals, including his entries from his early years on Read:

> I have now been an immigrant to Canada for a month. While not by any means settled or even finished moving my impedimenta hither, I have bought about 120 acres of Lot 780 and am camped in a shocking disorder of my gear in an open shed behind the house, my bed in a loft over the roothouse, pending completion of Mr. Symons' new cottage on the beach. . . . My approach, really my original principle to which I have but returned, is different and is the only one for me: NO DEBT! Regardless of what I have to give up for years or forever. Proletarian employment is in the long run intolerable, but I have found no other way of guaranteeing monetary income even to the precarious extent that the proletarian's income is guaranteed.

Mr. Taylor's wife and two children chose not to join him on Read Island, though his son and daughter visited during the summers. He was on his own a lot but he was no recluse. Taylor loved to visit and chat at length whenever someone was about.

Isabelle Hayes, Jim Edgett and some friends visited Mr. Taylor soon after he came to the island, and stopped at his garden gate in amazement. Classical music blared out from the trees where Mr. Taylor had hooked up speakers tuned into CBC Radio, but Mr. Taylor was nowhere to be seen. The group headed up to the garden in search of him, but Isabelle's friend held her back, saying they'd better let the men go on alone. True to her prediction, Mr. Taylor was happily at work in his garden wearing nothing but a pair of gumboots. In later years Taylor posted a sign at the head of his trail, Danger Man in the Buff Ahead. "He was quite a sight, bent over in the garden in nothing but his gumboots," recalls Brian Stevenson, who knew Taylor in the 1970s.

In 1949, with the South End school closed and the old log schoolhouse near Surge Narrows no longer fit to serve its fifteen children, a Quonset hut was erected as a new school on the edge of a field behind the Tiptons' store. The building, reminiscent of an airplane hangar with its arched roof of corrugated galvanized steel, still stands. "The interior is bright and roomy," said the *Campbell River Courier* when the school opened. "Large windows are flanked on either end by alaynite glass taking up an entire wall. Blackboards and built-in-cupboards cover the front and one side wall of the room." The school also had a cloakroom and "a modern washroom."

Dick Whittington, whose parents had both attended the old South End school in their day, rode his cantankerous horse several kilometres across the island to attend school at Surge Narrows. His father cleared a trail so he could go through the marsh in the centre of the island to connect with the public road. Thirty-six kids attended the school when Dick started there at the age of seven. He was already reading, thanks to Stephen Marshall's extensive library.

Many islanders supported themselves as loggers through the 1950s and 1960s, when the island's population hovered at about a hundred people. Changes to the school system requiring children to go beyond the grade eight education available on the island, though, forced some families to leave, including the Whittingtons. A new wave of settlers, the hippie generation, followed them. Over the next two decades, co-op groups purchased some of the island's early farms.

Mr. Taylor—and the others who stuck it out on the island after the population began to drop—welcomed these newcomers, while on nearby Quadra Island, long-haired youths met intense suspicion. Read Islanders, with a long history of embracing counterculture, readily accepted young men like John Toelle and his group of friends from Washington state, who built a squatter's cabin in Burdwood Bay. Toelle was joined a few years later by Ann, who fell in love with both the man and his lifestyle.

Most of these newcomers were city kids who revelled in the experience of living off the land and sea. The Toelles raised pigs and chickens, kept a large garden and ate lots of fish and seafood. "I even made head

John Toelle and his friends were among the wave of new residents who settled on Read Island in the 1970s. The island's population had dropped so low that many—but not all—islanders welcomed the long-haired youths. PHOTO COURTESY OF ANN AND JOHN TOELLE.

cheese," recalls Ann, "the first year we butchered a pig, canning it all, of course, because we had no refrigeration." Older residents like Marie Wilson at Evans Bay dock and long-time resident Alvina Poitras taught the young people how to can, salt and preserve food. When the Toelles made a trip to Vancouver, they'd stock up on staples, buying huge blocks of cheese Ann dipped in wax to preserve for later use.

A few of the long-time residents who stayed, like Louis Poitras, were models of adaptability and resourcefulness. When Harper Graham transported some calves to the island for Louis, he wondered how he would get them home. Louis arrived at Harper's Landing on his motorcycle and placed two or three calves at a time straddling his bike.

A few stores still operated on the island. Marie and Reg Wilson had a few things for sale in the living room of their house at the Evans Bay dock. The Dodmans had a well-stocked store on the former Tipton property in Surge Narrows, where you could buy all the basics, recalls Ann. For a few years they even had a gas dock, post office and liquor licence.

John Toelle went on from his first squatter's shack to build several more cabins, launching a successful career in construction. His main clients were people building summer homes on Read and elsewhere. "In those days," recalls Ann, "all we needed was about $500 and we'd be set for the winter."

Mr. Taylor stands out in Ann's memories as an island character. He wanted to buy one of Ann's chickens and showed up unexpectedly early one morning, waving an ancient frying pan loaded with grime and a jar of pancake batter to make them breakfast. It wasn't very appealing, says Ann, but a kind gesture.

Fern Kornelsen of Sonora Island also visited the old man, who had taken to wearing a battered hard helmet—to protect him from the falling timbers in his mouldering cabin, he said. Others said he took to a helmet to protect the bald spot on his head. As Fern recalls, Mr. Taylor had a long piece of PVC pipe sticking out through his front door. Before he could open the door he had to haul in his "pecker extender," his version of indoor plumbing.

An influx of new residents with kids on the west side of the island, and in the Okisollo area in general, led to the construction of a new school with an attached community hall that doubled as a gymnasium, and the two-room primary school. It took six years of wrangling to make it a "community school" embracing a different lifestyle from what school board officials in Campbell River considered the norm. "Islanders were intent on taking on the responsibility of construction," reported a Campbell River newspaper. In the end they reached a compromise with an outside contractor who agreed to hire locals. The school opened in 1989 with thirty-three students and two teachers, George Mann and Eileen O'Reilly.

George Mann, a much-loved teacher, stayed with the school for many years, though the enrollment steadily declined as young families gave up on the isolated lifestyle when their kids reached high-school age.

"I found it really hard to be on my own so much," says Ann Toelle, "after I had Marshall." She could hop on her motorcycle with her baby to go to the Moms and Tots gatherings on the island, but it was a long ride and ultimately unworkable. "I needed to be around other mothers with kids," says Ann. Ann and John moved their family to Quadra Island.

Marnie Andrews and Mike Bullock and their sons bought the old John and Florence Jones property in the 1990s and revived its orchard and gardens. The one-lane road to their place passed through a dense forest of fir trees and giant maples, saved by a community association to protect two salmon-bearing streams. From there the road continues through a stretch of broken rock and scrub alder on a large cut block that was only partially replanted.

Mike and Marnie were seasoned coastal folks, having lived for many years on Haida Gwaii, but it was too hard to get enough work on Read, so they moved to Cortes. Their experience has been repeated over the years, contributing to a fluctuating population and a continual fight to maintain a minimum enrollment at the school. A new teacher of the past few years has attracted children—who were being home-schooled—back to the Surge Narrows School. The school had an enrollment of thirteen in the fall of 2007 and a flexible four-days-a-week schedule.

When the census was compiled in 2006, sixty-two people lived on Read Island in thirty private households. The majority of residents were adults, but in a place where daily life requires hard work, no one was over sixty-five.

Some long-term residents have created their own employment, like Ralph and Lanny Keller, who turned an old homestead and logging site in the head of Evans Bay into a wilderness lodge. They offer mountaineering and kayaking trips from this and another lodge on northern Quadra Island. From their start with a few kayaks that Ralph made, Coast Mountain Expeditions now employs five guides plus other staff.

Minke de Vos opened a Taoist centre in Evans Bay about twenty years ago. At Silent Ground she offers week-long programs through the summer in Chi Kung, meditation and yoga. Others make a living from oyster leases or work off-island seasonally. Brenda Dempsey, along with her husband Rieko Sevigny, run a reiki retreat on a communally owned property on southwest Read Island.

The island has several large woodlots, small logging operations wholly managed by individuals, from planting and thinning to harvest.

Teresa and Doug Beyerstein kept the Surge Narrows Store open until 1997, clinging to an island tradition more than economic gain. A note on the chalkboard outside the store in 2007 said "we are closed for good."
PHOTO BY KEITH GUNNAR.

The Surge Narrows Store in 2007. PHOTO BY JEANETTE TAYLOR.

One belongs to third-generation Read Islanders Dick Whittington and Dorothy (Whittington) Nord. Another belongs to Harper Graham of Quadra Island. Harper logged on the island for Raven Lumber of Campbell River and then bought his own land in Evans Bay. As required, he added about sixty hectares (150 acres) of his own land to a woodlot of about 1,300 hectares (3,200 acres). Until the downturn in the logging sector in 2008, he cut about twenty-three thousand metres (seventy-five thousand feet) per year and kept about six employees at work, including three who live on Read Island.

With Surge Narrows just a twenty-minute boat ride away from a new dock on northern Quadra, it's hard for Read Island to maintain its own services. A population of a similar size eighty years ago had two or three stores and two schools, but Doug and Theresa Beyerstein had to close the old Surge Narrows Store in 2007. "Yes, the time has come," said a chalkboard sign at the front door. "We are closed for good. Thank you for your caring." In an age-old (if gender-reversed) pattern, Theresa now works as a first-aid attendant in northern BC while Doug maintains the home front.

Many full-time residents on Read Island bought or inherited their land long before the current real-estate boom. The culture of their community—maintained for many generations—embraces an alternative lifestyle, removed from consumerism and mainstream society. People from away sometimes misunderstand the social statement embodied in recycled clothing. Well-meaning yachters returned the next year with boxes of clothing for people they thought were needy.

But there are hints of change on the horizon. On all the islands the rarified real estate market threatens the life of a "working coast." This is magnified in a small community, where two old homesteads (one of them undeveloped) were listed for sale in 2008 at well over a million dollars.

For now life continues in an appealing blend of high ideals, individualism and a quest for meaning. The Read Island Book Club won a province-wide Canada Reads contest from among sixty entries. Up to thirty islanders read and discuss books in a wide range of genres. They've been meeting for twenty-five years. "In Surge Narrows, the VHF radio is busy on a book club Sunday morning," says their winning entry. Members arrange for rides and plan rotating locales for their gatherings to suit the season and the tides. "There are two sets of tidal rapids to pass to get to Renate's place so we must schedule that for a day of small tides with convenient slack times. We always go to Jeannie's in August so that, for most of the meeting, we can sit nude in the natural pool below the waterfall on the creek. We've learned to avoid Jenn's house when the outflow winds from Bute Inlet clog her bay with driftwood and the steep waves guarantee a wet-footed landing on the beach."

While the general lifestyle on Read Island is a holdout from a previous era, it could also be considered the cutting edge of change. The café and armchair talk among urbanites about ways to reduce one's carbon footprint is a quiet reality for many on Read Island.

CHAPTER TWO

Cortes, Marina, Hernando, Twin, Subtle and Mitlenatch Islands

Ritual Purification

THE WOMAN ON THE PAY PHONE AT THE CORTES MARKET WAVES an arm as she talks in a voice too loud to ignore. She has no intention of keeping her conversation private. "You can't believe this place!" she exclaims. "The people here are so cool, and it's so beautiful." The breathless intensity of her voice drives the point home. She may well move to the island, as she declares to her friend, but more likely she'll join the throngs who double the island's population in summer.

Cortes and its satellite islands—Marina, Hernando, Twin, Subtle and Mitlenatch—are indeed precious gems. Their tranquil haven seems far removed from the evils of an ailing planet. Cortes is the largest of these islands. It is about twenty-five kilometres (sixteen miles) long and has a permanent population of nearly a thousand. Many of the smaller islands are now in private hands as holiday retreats, and distant Mitlenatch Island is a bird sanctuary.

The majority of Cortesians live on the balmy southern end of the island. The annual rainfall is relatively low here, due to the rain-shadow effect that causes much of the rainfall to drop closer to the mountains of the mainland and Vancouver Island. Groves of heat-loving arbutus and manzanita trees overhang rock bluffs, and the sandy beaches on the western shores are loaded with farmed oysters. The tranquility of these islands has a soothing effect that's long been an attraction. Some residents, like 1890s settler Henry Hague, came for the healthful climate;

others, like contemporary author-activist Ruth Ozeki, came to visit a new friend and fell in love with him and his island home.

In February 2005, on a day of drifting fog and bird calls, we visited Channel Rock, the late Gilean Douglas's property. Douglas based her poetry and non-fiction on her observations of the seasons, birds, plants and animals of the coast. Thanks to restrictive covenants she placed upon her exceptional waterfront property, it remains much as she left it.

We made our way from Gilean's abandoned cabin on a rock bluff to her garden, where the current owners have built cottages and workshops. A young couple with great twists of dreadlocked hair, the winter caretakers, served us mugs of stinging-nettle tea. Their cob house, made from a mixture of straw and plaster, was built by a team of local craftspeople. It looks elegantly simple, but the project was complex. Below are a sauna built from log rounds set into plaster and a solar-powered outdoor shower skirted in elegant panels of woven twigs.

Channel Rock now belongs to a Washington state family that operates a college on Bainbridge Island where students develop eco-friendly and environmentally sustainable business strategies. Some classes come to Channel Rock to complement their studies. The college's philosophy is akin to that of the Hollyhock educational retreat across the island, where weary visitors rest their souls and engage in therapeutic workshops. Idealism runs high in both these places, buoyed by the sense of removal from the mainstream.

But other realities sometimes intrude. Just days before our visit at Channel Rock, three young Sliammon men pleaded guilty to harvesting clams on a Cortes Island beach. It seems the men had the appropriate licences, but some of their sacks weren't properly tagged. Leon Timothy received a two-hundred-dollar fine, while Charles Timothy and Dean Louie got eighteen-month harvesting bans. According to the *Powell River Peak*, these men support their families through marine harvesting as their people have done for thousands of years. "I think I should be allowed to dig clams on my own beaches," said Dean Louie, who couldn't afford to pay his two-hundred-dollar fine.

Dean Louie's people have a reserve called Paukeanam on the southwest shore of Cortes, though their current home village lies many kilometres to the south near Powell River. Their possession of this distant reserve hearkens back to a time when the Sliammon population was much larger. Anthropologist Homer Barnett, who interviewed elders in the 1930s, speculated that the Sliammon were once so numerous they encompassed two large groups spread over a vast territory.[29]

The Sliammon are closely related to two other groups. The Klahoose live on the east coast of Cortes at Squirrel Cove, and the Xwemalhkwu (Homalco) lived until recent years near Bute Inlet. Ethnographers have assigned the name Mainland Comox to these three groups to recognize their close linguistic and cultural ties. As the northernmost of the Salishan speakers, they also have ties with groups to the south.

The eastern Discovery Islands and adjacent inlets have been home to the Mainland Comox for thousands of years, as shown by the depth of their clamshell middens (refuse piles) at Carrington Bay, Mansons Landing, Gorge Harbour, Paukeanam, Squirrel Cove and Smelt Bay. Mainland Comox legends provide a glimpse into a complex society with a richly developed belief system based upon the elements, plants and animals of this coast. In spring, villagers divided into family groups to gather and preserve food. They dug and dried clams at Mansons Landing, and fished for salmon and hunted seals off Marina Island. They picked berries along the streams that feed into Whaletown Bay and Gorge Harbour, gathered soapberries (soopollalie) on Subtle Island, hunted ducks and deer on the shores of Gunflint Lake, and fished for cod and herring in Von Donop Inlet.

The supernatural world of the Mainland Comox was ruled by beings who inhabited the sky, land and sea. A mythic serpent and an eagle-like bird that brought thunder and lighting could wreak havoc upon humans or bestow incredible strength and prowess. It was possible to meet these beings during sleep, as the human soul travelled, or through the more determined effort of rigorous purification, fasting and bathing. However the encounter transpired, it took tremendous courage not to flee or shun such a visitation, for there was much to fear. The serpent could knock its beholder unconscious and cause bleeding from every orifice. On the other hand, it could endow heightened powers as a hunter or fisher and give songs and other talismans of magic guardianship.

According to a tale anthropologist Franz Boas recorded in 1886, the Sliammon people's use of Cortes Island reaches deep into the mythic past, when magic ancestors could change at will between human and animal form. A girl rejected such a man, Tlaō'k·ōk·t, so he tempted her with chewing pitch. The girl was wary but sent her sister to receive the pitch, given on the condition that the girl swallow it. That night the girl awoke with a swelling belly, and when her father discovered she was pregnant, he ordered all his people to abandon her. He told P'a (Raven) to extinguish all the fires before leaving, but the girl's grandmother, T'Ets (Crow), took pity on her and hid a glowing coal in a shell so she would have fire for cooking and warmth.

In due course the girl gave birth to seven puppies, six males and one female. Whenever she went to the beach to dig clams, she could hear her children's noisy play back in the house. Sometimes they sounded almost human so she crept up to the house, and indeed, as she had suspected, they had cast aside their dog skins to frolic in human form. She dashed in and threw their dog skins into the fire, where all were destroyed.[30]

Now the children were permanently transformed into humans, and as such they pledged to care for their mother. The girl said she would weave capes for her family, the eldest son offered to hunt deer, the second to hunt seals and the third to be a whaler. Each had something to offer.

One day the eldest brother, wearing a feather cape made by his sister, grew tired from hunting and went to sleep on a small island. The Sun descended from the sky and offered to exchange capes with the boy. "If you are hungry, dip the corner of the cape into the water and shake it a bit. Thereupon many salmon will come." The Sun climbed back into the sky, and thereafter the woman and her children became very wealthy.

The dog children were young adults when T'Ets came back to see how her granddaughter had fared. She was well received and given lavish presents, including seal blubber that she took home. As she roasted some of this blubber, Flea happened upon her and learned that T'Ets's granddaughter had become very wealthy. The news spread through the village, and the girl's father decided they should pay her a visit. P'a was the first ashore and ran into his former home, now occupied by one of the dog children. P'a was sent away from this and every other house he entered, for the children knew he had extinguished all the fires. They gave him nothing but red snapper to eat, so he made himself a herring rake and went fishing, but the eldest brother caused reefs to form wherever P'a dipped his rake into the sea. Thus P'a came home empty-handed, and "since that time the sea to the north-east of Cape Mudge," said the storyteller, "has been full of reefs." And this is how the eldest brother became the ancestor of the Tlaā́men [Sliammon] people.[31]

Many sites along the west coast of Cortes bear traces of these long-ago people. The narrow entrance to Gorge Harbour was a place of great significance. On the sheer rock face of the northwestern shore are intriguing painted figures, including a double row of ten marks that suggests tallies. Nearby are a whale or fish and human forms; one of these has sunburst rays around its head, and another has arrow-like projections suspended above it. On the opposite shore lie the terraces of a former village below a rocky promontory overlooking Sutil Channel. To one side, a jumble of massive rock slabs forms interconnected caverns where ferns and trailing vines overhang burial sites plundered in the last century.

Ned Breeze, who homesteaded at Gorge Harbour a century ago, saw skeletons laid out in boxes in these caverns. Some still bore traces of hair and clothing. Another early resident, a medical student named Charles Marlatt, found the skeleton of a female with a fully grown fetus within her pelvis on a small island at the Gorge. Over the years tourists and souvenir hunters have removed all of these human remains.

The Mainland Comox lost hundreds of people to smallpox a decade before the 1792 arrival of British and Spanish explorers. The pandemic started in Mexico and spread across North America, killing an estimated ninety percent of the aboriginal population. Historical geographer Cole Harris, referring to oral history and early exploration accounts, speculates the disease stopped among the Discovery Islands. To the north of this region, on the frontier of Salish territory, lived the Lekwiltok, who have close ties to the Kwakwala speakers of northern Vancouver Island.

The Lekwiltok had numeric advantage over the Mainland Comox. They also got guns from Europeans through trading connections at Nootka

Sound long before their southern neighbours. Armed Lekwiltok warriors travelled as far south as Juan de Fuca Strait to take slaves to sell to northern Native groups for European goods. To protect themselves, the Mainland Comox built elaborate defensive sites and later retreated deep into the mainland inlets of their territories.

Deep hollows in the field at Smelt Bay Park are house depressions from a Mainland Comox village, where houses were buried to the rafters and covered with bark and earth to keep them from view. As further protection, some houses had escape tunnels into the surrounding forest.[32]

There are other signs of a prolonged period of warfare on Cortes Island. Palisades and trenches defended the seasonal village at Mansons Landing, which had vast clam beds.[33] At Gorge Harbour, the Native people kept rocks piled on the cliff top to throw at enemies below. A Klahoose elder of the 1890s spoke of a retaliatory attack upon old enemies from the north—probably the Lekwiltok—whom they invited to a meeting at

Old George McGee and his family spent parts of the year at Paukeanam ("place where the maple leaves turn brown"), a reserve on the southwest coast of Cortes Island.
PHOTO COURTESY OF CORTES ISLAND MUSEUM COLLECTION, MAY ELLINGSEN COLLECTION, MCR 19,328.

the Gorge. When they were seated at the agreed place, the Cortes people used slingshots made from vines to hurl rocks at them.[34]

Old George McGee, born in about 1850, was the survivor of several slave-taking raids. When he was about seven, George's family camped on the southern tip of the island, where they were attacked just before dawn. George escaped to the bushes and hid. When he returned, all that remained of his family were headless torsos, a sight that haunted him for the rest of his life.[35]

The Klahoose people were a proud, generous and wealthy nation, as shown in an early account of their rescue of a survey party en route to Bute Inlet in 1861. "Indians from a distant tribe" boarded the surveyor's canoe with hostile intentions in Homfray Channel. As the surveyors readied themselves for the worst, a loud "war-whoop" rang out across the water, wrote survey leader Robert Homfray. "On looking behind us we saw a tall powerful Indian standing in his canoe waving his paddles in the air and calling out loudly." At the approach of this chief, the attackers fled. The Klahoose chief took the surveyors up a river to his encampment, where he fed them mountain sheep, beaver and bear meat. The chief and his people later came to their rescue again when the surveyors returned from Bute Inlet starved and in need of help.

In 1862–64 smallpox swept the coast again, this time reaching all Native groups. An estimated fifteen thousand people died. George McGee somehow survived, though as he told his friend John Manson later in life, he remembered seeing his relatives throw themselves into the ocean to quell the awful fever of smallpox. Some of them died on the beaches. Before smallpox, said McGee, the "beach was black with Indians." Afterward few remained. Mass graves, like one full of infants' and children's bones found many years later above Mansons Landing,[36] may relate to this tragic period. With a decreased population the Klahoose stayed in Toba Inlet during the late nineteenth century. They used their former village sites on Cortes sporadically, and all the Mainland Comox congregated in winter in "super villages" for protection at Grace Harbour—just inside Okeover Inlet on the mainland—and later at the Sliammon Creek village near Powell River.

In 1888, when Indian Agent George Blenkinsop set reserve boundaries, the Mainland Comox said attacks by the Lekwiltok had stopped. Blenkinsop took a census of the three Native groups, estimating their combined population at 189. He noted they lived in relative isolation from non-Native settlements, keeping them "from being contaminated by the evils to which those living nearer civilization have been exposed."

This insularity would change in less than a decade with the arrival of non-Native settlers, and the effects would plummet a rich people into poverty.

Whaletown and Gorge Harbour: The Early Years of Non-Native Settlement

The first Euro-Canadian activity in the Discovery Islands was in 1869, when whalers built a try-works to render the fat from whale blubber in large kettles on a site west of the present-day ferry landing in Whaletown. The Dawson Whaling Company of Victoria hunted whales throughout the Strait of Georgia.

Abel Douglas, working with his crew on the schooner *Kate*, sent reports to an eager audience in Victoria. On August 11, 1869 they killed three whales. In September they launched three "bombs," striking a whale that circled and went down before rising again to thrust its head onto the boat and pull it down. "All hands swam for their lives," reported Douglas. The whalers recovered their overturned boat and returned to the schooner to tow the whale to the try-works in Whaletown. There the blubber—used to make soap, tallow, cooking fat, candles and lubricants—was stripped from the whale. On September 17, the *Kate* returned to Victoria with 150 barrels of oil from fourteen whales.

Whalers, without restrictions or seasons, quickly fished out the Strait of Georgia. In the winter of 1870 they relocated the Whaletown station, and in another few years the Dawson Whaling Company went broke.

Logging was the next industry. Retired British army officer Captain H.E. Sturt of Nanaimo explored the Cortes Island area in search of timber and minerals in 1876. What he saw impressed him. The dense stands of massive Douglas fir on steep shorelines could be felled directly into the sea. Sturt needed a partner who knew logging, so in 1884 he teamed up with Moses Cross Ireland.

Ireland sold timber-cruising information (his expert opinion on the location and value of forest tracts) to entrepreneurs like Captain Sturt, R.D. Merrill of Washington state and W.P. Sayward of Victoria. He also ran his own camps,[37] starting in the mid-1880s, from his Cortes Island base. In 1889 he registered for a government pre-emption, taking over the site of the Dawson Whaling Company's old try-works in Whaletown.

Ireland was a larger-than-life character, raised in logging country in Maine. He had energy, courage and drive. Accounts of his rescues and near escapes appeared in provincial newspapers from his earliest years in BC, when he joined the Cariboo gold rush in 1861. His rescue of a group of miners lost in a blizzard is a gold-mining legend. Ireland and his friends left the diggings late that season. They were struggling through whiteout conditions when they happened upon men, women and children huddled together in a circle to stay warm. Ireland, with his innate bush sense, walked through the night until he found the nearest settlement and then returned for the group, carrying a fourteen-year-old girl to safety on his back.

With his gold earnings Ireland went into sawmilling at Moodyville in Burrard Inlet with his friend Sewell Moody, but gave up that chancy business to run freight on the Skeena River. In his early fifties he returned to logging and moved to Cortes Island.

Most loggers were single men involved in a hard-living, tough-talking man's world without the regulating influence of women and families. In this brawny atmosphere it was all too easy to squander wages on gambling and whiskey sold illegally by coastal traders. Loggers lived in temporary shanties and—as long as the grub was plentiful and good—endured cramped living quarters, hard cots, the persistent itch of bedbugs and dangerous work. Accidents were commonplace and often fatal. Injured men were rowed to the nearest doctor in Comox or Nanaimo. Most died en route. A near miss in William Blaney's Cortes Island camp was reported in a Victoria newspaper of 1889.[38] C.W. Birdsell was working on a boom of logs when he fell in with thirty-six kilograms (eighty pounds) of chain slung across his shoulder. His brave co-worker Fred Childs dove in, unhooked the chains from Birdsell and pulled him to the surface.

By the early 1890s a few other settlers joined Moses Ireland in what they called Whale Bay. They included bachelor Joseph Yowart in the northeastern corner in today's Huck Road area. To his south were Samuel Thompson and Poker Bill Robertson.

Some of these early loggers and settlers stayed on Cortes from spring through fall and went to Nanaimo or Victoria in winter. During a winter sojourn Moses Ireland met Julia Ward, a widow from Tennessee with two children. They married in Victoria in 1888, but for the first few years Julia remained in Victoria and worked as a seamstress. Julia's seventeen-year-old daughter Celia was the first to join Moses at his Whaletown camp, sent there in shame with a child born out of wedlock in 1890. The next year she married forty-year-old Poker Bill Robertson of Whaletown, a man known as a competent logger but an irascible drunk.

It may have been a need to be closer to her daughter Celia that finally brought Julia and her son Bernard to Whaletown permanently in 1892. The start of the Union Steamship Company's freight and passenger service from Vancouver that year also made the island more attractive.

Moses purchased and pre-empted various properties around Whaletown in the 1890s. In 1893 he relocated his family to Subtle Island, then called Camp Island. There he and Julia opened the Alhambra Hotel,[39] which included a saloon and store. They cleared land for an orchard, and the place became a lively headquarters for loggers who stayed at Irelandville between jobs.

In 1894 logging partners William "Drink" Drinkwater and Lawrence Rose opened a small store and post office in their home on the south side of the bay to the east of what's now the government dock. As both men were logging, William Drinkwater's wife Laura likely presided over the store and post office. Rumours of Laura's show-girl past impressed schoolgirl Rose (Ward) McDonald. She recalled the Drinkwaters had an impressive library in their "rickety" house when she and a friend stayed the night. Laura gave them satin and lace nightgowns to wear, a luxury that bordered on naughtiness.

When William Rose and the Drinkwaters left Cortes in 1897, Poker Bill and Celia Robertson took over the Whaletown store and post office. In the mid-1890s Robertson also had a rock quarry at the west entrance to Cortes Bay, then called Blind Bay, where he cut rose-coloured stone into building blocks.

Celia's young life was in tragic ruin by the time she and her husband took over the store. She died two years later "from the effects of a prolonged drunk," as her death certificate states. Moses and Julia Ireland adopted Celia's nine-year-old daughter Sadie (or Sarah Orline), and Bill gave over management of the store and post office to his friend Charlie Allen for a few years.[40]

In 1899 Bill's neighbour Samuel Thompson brought his family out from England and bought a hotel in Vancouver for them. He commuted back and forth between Vancouver and his homestead for a short while and then returned to Cortes to stay with his grown son Nicholas. Samuel's wife Agnes and the rest of the family were occasional visitors.[41]

The forerunner of one of Cortes's specialty businesses started in 1895 with the chance discovery of rich native oyster beds in Carrington Bay and at the head of Von Donop Inlet. The Victoria *Daily Colonist* said the oysters were of a good size and fine flavour. "In the fall a shipment of them was made to Vancouver, where they were pronounced to be as good as any oyster on the market. A party of gentlemen have now secured exclusive fishing rights on these newly discovered beds, and plans are being made to start work on a large scale."

The Allen brothers pre-empted neighbouring properties in Gorge Harbour in the early 1890s. Born and raised in Dacca, India, where their father was a missionary, they were of mixed British and East Indian parentage. Wilf, Charlie and Jim Allen were the first to come. Over the next decade they were joined by their brother Bernie and their married sister Alice Robertson and her family.

Charlie Allen's diaries give a complex view of a settler's life and the pleasures and pitfalls of being surrounded by family, including the inevitable sibling squabbles. Charlie cleared several hectares and planted over 120 fruit trees at what's now Gorge Harbour Marina. He replaced his original log cabin with a frame house just before he married Jane

Nick and Mary Thompson's home at Whaletown originally sat east of the current government dock. Near their barns (right) is the first Whaletown store, which opened in the 1890s. In 1921 the Thompsons moved their home and store to the head of the wharf.
PHOTO COURTESY OF MEG (ROBERTSON) SHAW, CORTES ISLAND MUSEUM COLLECTION, MCR 20349-21.

(Jennie) Selley of Vancouver in 1905. The couple arrived five days later on Cortes with Jennie's father, a canary and a dog in tow.

Most men worked away from home to earn an income, when work was available, leaving their families to run the homesteads. Neighbours depended heavily on each other and loaned tools, food, money, boats and horses back and forth. Messages were sent with children who hiked the rough trails to bring word of a party. Someone going to retrieve mail usually made the trip on behalf of three or four families, and likewise cooperated to row or cart goods to the steamship docks at Whaletown or Subtle Island.

This tightly enmeshed interdependence was both a blessing and a curse. Charlie and Jennie Allen enjoyed frequent gatherings, and there was always help at hand if someone was sick or in trouble. On the flip side, Charlie was regularly at odds with one or more of his relatives over the return of broken or abused tools, the trespass of free-range cattle or conflicting views over local politics.

Bachelors who could afford to do so hired help. Samuel Thompson of Whaletown had a Chinese man for general chores, and around 1901 Poker Bill Robertson brought his twenty-two-year-old niece Mary

McLeod to the island[42] as a housekeeper and to help with his store and post office. In 1904, when Bill was in his mid-fifties, he sold the business to his neighbour Nicholas Thompson. Two years later their bonds were further cemented when Mary and Nicholas married in 1906. Nick promptly signed the property over into Mary's name,[43] for reasons unknown, and the three lived out their days together at Whaletown.

Shortly before Nicholas Thompson and Mary McLeod married, a new family moved into the tight-knit little community of Whaletown. Alice (Allen) and David Robertson bought Joseph Yowart's homestead at the northeast end of the lagoon in 1905. It was an ironic coincidence that the new family shared Poker Bill Robertson's last name. The two families almost immediately became enemies and clashed bitterly over road access and fence boundaries. Old Bill seems to have been the most obstreperous of the lot, making loud denunciations of David and Alice.

Alice's brothers, the Allens of Gorge Harbour, also became embroiled in the dispute, which climaxed when Poker Bill and Nick laid formal charges

Alice and David Robertson's well-developed homestead, Burnside Ranch, photographed in 1917, lay at the head of the lagoon at Whaletown.
PHOTO COURTESY OF PAULA MARLATT COLLECTION, CORTES ISLAND MUSEUM COLLECTION, MCR 13,574.

of trespass against Alice's brother Wilf Allen for crossing their property. The policeman came to get Wilf, who was suffering a health problem that would soon claim his life, to take him to trial on Quadra Island. When the local judge didn't show up to hear the case, Hosea Bull of the Heriot Bay Hotel—who had several serious liquor offences and larceny charges to his name—stood in as judge. He found in favour of Nick and Bill, though Bill backhanded one of Wilf's witnesses during the proceedings. "Wilf was milched of about $22.00 cost and fine," wrote Alice in her diary.

Alice's husband David was the real target of Bill's and Nick's animosity, as they openly declared. "We must now be careful not to trespass lest [Bill's] 'friend on the bench' lands us also for a good sum," wrote Alice.

Alice started writing her diaries in her tiny, precise script on her arrival at Whaletown in 1905. They provide a compelling portrait of a pioneer woman's life and a glimpse into the mind and heart of a complex and

Charlie Allen (left) and his brothers Wilf and James were among the earliest non-Native settlers on Cortes Island, homesteading in the Whaletown and Gorge Harbour area. Charlie finished his new frame house in Gorge Harbour, current site of a marina, just before he married Vancouverite Jennie (Jane) Selley in 1905. The newlyweds returned to Cortes shortly thereafter, with her canary and father (right) in tow. PHOTO COURTESY MCR, 13, 689.

Alice Robertson's pioneer experiences, typical of many, are captured in her diaries. Her husband David worked away from home for extended periods to earn a cash income, leaving Alice to run the homestead and care for their family. She had to learn everything from scratch, from milking the cow to tending the garden and poultry.

PHOTO COURTESY OF MEG (ROBERTSON) SHAW, CORTES ISLAND MUSEUM COLLECTION, MCR 19,911.

fascinating individual. The hard work of Alice's life is almost impossible to fathom by today's comfortable standards. She managed the farm and her children on her own for long stretches while her husband worked in Vancouver and elsewhere as a carpenter and joiner.

Alice juggled a ceaseless round of pruning, calving, poultry keeping, planting and baking bread with finicky yeast tablets that had to be soaked overnight to proof. She was thirty-nine the year she moved to Cortes Island and pregnant with her fourth and last child.

Nothing in Alice's early life prepared her to run a pioneer homestead. Raised in India by her Indian mother[44] and Welsh father, a Baptist medical[45] missionary, she had the luxury of an ayah, or nursemaid, until she went to Britain to finish her education. Alice later returned to India to work in her father's mission, and during a work furlough in the 1890s, visited her brothers on Cortes Island. The place captivated her, but it was a decade before she was able to move to the island.

Alice married Indian Army officer David Robertson at thirty-one. They were a good match. David had an irresistible Scots sense of humour, a counterfoil to Alice's serious nature. They immigrated to Canada but lived in Vancouver until they bought the Whaletown homestead.

Like many other islanders of these years, the Robertsons went into poultry farming on a large scale. Tending kerosene brooder lamps for the chicks was a twenty-four-hour routine, and keeping predators at bay was a constant job. Once the chickens began to lay, Alice shipped eggs weekly on the *Comox* to Vancouver. She also sold pears, cherries, apples, plums and beef to local outlets such as the hotels on Read and Quadra islands. According to her youngest son Duncan, Alice sold upward of five hundred kilograms (eleven hundred pounds) of cherries per season. She also sold beef at nine cents per half-kilogram (one pound) to local outfits, or ten cents per half-kilogram shipped.

A substantial garden was a vital part of family life. In 1907 the Robertsons planted thirty-one rows of potatoes and a hundred tomato plants. They also grew peas, sunflowers, many kinds of beans, turnips, lettuce, onions, broccoli, Brussels sprouts, watercress, Jerusalem artichoke, melons, raspberries, grapes, two kinds of currants, gooseberries and strawberries.

The Robertsons added thirty-four apple trees to the orchard—including 'Transparent' (the first apples of the season), 'Northern Spy', 'Spitzenberg', 'Belle Fleur' and 'Ben Davis'—along with nineteen pear trees and peach, plum and cherry trees. There was time and space for flowers, too, including sweet peas, nasturtiums, mignonette, pansies, dahlias, honeysuckle and a bed of twenty-two roses.

Everyone in the family fished, and until Alice's son Allen was old enough to hunt, her brother Jim supplied wild game in exchange for canning. The family kept venison in a meat safe, an outdoor cupboard with a screened door that served as a refrigerator.

The Robertsons' livestock included a work horse, cattle and a cow that everyone had to learn to milk, including eight-year-old Allen. Alice also recorded her family's trials as they learned to churn butter and make cheese, which they kept cool in a small shed on pilings in a stream near the house.

It's impressive how much one family provided for its needs in a place that has now returned to trees and a small clearing. The few staples the Robertsons ordered from Vancouver included oats, flour, sugar, lantern wicks, ground ginger, bootlaces, cocoa, crackers, sago, tapioca and tea.

When the Robertsons had dinner guests, the evening often ended with singing, to Alice's great delight. There were community dances that lasted through the night and picnics at Mansons Lagoon, in Gorge Harbour, or at Shark Spit on Marina Island. Women on the west side of the island, like their city counterparts, held "at homes" for tea and chat. The problem, in those days before telephones, was that the hostess never knew whom or how many of her friends to expect.

The Robertson children, like other children of this time, had many daily chores and were expected to obey their parents without question. They helped pick fruit, carried freight to and from the wharf, cared for the livestock and worked in the garden. Toys were a rare treat. For Christmas in 1911, Allen received a subscription to *The Scout*, Meg a paintbox, Rankin an air gun and little Duncan a Noah's ark.

Alice, with her family background in medicine, was called upon to help with accidents and attend the delivery of babies, as on March 5, 1912, when Margaret Middleton of Bluejay Lake gave birth to a sickly infant. When the baby died, Alice organized a funeral. "[David] made a little coffin," wrote Alice in her diary, "and I fixed the wee thing up as nicely as I could. A good many neighbours came at sundown and I read a few verses and we said the Lord's Prayer together over the little grave."

Alice also diagnosed and treated her family's ailments, including the chronic sciatica that plagued her. Sometimes she was confined to bed for days. "Crawled down last Thursday to see to [chicken] incubators but had to go to bed again," wrote Alice, "and could not get downstairs again till Sunday afternoon—pain very severe at times—used laudanum and chloroform and took salicylate of soda and potassium bicarbonate."

With doctors at a great distance, islanders sometimes died from treatable problems. When Mrs. Barraclough of Gorge Harbour contracted erysipelas (fever and swellings caused by strep) in 1909, neighbours went to Marina Island to get a family with a motorboat to go in search of a doctor. They returned many hours later, and the doctor had to operate on Mrs. Barraclough in her home. She died a week later.

Alice held the title to the Whaletown property and managed her family's income to the penny. She sold about four hectares (ten acres) to a logger for a hundred dollars to rearrange her financing and sold the timber near the house. "October 25, 1910—Sent Mr. Barrett a note to say that if he really wanted our timber I wished to have his offer in writing and also a statement as to leaving what trees I point out." The next day she agreed to one dollar per approximately three hundred metres (a thousand feet), and logging commenced. "Fallers at work all day—sad to hear the old giants cracking down."

There was a surge in logging on the island after about 1905, thanks to a booming provincial economy and the technological advance of the steam donkey for hauling. In 1909, according to Charlie Allen's diary, six camps were at work from Coulter Bay to Gorge Harbour.[46] Japanese crews ran some of these. A Chinese crew also worked in the Whaletown area. Bill Barrett fired his regular crew to hire the Chinese loggers, who worked under a man named Jee Jong at a much cheaper rate. When Barrett's show was finished, Jee Jong went into partnership with Charlie

Allen to log his property in Gorge Harbour. Jee Jong shared the cost of hiring two horse teams and equipment, backed by a Chinese grocer in Vancouver. His workers, who lived on-site for eighteen months, put five to fifteen logs per day into Gorge Harbour to be towed to Vancouver.

After Moses Ireland moved his hotel and saloon to Quadra Island in about 1901, the only place to buy a drink locally was on the Union Steamship's *Cassiar*, but the crew were only allowed to sell alcohol while the boat was under way. To dodge this law, the skipper stopped at a float on one side of Whaletown to pick up loggers who bought their drinks as the *Cassiar* inched her way over to the Whaletown wharf. Sunday nights in camp, recalled Allen Robertson, who was thirteen when he worked in a logging camp, got really rowdy.

Young Allen probably didn't tell his pious mother about the exploits of the drunken loggers. Alice Robertson would not have approved. She spearheaded a project to build a church and school in Whaletown a few years after she arrived. The church did not become a reality for over a decade, but the school opened near what's

Mike Manson from the Shetland Islands was among the first non-Native residents to buy land on Cortes Island. He established a ranch at Gunflint Lake (now Linnaea Farm) in 1887 and bought a trading post site at what's now Mansons Landing Park. He was an ambitious and gregarious man who became a longstanding MLA for the North Island riding.

PHOTO COURTESY OF CORTES ISLAND MUSEUM COLLECTION, MCR 13,648.

now the old cemetery at the intersection of the Whaletown and Gorge Harbour roads in 1909, with Miss Ross as the first teacher.

Being a rural schoolteacher, governed by an elected board in a tightly knit community, posed many challenges for young teachers. School boards tended to be fractious, working with a minimal budget, and they were often governed by self-interest. Alice Robertson, who received a first-class education, was not impressed with either of the first two teachers. "Miss Ross has been out till late the last two nights," she wrote in her diary, "and today at noon the children had to stay in the rain till 1 o'clock, as she was sleeping." As always Alice spoke her mind and endured a maelstrom of criticism. Ironically Alice approved of the next teacher, but others did not. The school inspector interceded and said he'd close their school if they didn't get along.

Whaletown and Mansons Landing were settled by non-Native people as entirely separate communities, with no road connection for many decades, but they were close enough to breed a sense of rivalry. While Whaletown and the Gorge may have seen the first commercial activity in the region, Mansons Landing quickly took over as the dominant centre, purely on the strength of one man's vibrant personality.

Mansons Landing and Hernando: The Early Years of Non-Native Settlement

The opening up of logging camps brought a need for local food production. Government guide D.H. McNeil was sent in search of arable land along the mid-coast in 1885. In his report to the *Daily Colonist* of Victoria, he described the Discovery Islands as having a few "small patches" of arable land on southwest Cortes. This tepid report didn't spark a land grab. It wasn't until February 1, 1887, that Mike Manson became the first pre-emptor on the island, claiming a quarter section at Gunflint Lake, then called North Lake.

Mike Manson first cruised through the Discovery Islands as a trader in 1883 representing his Nanaimo store.[47] He was an exceptional man, endowed with incredible drive, charisma and ambition, along with the self-assurance of a natural leader. Mike was a Shetland Islander by birth, and though he was a crofter's son, he reaped the benefit of Scotland's egalitarian education system. The skills he learned at home, from sheep farming to seamanship, served him through his life, as did the fact his mother taught him and his brothers to run a household. All the Manson men could cook, bake bread "and even make a good cup of tea," recalled Mike's niece Rose (Manson) McKay. Their mother, the daughter of a tailor, taught them to sew a full suit of clothes, including the fancy shirt. They could spin yarn, knit garments, including socks and underwear, darn their own socks and cobble shoes. She also infused them with her strong Methodist faith, with its doctrine of temperance.

Mike arrived in Canada at seventeen, following a favourite aunt and her family to the Comox Valley in 1874. He worked there for a season and then got a job in the Nanaimo coal mines. Mike was only nineteen when he became the foreman of a Chinese labour gang laying railway

John Manson moved to Cortes Island in 1888 to work at his brother Mike's trading post at Clytosin, later called Mansons Landing. While Mike pursued a variety of careers, John was a quiet, thoughtful man who was content to work the land.
PHOTO COURTESY OF MCR 6046.

track. A power struggle ensued between Manson and one of the labourers, as he recounted in his memoirs, *Sketches of the Life of Michael Manson*.[48] The story reveals an impetuous side to Mike's nature that led to trouble throughout the first quarter of his life.

Mike allowed his Chinese crew to smoke on the job, but the men had to return to work as soon as their cigarette was alight. When one man insisted upon sitting down for his smoke, Manson hit him with a stick "and unfortunately broke two of his ribs," wrote Mike. "Then the row began in full swing. The other fellows came after me with shovels. I grabbed a shovel and jumped on the top of a stump and kept them off in that way until they calmed down." The Chinese man hired a lawyer but Manson was "let off with a smile and told not to hit them so hard next time, but get the road built as quickly as you can."

Mike was excited by the wealth of opportunities available in Canada. There were all sorts of delicious advantages, as he told his relatives back home. Chief among them was the fact he was eating meat twice a day, compared to once a week in the Shetlands. He urged his brother Laurence to immigrate and share a new house he built. "Come," he told Laurence, "there is nothing in Shetland for you to compare with this."[49] Several more of his brothers and a cousin were likewise persuaded to immigrate.

Mike was batching with Laurence and two friends when he fell in love with seventeen-year-old Jane Renwick, daughter of a blacksmith and wagon maker. Jane accepted Mike's engagement ring, but when she proudly showed it to her father he struck her hand with a poker and ruined the ring. The tale of the ring—with no mention of the harm he must have done to her hand—became family lore, as did her elopement with Mike.

Jane had just stepped out the front door with her small bag when her father happened along. He wanted to know where she was going, but she threw him off by saying she was on her way to a Bible class. Instead Jane met Mike in Nanaimo harbour, from where they went to Victoria in a hired canoe with six Native men as paddlers. They married on August 6, 1878, and soon returned to Nanaimo, where Jane's father became reconciled to the match, won over by Mike's charm and self-assurance.

The first decade of Mike's and Jane's married life was fraught with setbacks and heartache. Mike opened a general store in what's now downtown Nanaimo at about the same time as their first child Margaret was born. He wasn't in business more than a year before he ran into financial difficulties during a prolonged coal miners' strike in 1880. He sold the store to his brother Laurence,[50] who turned it into a family business propped up by his mine job.

Mike worked for a short while as a clerk for the city at sixty dollars per month, until he was hired as a salesman at a general store called The Red House. While in this job, Mike also served a one-year term as an alderman for Nanaimo, at the age of twenty-three. At this time Mike and Jane lost their second child, a baby girl who died within months of her birth in 1881.

After "three years and three months" at The Red House, wrote Mike in his memoirs, he bought a store on Commercial Street. His stock included furnishings, crockery, carpets, oilcloth and brooms. But bad luck still plagued him. His store was razed just over a year later in a suspected arson that caused about three thousand dollars in damage.[51]

With the courage of a stubborn Scotsman, Manson got financial backing from his father-in-law and rebuilt on a much larger scale in 1886, only to be burnt out again within a year. This time he lost about fifteen thousand dollars' worth of stock, a tremendous sum at the time.

A few months later Mike and his friend George Leask[52] went on a search for sheep-farming land on the Discovery Islands. He registered a pre-emption on Cortes in February 1887 at Gunflint Lake. At the same time Mike launched into a new career with the six-thousand-dollar purchase of the *Rustler*, a sixty-three-tonne (seventy-ton) schooner. He advertised his services in Nanaimo, offering to carry freight between there and the settlements and logging camps of the northern Strait of Georgia.[53]

The opening of gold mines on Texada Island to the south of Cortes made his new business an immediate success. Mike hired Captain LeBlanc and a crew for the *Rustler* and advertised regular runs. "The *Rustler* leaves Hirst's wharf for Texada, Willow Point, Cape Mudge, Seymour Narrows, Read and Cortes Island," read an ad in the *Nanaimo Free Press*. Mike ran

Mansons Landing, now a park, was a large First Nations village site and—when Mike Manson and George Leask established Clytosin trading post around 1887—Cortes's first non-Native settlement. In 1918 it had a government wharf, freight shed (right), trading post, steamship waiting room and Jane and Mike Manson's home.
PHOTO COURTESY OF MEG (ROBERTSON) SHAW, CORTES ISLAND MUSEUM COLLECTION, MCR 13,690.

the booking office at the wharf, worked shifts as captain and also oper-ated several logging camps on the Redonda Islands and in Jervis Inlet.

Though Jane suffered seasickness, she accompanied Mike on some of his trips around the strait. On occasion they made stopovers at their property (now Linnaea Farm) at Gunflint Lake.[54] On October 5, 1888, Mike bought a second property on Cortes at what's now called Mansons Landing. (The name Mansons Landing came into use many decades later. Mike retained the old Native name Clytosin, "land with water on both sides.") Mike built a cabin at Clytosin and opened a trading post, which his friend George Leask managed for the first few years. Soon they put a road through from the trading post to Mike's Gunflint Lake ranch and gave it the Native name Taka Mika, which means "clear water."

Not much is known about Mike's partner George Leask. He pre-empted sixty-five hectares (160 acres) in 1888 at the southwest end of Hague Lake, between present-day Seaford and Bartholomew roads. Leask was an engineer in Nanaimo and a recent widower in his mid-twenties when he moved to Cortes.

The main attraction of Cortes for both these men was a return to their sheep-farming roots. According to government records, Leask built a hewed log house with a shake roof and a lean-to kitchen on his homestead at the lake. He cleared four hectares (ten acres) of forest and brought 0.4 hectare (an acre) into cultivation.

It must have been lonely for Leask, with only sporadic visits from Mike and Jane. His nearest neighbour was Moses Ireland at Whaletown until Mike's twenty-year-old brother John Manson moved to Cortes Island in 1888. John pre-empted sixty-five hectares (160 acres) at the southern tip of Cortes, at what's now Tealcroft Road, but he lived for more than a decade at Mike's and Jane's cabin at Gunflint Lake.

The trading post was an imposing structure at the head of the present-day government wharf at Mansons Landing. Mike hired Native people to build it in their traditional "big house" style, using massive hand-adzed posts and beams.[55] In the early years the Native people throughout the region were Manson's and Leask's primary customers. They traded dogfish oil (used to grease logging skid roads and mine tracks) and furs for all manner of goods at the store. Mike noted in his ship's log that he sold deer hides for thirteen cents apiece and mountain goat skins and mink for fifty cents, and he got a government bounty of fifty cents for each seal head.[56]

Reserve lands were set aside for the Mainland Comox people in 1888. The Sliammon were given their dog-salmon fishing station to the south of Mansons at Paukeanam. The Klahoose got two reserves in Squirrel Cove, 263 hectares (650 acres) at their current village of Tork and another seventeen hectares (forty-three acres) nearby. The heartland of their territory is in Toba Inlet.

The Klahoose began logging as early as the 1870s. In the 1890s they hired Mike Manson to tow their log booms to Nanaimo or Vancouver sawmills. There were an increasing number of logging camps by the late 1880s. According to the newspapers of the day, W. Keddy and J. Elgeson shipped sixty-one thousand metres (two hundred thousand feet) of timber from Cortes Island to Haslam's mill in Nanaimo in 1887. A year later, partners Moses Ireland and John Leatherdale were "getting out an immense number of logs" in Lewis Channel.

Shipping goods for large potlatches, where Native hosts gave away hundreds of dollars in furnishings and dry goods, was a lucrative part of Manson's business. In the late 1880s and early 1890s, potlatches were numerous. On one occasion Mike filled an order valued at $1,748—the equivalent of two or three men's annual salaries—for a potlatch on Quadra Island.[57]

Things were on a steady rise for Mike Manson until he faced yet another reverse in 1889. Returning to Nanaimo from Vancouver, he spotted his crew from the *Rustler* rowing into English Bay. He called over the rails to the bedraggled men, who informed him the *Rustler* struck a rock near Powell River. She was a complete loss. "Mr. Manson informs us," said the *Nanaimo Free Press*, "he is not insured one cent for the *Rustler*, and he further states $6,000 will not replace her."

With his characteristic resilience, Mike was back in business within a few weeks. The *Nanaimo Free Press* announced he had leased a vessel to continue shipping and had financed construction of a new ship, the thirty-seven-metre (123-foot) *Thistle*.

Among Mike's earliest ports of call was a lively little non-Native settlement on 990-hectare (2,450-acre) Hernando Island. The island's prime attraction was a large natural meadow in its centre, surrounded by a fine stand of timber. Logging camp operator William Blaney is said to have been the first to pre-empt land there,[58] along with someone (whose name has been lost) who operated a trading post in Stag Bay on the north shore. Charles Baker and Henry Hearns shared a quarter section on the eastern shore. Next to them were Forest and Ellen Conant and their family, who came to the island from North Dakota in 1888.[59] In total about five homesteads were on the island by 1889.

Ellen Conant must have found her new life a challenge, raising a young family in the absence of other women and children. The year the Conants arrived was exceptionally long and cold, with about two and a half metres (eight feet) of snow through much of the winter. To make matters worse, Ellen's husband Forest died the next year.[60] Though Ellen had family in Ontario, she decided to remain on the island. Her economic situation may have given her no other choice.

Following her husband's death, Ellen registered for a pre-emption on the southern tip of Hernando, a privilege not available to women unless they were widowed. A sympathetic note in the land title records states they waived the usual registration fee because Ellen was "destitute and in receipt of government charity."

Dan McDonald lived on nearby Twin Island, then called Ulloa, in 1889. His legal name was Donald McDonald McArthur.[61] Dan was an intriguing character, a Gaelic-speaking Scotsman who served on the Liverpool police force before he immigrated to the US in about 1865. For a number of years he had a ranch in Wyoming, where he was a noted buffalo and "Indian hunter." He is said to have fought in the Battle of Little Big Horn, and a persistent rumour suggests he was part of the infamous Jesse James Gang, though his name doesn't appear on the list of known gang members. Whatever his past may have been, Dan lived in relative peace on Twin Island, raising sheep and growing fruit. In the early years he had a considerable flock that he moved about in a rowboat to graze on various sites on southwestern Cortes Island. He transported sheep "on the hoof" to Vancouver, where they fetched $2.65 per head for lambs and $3.65 for mutton.

Children who grew up on the islands liked to hear stories of Dan's cowboy past, but the really memorable thing about him was his peg leg. Everyone knew when old Dan was about by the loud tap-tapping of his homemade leg on the wooden floorboards. He'd lost his leg in Wyoming after his horse stepped into a gopher hole and fell on him some 145 kilometres (ninety miles) from the nearest town. By the time he got to a doctor, there was no way to save the leg, or so the doctor told him. He became incensed each time he recounted the tale, railing against what he thought was an overhasty decision to remove his leg.[62]

Mike Manson was a renowned storyteller too. He had a wealth of tales about his shipping adventures in the tricky waters of the inner coast, spiced by his lively sense of humour. Some of his scrapes were life-threatening, especially after he was made Justice of the Peace for the region in 1890. Being a JP required Manson to act as both a local judge and a policeman, and, as he owned a steamship, he was also hired to transport criminals and witnesses for trial. It was an honour to be selected as a JP, though it brought only a minor increase to his income.[63]

In 1890 Mike found himself in the thick of a murder scene in the Native village at Cape Mudge on Quadra Island. He had just delivered over a thousand dollars' worth of goods to the village for a potlatch when he was asked to intercede on behalf of a man accused of murder. An angry group, wanting to dispense justice on the spot, turned on Mike until he persuaded them of his authority to act for the Crown. Night was falling, so he stayed overnight in the village, leaving the money from his sale of goods in the care of a woman leader. The next day he took the accused man away for trial and raised money for his defence. The case ended in a manslaughter charge.

Mike's new steamship, the *Thistle*, arrived in the fall of 1890 just as he and Jane faced the greatest hardship of their lives. The Nanaimo newspapers carried endless reports of virulent cases of diphtheria. Some said it was in the water system, others said it resulted from the filth of overcrowding. Nine-year-old Robina Manson was the first of their children to succumb to diphtheria. She died on October 14, 1890, and three-year-old John died the next day. Ten days later their infant Martha Grace died, and five-year-old Barbara Ethel followed a month later.

Jane and their only surviving child Margaret were also terribly sick but managed to pull through. At one point, as Mike nursed Jane, she told him she didn't think she'd make it past midnight, so as she slept he set the clock ahead. When she awoke and saw she'd made it past midnight, she gained new hope.

As soon as Jane and Margaret were out of danger, Mike turned his attention back to his new ship. The *Thistle* was his largest ship to date. It was registered to carry seventy tonnes (150 tons) and required a captain and two engineers to operate. To make it pay, Mike branched out into sealing, travelling as far afield as the Columbia River and the Bering Sea. In May 1891 he described one of his sealing trips in the Nanaimo newspaper. "The weather was simply awful," said Manson. "Twice during the trip we had the glass in front of the pilot house blown in by the force of the gale and were only able to lower our boats three times during the entire trip and then I came near being drowned by the one I was in capsizing. We saw plenty of seals, any amount in fact, but were unable to take them merely on account of the bad weather."

He was fuelling up again, said the paper, to head out to Cape Flattery and then north to the Bering Sea. Jane and Margaret lived aboard ship with Mike. Storms and seasickness were better than being separated.[64]

When Mike started sealing, he and Leask closed their Cortes Island trading post, and George returned to Nanaimo and married. John Manson stayed on Cortes, however, earning his living by sheep and cattle ranching and as a caretaker for Toba Inlet logging camps in winter.

Mike's foray into sealing was short-lived. In 1892 he returned to shipping in the Discovery Islands and that December moved his family— which now included their infant twins Ethel and Robina—to Cortes on a permanent basis.[65] Along with their household goods they brought hay, six cows, twenty-four chickens and a pair of oxen.

Jane Manson knew enough of Cortes to realize her new life would be lonely, with Mike away for protracted periods and her brother-in-law John away sometimes too. Irish settlers Sam and Hillis Coulter lived reasonably close, and there were women and families on Hernando Island, but that was too far away for easy companionship. All considered, the Mansons' final move to the island likely was pushed by a desire to remove their children from the constant threat of diphtheria and other infectious diseases still prevalent in Nanaimo.

Jane's vulnerability in an isolated place was heightened by her husband's questing spirit. On one occasion Mike and John hiked into the mountains of Toba Inlet with a hundred-year-old Native man and his "great-great-great-grandson." The old man said he'd seen gold in the mountains and could lead the Mansons to it. When they reached the spot four days later, they found it had been covered over by a landslide. As the elderly man started up the broken rock to search for some trace of gold, he fell and broke a collar bone, dislocated a hip and broke several ribs. The Mansons made a sling to carry him out, but his young relative bolted. He was sure the Mansons would perish in their attempt to carry the old man out.

The party was already low on food before this accident. They rationed what was left to one and a half pieces of pilot bread each per day. "We didn't even see a sparrow we could shoot," Manson told historian B.A. McKelvie many years later. Eventually they shot a bear, and the old man lay by the fire all night to roast enough to get them through the remainder of their journey.

It was several weeks, from start to finish, before Mike and John returned to Mansons Landing. "When I arrived home," Mike told McKelvie, "it was dark and I could hear my wife crying inside. It was some time before I could convince her that I was really alive. The young Indian, after robbing our boat, had made straight for my place and told my wife that we were *memeloose*—dead—in the mountains."[66]

A census carried out some months before the Mansons moved permanently to Cortes gives a snapshot view of the island. In addition to their neighbours the Coulters, a couple of men, including a logger that old-timers called Nigger Bill, lived to the south in shacks at Smelt Bay. The liveliest place on the island was a logging camp where sixteen men from all over the globe—including the US, Eastern Canada, England, Norway, Quebec, Scotland, China (the camp cook), Ireland, Sweden, France and Germany—were at work. Among them was Alma Swift, an American woman, with her husband Benjamin and their eight-year-old son.

Jane's visits to Hernando would have been a special treat. There were eleven households on Hernando by the early 1890s, a surprising number for a small island. Some Hernando Islanders managed their livestock communally, suggesting that they came as a group. All the available land was under pre-emption by the early 1890s, though a surveyor named Drabble noted in his journal the only arable land was the central meadow and a bit on the southern end. The settlers did have about twelve hectares (thirty acres) under cultivation, however, according to an agricultural report, including fourteen hectares (thirty-five acres) fenced and another 243 hectares (six hundred acres) in pasture for three hundred sheep, ten cows, three horses and two pigs. They also kept, as a group, two hundred chickens, strawberry beds and a ninety-tree orchard of apples, plums and cherries.

It was logging that brought these settlers an income, as was the case throughout the islands.[67] Children who grew up on Hernando recalled the sound of men and oxen at work. "You could hear the ox skinners swearing at the oxen half an hour before they arrived," wrote Arthur Rorison to Cortes historian May (Freeman) Ellingsen. They slicked dogfish oil onto the skid road over which they dragged logs to tidewater. "It smelled terrible," Rorison recalled. "Everyone on the coast had a 20 gallon cast iron pot and boiled fish liver, which was used for dogfish oil in the woods and mills."

Arthur's parents, William and Louise Rorison, had two children when they arrived in 1891. Three more were born on Hernando within the next few years. The Rorisons converted the old trading post at Stag Bay into their home on property they shared with William's brother Basil, a prospector. Mr. Harris, a lawyer, and his wife lived on the neighbouring quarter section for a short time. In the centre of the island lived the Vernons with their two children. The Smiths had one child, and the McAdamses on the east coast had nine. William Blaney lived with a large Mainland Comox family of fishermen on the southern tip of the island.

Ellen Conant and two of her four children[68] from her first marriage were living in Charles Baker's home by 1891. Ellen and Charles's relationship had become a romantic liaison, and that year she gave birth to the first of their three children. She was pregnant with their second child when they were officially married in Comox on May 18, 1893,[69] with Mike Manson as a witness. It was likely pre-emption requirements that caused their delay in marrying. Ellen gained full title to her pre-emption just months prior to their marriage.

An influx of new settlers arrived on the island after the Union Steamship freight and passenger service from Vancouver started in 1892. Pre-emptions and purchases of land more than doubled on Cortes and its satellite islands, from ten in 1891 to twenty-two in 1892. The next year, as an anonymous Cortes Island columnist for the Comox *Weekly News* noted, Mike Manson (with John as an assistant) reopened the store, "which comes as a boon and a blessing to the settlers."

The region's population increased as the result of a deep economic recession in the early 1890s. It was difficult to find jobs in the city, so a few out-of-work families moved to the islands to farm and "live off the land."

With the population on the rise, Mike opened a post office at the store to serve the general region in April 1893. His petition to the government noted there were approximately twenty-five households on Cortes. A few months later a post office also opened on Hernando Island.

In 1894 Mansons Landing and Hernando Island were listed for the first time in the British Columbia Directory. Forty-two men (only men were listed in most communities) from as far away as Bute Inlet were on the list for Mansons Landing. There were also three traders and an engineer. Fourteen men were listed for Hernando.

Farming was John Manson's calling, and by the mid-1890s his future showed enough promise to allow him to return to the Shetlands to marry his childhood sweetheart Margaret Smith. She was four years his senior, a delicate woman who escaped the TB that took both her parents. When Margaret was orphaned, she was raised among the twenty household servants who managed the large stone house of two genteel spinsters. She

Margaret Manson was considered "as pretty a girl as ever passed through a church door," recalled her daughter Rose McKay. John courted his childhood sweetheart by mail, and once he was well established on Cortes Island, returned to the Shetlands to marry her in 1895.
PHOTO COURTESY OF ETTA BYERS COLLECTION, MCR 9362.

maintained a polite correspondence with John in Canada. "My mother was a very proper woman and she was careful never to answer his letters in less time than it had taken him to write to her," wrote their daughter Rose.

Margaret was a servant in her adoptive home when John returned to claim her as a bride. The newlyweds arrived on Cortes in February 1895. Her first sight of the island was of the blackened skeletons of trees left by a recent forest fire, surrounded by the dark green of the foreboding forest. It was a stark contrast to the treeless hillsides of the Shetlands. Margaret never stopped longing for home, as she later confessed, but with her kind-hearted and steady husband, she became a beloved member of the community.

Though John got full title to his pre-emption on the southern end of the island before he married, he wasn't convinced it was the ideal farm location, so it was about six years before he and Margaret moved there. In winter they lived at Toba Inlet, as logging camp caretakers. In spring and summer they stayed at Mike's and Jane's farm at Gunflint Lake. And for about a year in the 1890s they lived on Mitlenatch Island, pre-empted by the Manson brothers in 1895 as browse for their sheep.

Mitlenatch Island is an extraordinary place, floating in a rain shadow on the horizon at the top end of the Strait of Georgia. The island's annual rainfall, at seventy-five centimetres (thirty inches) per year, is half that of Campbell River. Hundreds of gulls, cormorants and other birds nest on the island's bald headlands, filling the air with constant sound. The gulls lay their eggs on the bare rock near prickly cactus plants that sport soft yellow blooms in early summer. In spring, the huge natural meadow in the centre of the island is awash with purple camas and white and orange lilies.

Mitlenatch's rocky shores and small stands of scrub trees reminded the Mansons of home. "Michael and John had loved the windswept isle from first sight," wrote Rose (Manson) McKay. John and Margaret moved there in 1897–98 with their young son to secure their pre-emption claim, which required permanent residency. The rocky island filled some of Margaret's longing for home, but John's frequent absences to transport sheep to market were a hardship. "Imagine my mother alone on this island with her small son watching her husband row away in a skiff to be gone for a week," said Rose. Once their pre-emption was secure, the couple again divided their time between the Gunflint Lake ranch and caretaking in Toba Inlet.

By1894 Jane and Mike Manson had four children, including Margaret—the only survivor from "the first family"— the twins Ethel and Robina, and baby Wilf. When both of the Manson brothers had to be away, their Klahoose friend Old George McGee looked in on Margaret and Jane. Old George had his own extended family to care for as well. He and his wife Sophie and their grown son Harry and his family fished along the west coast of Cortes, staying in cabins at Paukeanam. They also harvested herring in Von Donop Inlet, where they had a shack near the rapids, and they dug clams at Mansons Landing. The clams were strung onto thin cedar stakes and barbecued over hot coals or dried in the wind and sun. Old George paddled his canoe along the coast to sell or trade cod and salmon to settlers and logging camps. Sophie wove cedar-bark baskets decorated in geometric patterns to trade with non-Native women for clothing.

George McGee was a small man, standing just one and a half metres (five feet) tall, but he was a striking figure. In his senior years he kept his long, silver-white hair off his face with a headband made from a long strip of fine black cloth. On top of this he always wore an expensive brown Stetson hat, and at his side he carried an impressive butcher knife.

His relatives in the Klahoose Band made a permanent shift in 1896 from their winter villages in Toba Inlet to their reserve in Squirrel Cove, where the Oblate Mission financed the construction of a church. The band made the move at the urging of the Catholic Church, to make it easier for priests to visit them. Some also said the move was necessary to escape the constant flooding they experienced in Toba Inlet.

Though there were enough children on the Klahoose Reserve for a school, the Native people were likely unaware of this option. The non-Native community on the opposite side of the island, at Mansons, began to think of a school when the large Hague family arrived in 1894.[70] They came at the urging of their relatives the Heays, as Henry Hague needed a place to convalesce from a lingering illness. Henry was born in BC in

1859, in a tent outside Fort Victoria, where his Anglo-Irish parents came en route to the Cariboo gold rush. His family settled in Victoria, where Henry became a merchant and store clerk. He worked in Vancouver and Victoria, for the first few years after he and his wife Lydia moved to Cortes, as a furniture salesman for Weiler Brothers.[71] In 1899 Henry gave up this job to make Cortes his permanent home and pre-empted the east end of Mansons Lagoon and Hague Lake.

The community was short three children for the required minimum of ten students to qualify as a "rural assisted school," which would pay the teacher's salary. The Mansons persuaded Knight Inlet friends to board their children on Cortes, and John Manson offered to row upcoast to get them. The 160-kilometre (hundred-mile) journey in a 2.4 metre (eight-foot) homemade skiff took six days for the round trip, with John and the children sleeping on the beaches at night.

With these new youngsters to swell their ranks, school started in September 1895 in Alex Heay's log cabin near the corner of Lagoon and Seaford roads. The kitchen became the classroom, with its cookstove as a heater.

The island's first teacher, Miss B.E. Ward, boarded with the Hagues at Mansons Lagoon. The government paid her a salary of fifty dollars per month and provided some books, for a total annual cost of $37.39 per child. Miss Ward taught writing, spelling, mental and written arithmetic, geography, Canadian and English history, anatomy, hygiene, music and drawing.

Hernando Islanders opened a school a year before Mansons Landing, making theirs the first school on the Discovery Islands. A total of seventeen children lived on the island when an abandoned shack on Hidalgo Point in Stag Bay was converted into a school in 1893.[72] Ellen (Conant) Baker's children Abner and Cora were among the students. As Abner later wrote to historian May (Freeman) Ellingsen, his few years in this school were his only education. "Please excuse my mistakes and poor writing," wrote Abner. "I received my little schooling on Hernando in 1893-1894; finished in 1895."

William and Cecilia Wildgrube took over the McAdams property on the southern tip of Hernando the year the school opened. William was attracted to this part of the coast to log and farm, though he was an unlikely candidate for either job. He was a classical pianist by profession, trained in the famous Leipzig Conservatory in Germany. The Wildgrubes moved here from Vancouver, where William earned his living by playing piano in a combination of the new opera house and the bars and brothels of skid road. The loggers who frequented the bars impressed William with their lavish tips, so he figured logging must be lucrative and decided to give it a try.

William took his family to Hernando, where he and a partner worked hard to put together a boom of logs. At season's end his partner offered to take the logs to Vancouver as William was not fully fluent in English. When his partner didn't return, William wrote to a prostitute he'd befriended while working in the bars, and borrowed enough money to pay for a trip to Vancouver to search for his partner.

Whether or not Wildgrube recovered his share of the earnings is not part of family lore, but he and Cecilia continued to make the Discovery Islands their home until about 1900. After this William returned to his original profession as a pianist, and his talent permitted him to make a small fortune.

A post office opened on Hernando in 1893 with William Rorison as postmaster. The crew of the *Comox* passed mail and freight into a waiting rowboat until a government wharf was built at Stag Bay in 1895.[73] But within a few years the little community on Hernando fell apart. The post office closed in 1899, as did the school a few years later.[74] Where the British Columbia Directory listed thirteen men's names in 1898, by 1905 only farmer Norman Smith remained.

Hernando was not the only community to experience a sudden decline at this time. Cortes also went into a slump in response to the excitement of the Yukon gold rush. Some left to try their luck in the goldfields. Others moved to the burgeoning new city of Vancouver, where the economy was booming. Three families left Cortes Island all at once in 1898, according to Henry Hague's memoirs, and as a result the Cortes Island School, Manson's trading post and the post office all closed.[75]

Mike and Jane Manson were among those who left in the late 1890s. Mike took a job in 1899 with the Dunsmuirs' Cumberland mines

The Hagues opened a co-operative clam cannery in Mansons Lagoon in about 1897. Lydia (Heay) Hague and her children managed most aspects of the work. The cannery closed in about 1904. PHOTO COURTESY OF MAY ELLINGSEN COLLECTION, CORTES ISLAND MUSEUM COLLECTION, MCR 13, 890.

to manage their Union Bay wharf. Jane and the children remained on Cortes for a year and then followed Mike to Union Bay, though they returned to the island in summers.

Those who stayed after the slump of the late 1890s cobbled together an income from a combination of logging and fishing, but always with the fond hope that their homesteads would some day prosper. Many more people with these unrealistic agrarian dreams were to arrive over the coming decades. Those with family money to support them could enjoy their homesteads as a rural adventure. The rest lived a hand-to-mouth existence on subsistence farms.

A Touch of Eccentricity

The Hagues were among those who stuck it out at Mansons Landing after the school, post office and store closed. One thing that kept them here was the co-op clam cannery they opened with Daniel Lowe in Mansons Lagoon in 1897. Lydia Hague and the children were in charge. They packed 0.4-kilogram (fifteen-ounce) cans and shipped them to the Hudson's Bay Company in Vancouver. Their granddaughter Mabel Christenson recalled the cannery as a large structure you could row beneath at the right tide to unload your clams. The deep lagoon had an incredible clam bed, but the cannery didn't prove profitable enough to maintain beyond about 1904.

Margaret and John Manson also stayed, and in about 1900 they moved their two children to their own homestead on the southern tip of Cortes. The place faced directly into the prevailing storm winds, but as their daughter Rose recalled, John had a Shetlander's love of southeasters. To cut the wind from his fields and their new house, he clipped alder trees into a hedge along the steep bank that overlooked the sea. The Mansons had two more children after they settled at Sunny Brae. Rose Anna was born on September 6, 1900, and a few years later their last child Nicol Bain Manson was born.

Clearing Sunny Brae of its trees, stumps, roots and rocks was the work of many years. As a schoolgirl Rose sat by the towering light of her father's endless brush fires to do her homework. John specialized in raising sheep and growing potatoes and fruit. He was a skilled shepherd, but it was a challenge to keep sheep in a place with limited browse and a resident wolf pack. The sound of the wolves howling around the house terrified Margaret. John kept the wolves in check by setting poison traps right across the narrowest part of the island at a place they called Poison Bay.

Another stalwart was one-legged Dan McDonald of Twin Island. In addition to sheep farming, he worked at road building whenever a government contract was available.[76] He camped in John and Margaret Manson's farm field while doing road work. The sight of Dan's nightly campfire was the signal for the Manson children to join him and watch with interest as he cooked frying-pan-sized bannock cakes and to beg a story from his ready stock of Wild West adventures.

Islanders were pleased to see the population slowly rise again after 1901, when a census showed a hundred people lived on Cortes and its satellite islands, including thirty-three women and girls. Logging was the dominant occupation, with twenty-eight men at work in the woods compared to fifteen farmers. There were four small camps on the island in the spring of 1901. The rest were handloggers, working on their own with no animal power or other means of hauling. The census also listed two woodcutters, a fisherman, a machinist and three engineers. Most earned from five hundred to seven hundred dollars per year. There were three Chinese men of various ages. One worked as a farm labourer at two hundred dollars per year, and the others were cooks in logging camps, earning three hundred dollars annually.

Cortes came to have a decidedly British feel over the next few decades, with an influx of moneyed immigrants. The 1901 census, however, showed only twelve of the hundred residents came from Britain, though seventy percent had British roots. The majority, as in other Discovery Island communities, came from the US and Eastern Canada.

A distinctive feature on Cortes at this time was the number of large extended families. Some, like the Mansons, created close-knit community enclaves, each with its own clan-like culture. This, and the fact there were no roads to connect the various settlements until many decades later, left communities like Whaletown and Mansons Landing to develop as separate entities.

The Smiths, Heays and Hagues of Mansons Landing are examples of one extended family on the island. When young Cora Smith of Read Island married Horace Heay of Mansons in 1897, her father and fourteen-year-old brother moved to the island too.[77] Most of her husband Horace Heay's family were at Mansons: Horace's mother Eleanor; his brothers Alex, Walter, James and Frank Heay with their families; and his married sister Lydia with her husband Henry Hague.

August Tiber (spelled Teuber on his death certificate) was the first to arrive of yet another large island family. August was born in Glatz, Schlesing, in what's now Germany, and served in the Prussian army. He and his wife Mary Theresa immigrated to North Dakota, but when she died prematurely in about 1891, August boarded out his three daughters and son Henry and moved to Canada in search of a new life. Henry Tiber followed his father in 1893.[78] Each pre-empted land, August at what's now called Blue Jay Lake in 1895 and Henry across the passage at Burdwood Bay on Read Island. Henry later moved to Tiber Bay on Cortes.[79]

August was a decided character. He was a short, sturdy man, as Rose (Manson) McKay recalled him in his senior years. She was impressed by his snow-white complexion, rosy cheeks, startling blue eyes and curly white hair. But he was most noted for his rambling chatter in inscrutable broken English with a thick German accent. Islanders could follow most of what he said, but newcomers were lost.

Mary Tiber, whom Rose (Manson) McKay described as a great beauty "with hair as black as a raven's wing," was the first of August's daughters to move from Dakota to Cortes, where her skill as a seamstress was in demand. Mary boarded with a large French Canadian family named Marquette in about 1901. Her sisters Olive and Annie soon followed.[80]

The fluctuating population of these years can be traced in the opening and closing of stores and the school. In about 1902, for instance, John Manson reopened the trading post at Manson Landing, probably on a very limited basis, and two years later he revived postal service there too. He rowed out to meet the Union Steamship boat as it approached his home on southern Cortes to retrieve the mail in mid-stream and then

Rose Manson (McKay), daughter of John and Margaret Manson, is in the centre rear, the shorter woman with a hat in this Mansons Landing School class. The school was across from what's now the Mansons Community Hall, where much-loved teacher Katharine Lettice planted a dogwood tree around 1914. PHOTO COURTESY OF ROSE (MANSON) MCKAY COLLECTION, MCR.

rowed to Mansons Lading to sort and distribute it. School also reopened near the Landing in 1902 in an old log cabin outfitted with homemade desks near the meeting of Sutil Point and Bartholomew roads. Miss Margaret Bonis was hired to teach fifteen students, but the next year enrollment dropped again, and the school closed. Five years passed before there were sufficient children for it to reopen.

August Tiber played a role in the reopening of the school when he married twice-widowed Anna Doering of Minnesota, who had four children. Anna, a family friend, brought her children to Vancouver by train. Islanders smiled when the fusty old farmer complained about the need to don his best clothes to meet Anna and her children, but the couple married on October 29, 1908.

A welcoming party awaited the newlyweds at the Mansons Landing dock. "I don't know how we came to have fire crackers," recalled Rose (Manson) McKay, "but we did, as well as rice (not too much of the latter because it was food). I was never able to hit anything I aimed at, so the fire crackers I threw landed at Mrs. Tiber's startled feet. She took it very well but I still feel guilty." August had recently purchased the Heay place[81] at the intersection of Lagoon and Seaford roads, so the revellers followed the Tibers to Hague Lake for a picnic.

It was a bit of a squeeze for Anna and the kids to fit into August's log house. He was proud of the place, as he built it entirely without nails. Anna's daughters took over the attic, climbing to their room by a ladder that ran up one wall. They found island life an adventure, but Anna was used to urban comforts and had to adjust to both pioneering and the peculiarities of a middle-aged man who was set in his ways. It was a long time, for instance, before she could cure him of stuffing his shoes with newspaper in place of socks.

Mike and Jane Manson's family also swelled the ranks of the school population when they moved back to the island in 1908. His first venture was poultry raising, a branch of farming that showed great promise in areas lacking arable land. Mike built large sheds for the poultry, as noted in the Columbia Coast Mission's magazine, *The Log*. "He already has his brooder 100 feet long, hot water heated, and containing, at the time of our visit, over 1,200 chickens. This is wonderful work, considering the short time he has been at it." Mike also raised sheep, keeping them on Hernando, where he owned many hectares of land.[82]

With the population on the rise again, islanders built a new log schoolhouse in 1908 on Sutil Point Road across from Beasley Road. As August Tiber's stepdaughter Gertrude (Mundigal) Lambert recalled, their homemade desks were only fifteen centimetres (six inches) wide, which forced students to sit ramrod straight.

Fourteen pupils enrolled in the new school. The teacher boarded at John and Margaret Manson's, as did a Whaletown student who walked with the Manson kids along the dirt track that's now Sutil Road. The kids went barefoot in all but the worst weather to spare their precious shoes, swinging their lard-pail lunch tins and a lantern during the short days of winter.

Chicken ranching didn't deliver on its great promise of prosperity for Mike or many others who invested in it. He turned over his huge flock to his daughters when he was elected as the Conservative party MLA for the Comox-North Vancouver Island riding in 1909.[83] Businessmen like Hosea Bull of the Heriot Bay Hotel on Quadra Island[84] urged Mike to stand, since the Conservatives didn't support a proposed ban on alcohol consumption. The Conservatives also opposed giving women the vote and were anti-union, a position Mike supported after years in management with the Dunsmuirs.

Mike Manson was a natural for the job of MLA. He had a huge network of friends and acquaintances throughout the region and he was an outspoken man with strong convictions, high principles and a good record of community service. He was also no stranger to political life. Mike had served as a Nanaimo alderman and school board trustee, and one of his brothers and a cousin were also MLAs in Premier McBride's powerful government. The Conservatives were so popular in the flush economy prior to World War I that they took nearly every seat. With three members of the Manson family in his cabinet, McBride tossed off a saucy quip that there were more Mansons in the house than there were members of the opposition.[85]

Cortes Islanders were pleased to have direct political representation, but even without Mike's considerable pull, the island's population and community services shot up again after the school reopened in 1908.

Islanders today might envy some of the conveniences available a century ago. A twice-weekly steamboat service connected Vancouver with Mansons Landing, Whaletown and Hernando.[86] The boat also stopped at Subtle Island, tide and weather permitting. A return trip to town took about nineteen hours and cost seven dollars and fifty cents, including a meal presented on monogrammed service by a uniformed waiter. The *Comox* stopped along its route at every settlement and camp, where a crowd awaited it "a'talkin and a'criticizing," as settlers and passengers swapped news.

Rose (Manson) McKay remembered the *Comox* with great fondness. It had a nicely appointed dining room, a social hall, a comfortable smoking room and eight cabins with double berths. "What a grand deck she had," wrote Rose. "The smoke stack came right up through the middle of the deck and there was a lovely seat all around it so [it] was always comfortably warm. It was such a grand ship."

In 1908 the Whaletown dock was on the southeastern side of the harbour, near the site of the current dock and post office.

Some freight the Union Steamship boats carried required special treatment. The crew had a hard time getting John Manson's horse Barney on the boat in Vancouver, for example, and when it came to getting him off at the Hernando dock the horse wouldn't budge. In desperation they took Barney around to the freight door on the opposite side of the boat and backed him into the saltchuck. The wild-eyed horse swam for one of the nearby islands, where it would have been impossible to retrieve him, but a brave lad watching from his little fishing boat jumped in and swam after Barney. He heaved onto the horse's back and took the dangling reins to guide him to the beach on Cortes just below Sunny Brae farm. "From that day forward," wrote Rose (Manson) McKay, "Barney refused to back up except under extreme circumstances."

Barney was one of few horses on the island, and the Mansons were generous in loaning him. Their cash-strapped neighbours sometimes abused their kindness, recalled one of the Mansons, since they didn't seem to think Barney needed to be fed while in their care.

The need for better roads became an issue for farmers who lived at a distance from steamship docks. In 1900 just two trails ran east–west across the island. The Tiber Trail (now in part Carrington Bay Road) went from Whaletown to Blue Jay Lake, and the difficult Allen Trail (now part of Whaletown Road) cut across from the Gorge to Squirrel Cove. John Manson led a crew in 1908 to hack and grub a wagon-road connection from Mansons Landing to the farms at the southern tip of the island.

Islanders were excited when the Powell River pulp mill went into operation in 1910, providing an outlet for their produce and easier access to medical care. The mill town brought other conveniences too. In 1910 telegraph and telephone lines were extended from Powell River to Cortes and Marina, where stations were opened in 1911.

Life had finally settled into a more stable and comfortable pattern for John and Margaret Manson when their home at Sunny Brae, built just a few years earlier, burned in July 1912. They salvaged very few personal possessions. Rose (Manson) McKay blamed herself, having urged her father to pull their precious piano from the burning house so little else was saved. Unfortunately their house insurance, carried through a

The Marlatt family of Manitoba bought Marina Island in about 1907 and built several houses on the western shore. The island was named Marina by Spanish explorers, for conquistador Hernando Cortes's Mexican mistress. Pious Cortesians of the last century adopted the name Mary Island for many years. PHOTO COURTESY OF PAULA MARLATT COLLECTION, MCR 20349-6.

relative, had expired unnoticed just three months prior. The community helped the Mansons erect a temporary dwelling that wound up being their home for five years until they could afford to build a new house, which remains on-site.

John was ready to give up on Cortes Island after the fire. He wanted to try ranching in the prime cattle country in the Cariboo, but Margaret wouldn't hear of it. There were rumours that a cougar killed a child there, so she flatly refused to leave Cortes Island. John could have worked in the fishing industry, as an expert net mender, his daughter Rose recalled. But if he was determined about anything, it was to not work under someone else's rule, as he put it, "a prey to the whistle" so they remained on their marginal Cortes Island farm.

The Marlatts of Portage la Prairie bought Marina Island, then called Mary Island, in 1907.[87] They had big plans. The editor of *The Log* in 1908 said they cleared a large garden around the house and another for "experimental purposes" to test various grains. "He plans to build a mill on the northeast side of the island, and when the timber is cut in about ten years' time, he will divide the island up into forty acre plots and sell to settlers."

The Marlatts—Sam, Elizabeth and their daughter Hannah—built a log house facing into a deepwater bay on the west side of the island, "within earshot of the lapping waves." Their house had a fireplace and a row of gable windows upstairs that overlooked their prized monkey puzzle tree. Their son Roy and his wife Mabel built a house nearby. In back was a four-hectare (ten-acre) field and an orchard of apple, peach, apricot, cherry, plum, pear and quince trees.

In 1910 the Marlatts opened a post office on Marina, registered under the island's Native name of Chamadaska, and in 1911 they began to log with a crew of twenty-one men from Russia, Germany, Finland, Iceland, Norway, Sweden, Canada and the US. But within a year they gave up on the island and their dream for a farm community. Disheartened by the vagaries of the logging market and a slump in the

By 1910 enough people lived near Marina Island to open Chamadaska post office and telegraph station, using the island's Native name. In about 1912 the Milnes, Scottish industrialists, bought the island and built houses, a barn and a larger dock (seen here) on southeastern Marina.
PHOTO COURTESY OF MEG (ROBERTSON) SHAW, CORTES ISLAND MUSEUM COLLECTION, MCR 13,581.

economy, they moved to Powell River, where two sons were in practice as a doctor and a dentist.

The next owner of Marina Island was James Milne, a large man with an impressive black beard. Milne came to the area for sport fishing after a business trip to sell paper-mill equipment in Port Alberni and was smitten by the coast. He arranged for a middleman to buy Marina on his behalf, but the man resold it to James at an inflated price on the strength of its logging potential, which didn't pan out.

James Milne came from a Scottish family of biblical proportions, one James begetting another in a long line of successful foundry owners, but by the early twentieth century the business was beginning to fail. James moved his housekeeper Bella and three daughters to Marina in 1912.

As James Milne Jr. wrote in a family history, Marina Island had one of two telegraph-telephone stations in the area, as well as a post office and steamship dock. "The settlement on the northwest side of the island facing Quadra," he wrote, "consisted of a main house, barn, a second cottage for guests and a third shack for the hired man Harry Bourman [Bowerman] who proved to be a surly man who kept two vicious dogs and a number of smelly goats."

It may have been a fishing paradise for James, but the isolation was boring for his daughters and ultimately too much work for an aging man. The Milnes, like the Marlatts, gave up on the island within a few years.

Across the water at Smelt Bay lived the Padgetts, who bought their property sometime before 1906.[88] Their farm included pigs to clear the land, leghorn chickens and goats. Herbert came from a well-to-do background that islanders called "top drawer." His father, who had owned a woollen mill and several estates, amassed a fortune making uniforms during the Crimean War. Herbert's wife Patty Shackleton came from an old family and was presented to Queen Victoria as a debutante. James was a good match, but his propensity for gambling on chancy gold mines and land deals beggared his estate, so they immigrated to Canada to rebuild their lives.

Patty Padgett was an exceedingly lovely woman who enchanted young Rose (Manson) McKay. Patty brushed her floor-length auburn hair at least twice a day, Rose said in a perhaps romanticized recollection, but only washed it once a year, always on the same day in August. Rose was also intrigued by the woman's fine clothes and white kid gloves that bore the marks of her heavy rings, studded with diamonds, rubies and sapphires. Rose recalled the day she arrived at the Padgett's place just as Patty returned from a dance on Marina Island. "Mr. Padgett met her at the beach and carried her ashore from the tender. She was gowned in a beautiful black silk evening dress, complete with a train. I thought that was the living end! She looked so beautiful."

The Padgetts had at least one distinguished guest during their few years on Cortes. Young Rose was fascinated by the amazing stories Patty's relative Ernest Shackleton told of his Antarctic explorations.

Some people who arrived on Cortes in these years were decidedly eccentric. Fred Hawkins discovered Cortes on a hunting trip and longed for the day when he could leave his job as the foreman of a Vancouver shoe factory to move to the island. He bought Horace and Cora Heay's property at Mansons Lagoon, at the west end of Taka Mika Road, in 1908.

Fred was a bit of an oddity, being completely hairless. Everyone knew his thatch of red hair was actually a wig because it was often askew. "But you dare not say a word about it," recalled George Griffin in a taped interview.

As Fred was not a robust man, most of the farm chores fell to his children and wife Sabina, who looked after the chickens, pigs and a cow under Fred's watchful eye. To control household expenses he hung a notebook from the doorknob of the pantry and expected Sabina to jot down "every speck" of food she used. "There was a to-do if she used too many eggs or more of anything else than he thought she could get by with," wrote Rose (Manson) McKay. As it turned out, Sabina was no more fit for hard work than he was. She succumbed to a stroke early one morning as she scrubbed the family laundry in 1913.

Dan McDonald, the crusty old Scotsman of Twin Island, moved to Coulter Bay in about 1911[89] when he sold his homestead to Reverend Harpur Nixon of Denman Island. The minister was an occasional resident, but his son James and his wife Margaret moved into Dan's cabin after they were married in 1912.

Margaret Nixon of Twin Island left a very different life as a missionary nurse in India when she married James Nixon. Her first husband and children died of tropical diseases in India, and she was attacked by a parasite that entered her nose. Surgery failed to remove the parasite but she lived for many years. PHOTO COURTESY OF ROSE (MANSON) MCKAY COLLECTION, MCR 5424.

James and Margaret were an unconventional couple, and as his many excellent photographs demonstrate, they were very much in love. He was twenty-three and she was forty-eight when they were married in Vancouver. They took to their new life with gusto, enjoying the social scene on Cortes, hobby farming, hunting, fishing and boating.

Like many others, the Nixons came to the area so Margaret could convalesce. She lost her first husband and both her children in India, where she'd served as a missionary nurse. She inhaled a parasite or insect that entered her nose and burrowed into the left side of her face, causing continuing problems and a need for complex surgery.

James, on the other hand, grew up in ease. His father was an Anglo-Irish nobleman and an Anglican clergyman who immigrated to BC with his English wife and children in 1891. They built a fine house on a Denman Island homestead, where James followed his father's passion for sailing and became a marine engineer.

Newlyweds Captain James and Margaret Nixon moved to Twin Island when James's father Harpur bought it as a retreat. Shortly after the couple left the island, Harpur Nixon died under mysterious circumstances.
PHOTO COURTESY OF ROSE (MANSON) MCKAY COLLECTION, MCR 5894.

James and Margaret lived in Dan McDonald's cabin on Twin Island for about a year until Harpur built an attractive bungalow on a rise that overlooked a swale where sheep grazed in the orchard.

The couple left the island in about 1915, and about a year later Reverend Harpur Nixon came to a mysterious end. He was resting on board his boat at dusk when he was hit by an inexplicable blast that tore away most of the lower part of his face. He swaddled his jaw in a towel and went to John and Margaret Manson's home on southern Cortes. In a note he explained he'd inadvertently put a blasting cap in his pipe. John took him to the Powell River hospital, but he was transferred to Vancouver, where he died a few weeks later.

Shortly before his death, Harpur Nixon changed his statement on the cause of the accident, saying he didn't know whether it was a blasting cap in his pipe or a shot from a hunter who mistook his glowing pipe for the eyes of a deer caught in a pit lamp. An investigation ensued but with no results. When the *Belfast Chronicle* in Ireland reported the story, it noted that Reverend Harpur Nixon's father, also a minister, died of a similar injury in 1859. He was leaving the church on his Donegal estate when a party of armed and masked men shot him in the jaw.[90]

The Froud family of England heard about Cortes's healthful climate from one of the Mansons and sent their son Frederick, who was slow to recover from rheumatic fever, to live with John and Margaret. The climate proved so efficacious that most of Frederick's family followed, including his parents and various grown siblings. "We were so sure we were all going to be happy there," wrote one of the Frouds in later years, "that we ordered the materials for two houses, making sure to miss nothing and it all came up on a scow in July of 1914."

Frederick's parents had strong and somewhat unconventional convictions. They were both vegetarians, and his father was a Theosophist,[91] following a new religion that embraced the occult. The Frouds were rather highbrow, as Rose (Manson) McKay recalled, genteel folk whose lifestyle was out of sync with most of the young people raised in a poor logging and farming community. "The music was parlour music, so different to the 'hoe downs' islanders normally enjoyed," wrote Rose.

Fanny Froud was in delicate health, like her son, so her husband built her an indoor toilet in what looked like a large cupboard. It had a back panel that hinged open so the galvanized bucket beneath could be removed. The toilet seat was covered in deer hide, complete with bristling fur. Fanny was anxious to make her special toilet available to her lady guests. "As the evening wore on," recalled Rose (Manson) McKay, "Mrs. Froud would draw each lady aside and inquire softly, 'would you like to make yourself comfortable?' [The toilet] was a bit of a shock at first, but a very kind gesture nevertheless."

Eugene Paulson also came to the island to recuperate. He had made the mistake, or so his parents thought, of marrying beneath his station, so they cut him off until they learned he was ill with meningitis. Eugene's wife Sarah worked as a housekeeper to support them until his father bought the couple land on southeast Cortes Island, now the Hollyhock retreat centre. "They arrived one spring evening on the Union Steamship boat," wrote Rose (Manson) McKay, "complete with tents, provisions and lumber. A very well constructed house was built that summer and it still stands today."

The property was cleared and some of the trees were limbed to create what the Paulsons called a park, a pretentious term that made the neighbours titter and puzzled young Rose, who expected to see exotic animals like those she'd seen in Stanley Park in Vancouver. It wasn't long before the Paulsons decided their new property was too exposed to southeast storms and not congenial to Eugene's delicate health, so they moved to Chris's Lagoon near Cortes Bay.

Another well-to-do couple of these years were Mabel and Robert Houlgate, who first came to the area on sailing trips. They bought Subtle Island from the Strange family in 1909 and built a modern bungalow near the government dock, where the two parts of the island join.

Robert was the son of a prominent banker and had many business concerns of his own, including a position on the board of the Union Steamship Company. He was only an occasional resident but Mabel and Robert's brother Alfred lived on the island year-round with two Chinese servants and a farmhand.

Cortes Island became a destination for Seattle and Vancouver boaters at the start of the last century, according to Charlie Allen's diary. Some returned every summer for years. They anchored in Gorge Harbour for a few days or more, bought produce and baking from the locals and hired them as fishing and hunting guides. Charlie crowed in his diary over the pleasure of the occasional glass of gin and relaxed chat aboard the finely appointed boats of these summer visitors.

When the middle-aged Strange siblings sold Subtle Island to the Houlgates they moved across the channel to what's now Sawmill Bay, where Charlie had a steam-powered sawmill. There was a steady market for their lumber in the pre–World War I boom years. Patty and Alice Strange fired the steam boiler and helped stack lumber. They also hired out to do sewing and fancy baking. Up the road from the Stranges were their nephews the Houghtons, with a house on the corner of what's now Sawmill and Carrington Bay roads.

Charlie Houghton came to an untimely end on Christmas Day in 1912. His hunting party on Read Island fanned out, as was common practice, to flush out deer. At the end of the day Charlie didn't meet the others at the beach as planned, though his friends heard a shot from his direction earlier in the day and assumed he'd bagged a deer. Their search for Charlie proved futile, so they went to Cortes for help. "Miss P. Strange came over before we were up," wrote Charlie Allen in his diary, "and wanted me to go and look for Charlie Houghton, so I got ready right away. Then 10 men came from Mansons, so they took them all over to Read Island. Bill Robertson was there with his launch and they were hunting all day, but found nothing of him." The search continued for two days, through a wicked southeast storm, but the only clues they found were a few bullet casings presumed to have come from Houghton's rifle.

Twenty-six years later Charlie Houghton's mysterious disappearance was explained when a man on the point of death in a Victoria hospital confessed he'd shot a man by accident on Christmas Day on Read Island in 1912. He panicked when he realized what he'd done and rolled Houghton's body off a bluff into the sea.

Apart from this tragedy, island life had become much more comfortable for Cortesians. War and recession loomed on the horizon, but the island's population would flourish, along with its distinctive culture of companionable eccentricity.

A Proliferation of New Communities

News of the war in Europe started to filter into the diaries of Charlie Allen and his sister Alice Robertson in the summer of 1914. Just days after Alice noted the fall of Antwerp, her sixteen-year-old son Allen and her brother Bernie set off to Vancouver to enlist. Alice's son had been out of school for several years and worked on the road crew, in construction with his father, in logging camps and more recently on a new dock at Whaletown.

Alice's strong sense of patriotic duty is clear in her diary, but she gives no clue of what she felt as her young son set off to war. She used double exclamation marks in the spring of 1915, however, when the boy got a short leave to visit home before going on active service overseas. He looked "fit and bright," wrote Alice in her diary.

Allen Robertson of Whaletown was adept with a rifle, like many country-bred youths, and was sent to the front lines in World War I. He was gassed and needed many months' treatment in a sanatorium before he was finally released toward the end of the war.
PHOTO COURTESY OF
CORTES ISLAND MUSEUM.

Once the apple harvest was over that year, Alice's husband David became restless. As a former army officer, he too wanted to enlist. David waited in the wharf shed through a chill November night for the Union Steamship boat, with Alice watching from the kitchen window where she could see David's lamplight. A few days later he wrote home to say he'd been refused because of his age and health, but he persisted and was finally accepted.

While David waited in Vancouver through that winter for an over-seas posting, young Allen was in the thick of battle in the trenches in Flanders, where he was gassed. "The chemicals have settled in his lungs," wrote Alice in her diary, "and he was unable to walk the four miles from the trenches to his billet." Allen was transported to a sanatorium in Calgary to recuperate and some time later paid a surprise visit home. When Alice came downstairs to light the fire in the morning she found the lad sitting quietly in the kitchen. "The dear boy is thin and his voice is weak but otherwise he seems well, and does not cough much," she wrote. Allen was far from well, however, and it was many months before he was deemed fit to return home again.

The same day Alice learned her son would soon be home for good, she got word David was going into active service. "D writes from Seaford, Sussex," she wrote. "He is now in the 16th Reserve Battalion. I am a happy woman this day."

A number of other islanders enlisted for the Great War, but most were urged to remain at home, as they provided essential services such as logging, fishing or farming. Mabel and Edward Huck, with their five children, had just settled into an old one-room cabin on their remote Green Valley home-stead at Blue Jay Lake when Edward enlisted. Mabel saved her husband's letters from boot camp and overseas. "You say I talk as if you forced me to enlist," he wrote. "I never meant it that way but I had to do some-thing to protect you and the kids and that was all there was to it."

Edward's letters ring with affection for his wife and family. He glossed over the horror of the trenches, but in September 1916 he gave a few more details: "I have been to the trenches and had some pretty close shaves but come out OK though we lost a few. I was in the trenches on the anniversary of our wedding. It does not seem like thirteen years since we were married."

A month later Mabel received an envelope bordered in black to tell her Edward had been killed in action. This left her a widow with five children to raise on her remote homestead. Mabel's neighbours—the Barretts, Middletons and Taits—helped her through that harsh winter of heavy snow. They brought her venison and shovelled the snow from her house and outbuildings. About a year later Mabel's brother Jack Wells moved in with her. Though he was debilitated by a serious head injury and the loss of sight in one eye from his war service, he was still able to follow his trade as a farrier and blacksmith.

Alice Robertson was luckier than some. Both her son and husband returned from their war service to remake their lives on Cortes Island.

Everyone got involved in the war effort, whether or not they had family enlisted. The community raised money, wrote letters to homesick soldiers and knitted for them. In the summer of 1915, Cortesians arranged what they called a Tobacco Concert, a version of today's coffee house, as a fundraiser to send tobacco to soldiers.

War also disrupted the lives of new residents John and Elizabeth Poole, who were married in West Africa some years before their move to Canada. They had just moved into a cottage they bought from Charles and Jennie Allen in the Gorge when John was conscripted. When he returned, John bought a large acreage at what's now called Channel Rock, but Elizabeth was content in her cottage, so they moved back and forth between the two places. The house John built on a rocky bluff at Channel Rock still stands, though long abandoned.

With no children to care for, John indulged his passion for reading and botanizing. "Listening to Bernie Allen and John Poole discuss wild flowers was like a mental minuet," said one of their contemporaries. Poole's library included lofty tomes by Tacitus, Gogol, Darwin, Gibbon and others. His letters about his plant discoveries remain on file at the Royal BC Museum in Victoria.

Very little changed for the Klahoose people of Squirrel Cove as a result of the Great War and the nasty recession it sparked. Their lives had long been a struggle with poverty, dominated by racist legislation that robbed them of their traditional economy. Their population was dangerously low, but it held at between sixty and seventy people through the first decades of the twentieth century.

The 1901 census listed seventy-two band members, of whom only Chief Julian and a fifty-year-old man named George spoke English. Unlike the We-Wai-Kai Band on Quadra, which had a low ratio of children, more than half of the Klahoose population were children aged fifteen and under, but only three were in their teens. There were eight seniors of sixty years or over, some of whom retained their Native names, including a seventy-year-old blind man named Sai-quo-sheen and sixty-five-year-old Klikamie. The rest were simply listed by Christian first names like Ignace, William, Rose and Agnes, with no surnames. The band also likely had other members, away for seasonal work or staying on other reserves.

The band's population dropped to sixty by the time of the 1911 census. There were now just twenty-one kids fifteen and under, suggesting a high childhood mortality rate. The heads of the households listed their occupations as loggers (ten), fishermen (five) and farmers (two), and by this census band members had adopted Christian surnames like Louie, Hill, McGee, Peter, Dominick, Old, Beal and Harry. A few blended their Christian names with Native names like seventy-year-old fisherman Harry Carchit. Three band members could read and write English, including fifty-year-old Sophie McGee, seventeen-year-old logger Joe Dominick and sixteen-year-old Alex Louie.

When a Royal Commission toured the province to hear grievances, they visited the Klahoose on Saturday, February 20, 1915. Chief Julian spoke on behalf of the band, saying there were seventy-one Klahoose people, with thirty-one buildings on their reserve at Squirrel Cove, about ten at Toba Inlet and a few more elsewhere.

Chief Julian and his wife Mary were born just before the huge smallpox epidemic of 1862. At the time of the commission's hearings, he was fifty-four and supported himself as a fisherman. He'd seen and experienced too many heartbreaks. As a very old man, when anthropologist

Homer Barnett recorded his memories in the mid-1930s, he was in the grip of alcoholism, a habit encouraged by loggers and whiskey traders through most of his life. Barnett noted Chief Julian's uncontested right to chiefly lineage. His memory stretched back to his childhood, when he wore a goatskin robe at the winter ceremonials.

"I am glad to see you Commissioners come here this afternoon," said Chief Julian at the 1915 hearings. "It is about two years since we have been hearing that some day you would be up here and we had been waiting ever since. We are very poor Indians, and that is why we are all glad to see you Commissioners because we know you will help us." Julian spoke at length about his band's willingness to engage in agriculture, but the Department of Indian Affairs blocked their plans to log their land and they couldn't afford the tools they needed to clear and break farm land. What kept them in a famished state, said Julian, were restrictive hunting laws. "If we do not kill deer out of season we have nothing to eat, only bread and tea. We would like to be allowed to kill deer out of season."

There was also talk of requiring the Native people to buy licences to fish. "We fish, and we hunt for deer and for clams—and that is how we make our living," said Julian. "We do some trapping and we work out-side for white men. We sell some logs at the camp and get a little money."

When asked about education, Chief Julian said there were twenty-two school-aged children but only one had attended the school at the Xwemalhkwu (Homalco) Reserve at Church House. Julian agreed he would like to see all the children educated, if there was a school within a reasonable distance.

Religion was important to the Klahoose people. They had converted to Catholicism in the early 1860s, and though a priest visited the reserve only a few times a year, Julian said band members attended church every day, once in the morning and again before bed. Homer Barnett said that Johnny Dominick conducted church services. "He was of a retiring nature, without enmities or pretensions," said Barnett.

For the Klahoose, as for most bands involved in these hearings, not much changed as a result of them. The commissioner said he intended to talk to the Indian Department about restrictions on logging, but when it came to their traditional pursuits like hunting and fishing, he was inflexible and simply defined how and when they could hunt according to legislation.

Education for Native and non-Native kids was segregated. When a small non-Native community sprang up at Squirrel Cove across the bay from the Homalco Reserve, Native children could not attend the school that settlers opened in 1916.

Whaletown and Squirrel Cove disagreed over which school was closest to Blue Jay Lake, then called Green Valley, should attend. Bill Barrett settled the debate by tying a rag to the wheel of his wagon and counting the revolutions on a trip to each school. Squirrel Cove won.

Mr. Ewart opened a store at Squirrel Cove in a tent in 1914 and later replaced it with a frame building that forms the core of the current Squirrel Cove store. David Forrest took over the store and in 1916 became the first postmaster, holding the position until 1940.

Oyster leases on beds of small native Olympic oysters formed a minor part of the island's economy. Helen Bull of the Heriot Bay Hotel on Quadra Island owned two twenty-one-year leases in Squirrel Cove until 1924. A character named Dave Logan also had an oyster lease at the head of Von Donop Inlet. (The ladies of the island avoided Dave at dances because he only knew how to do "the chicken dance," whether the music was a waltz or the jitterbug.)

A World War I vet named Peter Antonio Police of Carrington Bay was another character, with his thick Italian accent and particular ways. He was badly injured in the war with shrapnel in the head, so a Montreal doctor told him he'd have to have surgery. Peter said that first he wanted to see his mother. He looked at a map of Canada and decided Haida Gwaii was the farthest away he could get, so he told the doctor that was where his mother lived. Peter fished for a few years at Haida Gwaii and then traded his boat for land in Carrington Bay.

Peter kept a sign at the head of his driveway saying there were people who were welcome and some who were not. In 1923 Peter married Violetta Woodhead, but the union ended within three weeks, so he never tried marriage again. "I will not be responsible for any debts incurred by my wife, Violet Police," Peter announced in the *Daily Colonist* in January 1924, "who has left my bed and board."

Another new little community sprang up during the war years on the east coast of the island at Seaford, which had a trail across to Mansons Landing. In 1917 Seaford became an official port of call for Union Steamship boats, and a post office was opened there with Captain Marian E. Smith as postmaster.

Herb and Mary Aldrich moved to Seaford in about 1914, attracted to the area by their Read Island relatives, the Wylies. Mary had trained under her father, a doctor with an in-home clinic in Rochester, Minnesota, where she went to school with the Mayo brothers. (Mary's sister Ida managed the Mayos' convalescent home, which later became the famous Mayo Clinic.) Mary's skill as a midwife and in basic medicine was a boon to her neighbours.

Mary Aldrich was the backbone of her family, as Etta (McKay) Byers recalls. "Herb was more of a talker than a doer," wrote Etta, "consequently money was often short. Mary would milk the cows, tend the garden, look after the children as well as be available whenever her medical knowledge was needed. They never owned a horse, so she had to walk or row wherever she went. She'd say, with her American twang, 'you'll-a do it!' and everyone would listen."

Mary Aldrich kept her doctor's bag at the ready, stocked with herbal medicines she ordered by mail. When Mary advised Robina (Manson) Freeman her pregnancy had terminated, Robina went to a Powell River doctor. Mary was outraged when she learned the doctor said all was well with the pregnancy. In twenty-eight days, said Mary, Robina would be really sick—but the Freemans decided to wait. As Mary predicted, twenty-eight days later Robina had to be rushed to hospital in Vancouver. She almost died en route and never fully recovered her health, dying about nine years later.

Also at Seaford were the Jefferys. Mary Jeffery was a gregarious woman who found the isolation of her new home a hardship. To get anywhere she had to walk a long distance inland or travel by small boat, but that didn't stop Mary, who walked for kilometres by the light of a "bug," a lantern made with a candle set into an old tin can, to attend dances and social functions.

The Jefferys were an anomaly for their time. Mary's war-vet husband took charge of the household chores, children and cooking, giving her time to organize social and religious functions. She was the moving force behind a church that opened in Squirrel Cove and she initiated the formation of a branch of the Women's Institute, a rural organization providing health care information and an outlet for socializing and community work.

Before the war ended, the Aldriches' daughter Ruth and her husband Henry Byers followed them to Seaford, where they formed a logging partnership with Tom Lambert of Sutil Point. Henry Byers was a lively new addition to the community. In his native Cape Town, South Africa, he learned to play the guitar in an infectious style he credited to his South African teachers. With his brother-in-law Wallace Aldrich on violin, Henry was in constant demand for dances.

Boat day at Mansons Landing, a social event, brought settlers together once a week to catch up on the news as they waited for the arrival of their freight, mail or visitors. The same scene played out in many coastal communities. PHOTO COURTESY OF MCR 19,332.

Henry had a livery stable before he moved to Cortes, so he was a natural for horse logging. He logged at Sutil Point on the Lamberts' place in 1917, using a massive landing made from logs and boulders that remain on-site. The landing had to withstand the southeast storms, recalls Etta (McKay) Byers, and support a team of horses with a load of logs. The logs were unhooked and rolled with a peavey—a spiked pole with a moveable clasp near the end—down the log structure and into the water to be boomed. An unexpected job hazard was Tom Lambert's infernal billy goat. Henry managed to avoid him until one day the goat caught him unawares and gave him a mighty butt that knocked Henry "ass over teakettle" into the sea.

Henry Byers's brothers Charlie and Andy followed him to Cortes. By 1919 they were all living at Seaford in shacks built from logs and shakes. Ruth's and Henry's house went up in one day, and though it was unbearably cold, it remained their home until 1922.

First Nations families were forced to send their children to residential school after 1915. They wanted their children to have an education, but not at a distant school in Sechelt or elsewhere. They had no choice. The children, who spoke limited English, were punished for speaking their own language. Tom Hill started school in Sechelt at thirteen and stayed for several years. "It was terrible," he recalled in later years. Religion was "pushed down their throats" and most other subjects were covered in a basic way. The generations of children who followed, raised in institutions, gained no practical experience with parenting, feeding and caring for themselves. Kathy Francis, who has served as band chief, says there is a spiral of after-effects. "It destroyed people and it doesn't just end because it's no longer happening."

Mike Manson remained the MLA for this region until the Conservative Party lost the election in 1916,[92] their popularity falling with the deep recession of the war years. The provincial government that followed gave the vote to non-Native women. At the same time, in 1917, the federal government banned alcohol sales in what was called Prohibition. This ban created a lucrative business opportunity for families like the Conlins, who sold moonshine at Smelt Bay. The Conlins took over the Padgett property just before the war and hired young Wally Aldrich to transport their illegal hooch to Vancouver, where Michael Conlin owned a hotel. From there some of the liquor was also smuggled into the US.

Michael Conlin was among the lucky few who made some money in the Yukon gold rush and used it to start a logging company and buy a Vancouver hotel. His exotic wife Ellen was intriguing to islanders. Some said she was part First Nations and Afro-American, while others said she was part Hawaiian. Ellen and her children stayed at the Vancouver hotel while Michael worked away as a logger. The wild lifestyle at the hotel exposed their boys to the "seamier side of life" and broke apart their marriage. The couple separated before Michael moved the boys to Smelt Bay, accompanied by their mother and her new husband. Michael hoped they'd become farmers, but as Rose (Manson) McKay recalled, they weren't cut out for it. Michael Conlin Jr., Edmund, Parnell and Patrick continued to drink and make merry, dipping into their still. When their father went broke a few years later, the boys—and eventually his ex-wife and her husband—gave up on farming and went their own ways.

The World War I recession continued well into the early 1920s. With jobs scarce and no welfare system available, new families came to the island to live off the land. Some were veterans the government placed on sixteen-hectare (forty-acre) plots on soldiers' settlements. The Conlins' property at Smelt Bay became one of these settlements, where Henry and Mary Jeffery of Seaford got land on the strength of his war service.

Several railway logging shows started work on the islands after the war. From 1920 to 1924, logs were dragged with a cat along a narrow-gauge line from Carrington Lagoon to the base of Green Mountain. An outfit called ABM logged with conventional railway logging trains on southern Cortes through the 1920s. Their camp was at the corner of Seaford and Gorge Harbour roads. ABM's steam donkey lies half-submerged in Gunflint Lake—the current Kw'as Park trail—where it blew up, taking the life of young Hazen, who was about to be married. The third railway outfit, Campbell River Timber Company of the Lower Mainland, logged Mike and Jane Manson's property on Hernando with a Japanese crew, starting in about 1917. Their camp and log dump were at Stag Bay, not far from the Manson families' homes.

Mike Manson turned his attention to sheep farming on Hernando after he lost his seat as an MLA in 1916.[93] The island now belonged entirely to the Mansons. Mike and Jane and their grown children Wilf and Robina moved there during the war. They may have seen the island as a temporary home for the duration of CRT's logging operation, as Mike and Jane had just built a fine new home at Mansons Landing several years prior. They rented out their new home and loaded their old house onto a barge to relocate to Hernando, but as they rounded Sutil Point, the house slid off the barge into the sea. They had to move into an old settler's house in Stag Bay. The beautiful location—surrounded by fields, fruit trees and a fenced garden that faced a broad expanse of sandy beach—made up for some of these losses. The old Rorison house was to remain Mike's and Jane's home for the remainder of their days.

By 1920 the population of Cortes and its satellite islands was around five hundred people.[94] Whaletown, including Blue Jay Lake and Gorge Harbour, had about sixty people, according to the British Columbia Directory. In 1929 the settlers at Whaletown built a church hall near the school on Alice and David Robertson's land next to the old cemetery at the corner of what's now Harbour and Carrington Bay roads. The church was officially opened at a fair with food booths and a quilt raffle. "The afternoon proceedings were succeeded in the evening by a real, old-time dance, which was enjoyed by all," reported the *Comox Argus*.

As most settlers owned huge tracts of land, community services were built on donated land in a random fashion. At Whaletown the school and church hall were in the northern part of Whale Bay on the Robertsons' land, for example, while the government dock and store were at the south entrance to the bay. Mary and Nick Thompson built a new store at the head of the wharf in 1921.[95]

The Mansons Landing community was also scattered rather than consolidated as a village. According to the provincial directory, about seventy people lived there in 1920, when a new wharf was built there near the current location at Mansons Landing. As the Mansons owned many hectares at the dock, community services like the school were built several kilometres to the east along a dirt track. Residents pooled their money and labour in 1920 to build a new community hall across from the log schoolhouse at the intersection of Sutil Point and Beasley roads on land donated by Fred Froud. It was a proud achievement in those recession years.

Little pockets of settlements sprang up throughout southern Cortes Island from Von Donop Inlet in the 1920's, at Carrington Bay, Cortes Bay, Squirrel Cove and Seaford. The latter two were large enough to have their own schools, post offices, stores and steamship docks.

In 1925 a young journalist with the Vancouver *Province* visited Cortes and several other Discovery Island communities to write a four-part article on coastal living. Cortes Island enchanted Lukin Johnston, who predicted one day it would become a tourist haven:

> Tucked away in Gorge Harbor, on Cortez Island, one of the beauty spots of the Coast, are more small farms, where settlers are struggling hard and making good. There is no more picturesque spot in all British Columbia than the narrow entrance to Gorge Harbor. The channel is not more than 200 yards wide, and on one side a bold cliff rises to a height of 100 feet, sheer up from the water. On the other side the land slopes down to the waters' edge and is clothed with splendid maples which, in the fall of the year, presents a magnificent spectacle in their mantle of red and gold. Nearby is the pretty red-roofed cottage of Edward Breeze, nestling among the trees.
>
> Some day Cortez Island will be "discovered" by the tired business-men of Vancouver and Victoria. Every bay on the island presents vis-tas of beauty, where one feels a desire to erect a summer home. There are lovely prospects of sea and foliage at every turn—an ideally peace-ful place to forget the noise and cares of city life.

Johnston, whose article tracked the success of subsistence farming on this part of the coast, also visited old August Tiber at Gunflint Lake:

> Tucked away in the heart of the forest, August has spent 30 years clearing one of the most productive small farms you could wish to see. We entered his gate and saw the old man approaching across his big garden. In his hand he carried a heavy pail full to the brim with fine

potatoes. Search where you may you will not find a more picturesque figure than this old Cortez Island pioneer. White-haired and white-bearded, but with ruddy cheeks and an eye as clear as ever, old August greeted us with a cheer shout:

"Oh aye-by golly, by jove—good morgen to yer, good morgen," he cried as he approached.

"Why don't you take a rest at your age, Mr. Tiber?" we asked him.

"Rest, by golly? How can I rest? Tirty year I vork to make a fine farm, by golly, I get 'em all fixed up an den, by golly, by jove, de whole family dey up and go avay, by golly, by jove. Rest indeed!" snorted the old man.

He laughed as he told how he had been suspected of being a spy "or some fool ting," as he put it, during the war. "Yes, I was born in Germany, by golly, by jove," he said, "but whose fault was dat?"

Johnston was also impressed by John Manson, whose wife Margaret had recently passed away. He lauded the old settler for his integrity, saying there was no more respected citizen in British Columbia. "Today is to be seen the reward of long years of toil in John Manson's fine farm, his

Margaret Manson in the fine new home John built for his family in 1919. Fire destroyed their first house just three months after their fire insurance had, unknown to them, expired. Margaret was well loved for her kind nature and hospitality. A stained glass window in the little church beside the Mansons Community Hall is dedicated to her memory.
PHOTO COURTESY OF CORTES ISLAND MUSEUM COLLECTION, MCR 13,556.

solid house surrounded by orchards and fields," wrote Johnston. "His brother, who lives within sight on Hernando Island, raises sheep and also has prospered."

"Margaret Manson was much loved by all who knew her and when she died suddenly in August 1925," wrote her daughter Rose, "everyone was shocked and grieved." Three young men built her a fine casket, and the community hall at Mansons overflowed with mourners who brought lavish homemade bouquets as a tribute to a fine woman.

· Mike Manson returned to politics in 1924 when he was elected in the newly formed McKenzie riding, a sprawling stretch of coast that included Cortes Island. Several of Mike's and Jane's grown children took over his activities on Hernando Island. Their daughter Hazel and her husband Henry Herrewig got the property at Mansons Landing, while Florence and her husband Ervin McKay got the farm at Gunflint Lake in 1929.

Wolves and cougars remained a problem for stock raisers. One winter a predacious cougar killed sheep night after night, but islanders couldn't track it, so they sent for Cecil "Cougar" Smith, who worked for the game department. Smith had only two bullets on him when he rushed to Cortes but expected to get more from an island farmer.

Smith arrived in early evening and got old Dad Sutton to take him to the cougar's last kill so he could get a sense of the animal's methods before he started tracking it at first light. There was a dead lamb in a stream and in the field beyond were many more sheep, killed and left. Sutton fed Smith a late dinner and sent him up the road to his overnight accommodation in the pitch black. He felt his way along the road until eventually he saw a few lights in a valley below. On a whim he released his hunting dogs, and almost instantly one of them charged into the brush barking.

The baying of the dogs told Smith they'd treed a cougar. He shouted down to the valley and fired off one of his two bullets to attract their notice, then plunged into the bushes after his dogs. When he reached them he lit a match, and sure enough, there was a flash of light from the eyes of the treed cougar.

He fished around in his pocket for his last bullet and was pleased to discover a second one hidden in a corner. He tied his dogs out of harm's way

Cortes has more churches than any of the other Discovery islands. St James Church, next to the Mansons Community Hall, was built in 1927. The next year Mike and Jane Manson celebrated their fiftieth anniversary there, followed by a dinner for eighty and toasts with brandy Mike bought forty years prior for this event. Their family presented gifts in a model canoe as a reminder of the Mansons' elopement to Victoria from Nanaimo. PHOTO COURTESY OF GODFREY BALDWIN, MCR 3012.

and loaded his rifle, backed up against some fencing to brace himself, lit another match and fired. The roar of the gun was followed by a tremendous crashing in the trees. As Smith tried to pull away from the fence post, his mackinaw caught in the barbwire and sent him sprawling onto his face. Just then the cougar fell on top of him. He could tell the animal wasn't dead but he was able to wriggle from beneath it to grab his rifle. He took aim by the light of a match just as the animal steadied itself to pounce.

Smith headed down to the settler's home in the valley below and asked why they hadn't come to his aid. They heard the row, they said, but were too afraid to respond.[96]

There was no warning for the majority of Canadians that their economy was about to fall flat in the stock market crash of 1929. It took Cortesians by surprise, but it didn't impose the hardship so many other Canadians experienced. Islanders were adept at making do, and there were always clams, fish and venison to eat. In fact some residents of the day recalled the Depression as one of the best times of their lives.

The Great Depression

Tourism began on Cortes when the Union Steamship Company ran scenic cruises from Vancouver to the island from 1919 to 1924, but it wasn't until just months before the stock market crash of 1929 that a summer lodge opened in Gorge Harbour. Sarah Corneille, a widow, bought the recently constructed lodge in the extreme northern end of the harbour for six thousand dollars, with its five bedrooms, dining room and campground.

Sarah was an energetic promoter. She printed a brochure, advertising her rates at eighteen dollars per week, or ten dollars for children under ten, including food and lodging. The lodge had a tennis court on the front lawn, a badminton court in back and a high diving board on the dock. Sarah organized an annual midsummer regatta that was the big event of the season for both residents and visitors.

Sarah's daughters Bobbie and Mabel were integral partners in her business. Mabel picked up their guests in the wee hours at the Union Steamship dock in the launch and kept its motor in order. Both girls helped with the endless chores. "I seemed to only get [school] work done between October and May," recalled Bobbie in a taped interview, "because there were always things to be done. My sister and I had to put the resort to bed [and then] in spring you had to start the painting and getting the boats fixed up, and the tennis court fixed up and the badminton court, lawns cut and porches painted."

Sarah managed to eke out a living from the lodge. "You might live on $50 to $100 for a winter during the Depression," recalled their friend Duncan Robertson in a taped interview, "but we never missed a meal. In fact we had more fun in the Depression than before or since."

Mike Manson retained his seat in the legislature through the start of the Depression when then his health began to fail. A doctor warned him to slow down, but that wasn't possible for a man accustomed to a robust lifestyle. He and Jane were staying at a hotel in MacKenzie on a tour of his riding when Mike passed away suddenly in July 1932. He spent the day teaching a man to butcher sheep, recalled his granddaughter Etta (McKay) Byers. "He went up to the hotel room to see

Jane and tell her about his day, when he passed away quite suddenly at her side."

Jane was devastated. A friend helped arrange for Mike's remains to be sent to Nanaimo for burial next to the children they lost so many years earlier. Jane returned to her home on Hernando, where she passed away within a few years. She too was buried beside her family in Nanaimo.

It was the end of an era for the first generation of the Mansons, but the start of a lively new decade for the many young people who lived on Cortes during the Depression. They banded together to make the best of things, as Bill Ballantyne recalled in a taped interview. He and his mother and sister came to the island in the early 1920s and then scattered in various directions, his sister to California and his mother to a teaching job in Montreal. They were enjoying a family reunion on Cortes in the summer of 1929. "We were going to build a summer cottage and then go back to our occupations," recalled Bill, "but this was when the Depression hit and boom we discovered we had no occupations to go back to. Mother didn't want to go back to Montreal because my sister and I were sort of stuck here, although we were old enough [to be on our own]. So we got caught on Cortes Island for the duration of the Depression."

Bill and many others had to go on relief. "If you shot a deer you could trade it for chicken and you ate a lot of clams!" said Bill. "But we had a lot of fun. When we look back it was the good old days. Everyone was happy. Clothes were what really suffered. It was hard to get clothes, but everyone was in the same boat."

Bill and his friends formed a dramatic club and put on elaborate productions at the church hall in Whaletown, where they also held dances, until they outgrew the little hall. In 1933 they built a hall in Gorge Harbour on property donated by George Beattie, who inherited the Charlie and Jennie Allen homestead. Fundraising dances and cabarets brought in just enough to build the hall from cedar poles and shakes. Cardboard cartons lined the walls, and the stove was made from an oil drum. The hall, still on its original site on Robertson Road, has been renovated and expanded over the years but continues to host many dances and events.

Another hall was built in Squirrel Cove in 1934 by the CCF Club (the Co-operative Commonwealth Federation was the forerunner of the New Democratic Party). It was a large hall on the Middletons' property on Whaletown Road to the west of the current store at Squirrel Cove. Everyone pitched in. Clarence Byers dragged the fifteen-metre (fifty-foot) rafters to the building site with an old Model T. "Once I got going down the hill with those big timbers there was no stopping!" The Squirrel Cove folks enjoyed some wonderful dances in the hall, where the stage was large enough to accommodate a five-piece orchestra.

Whaletown lost several of its earliest pioneers during the Depression. Nicholas Thompson passed away in 1927, and his wife Mary, after thirty years as the unofficial postmistress, finally got the job in her own name. She continued to care for old Bill Robertson until he too passed away in 1930. "Well Roy," wrote Mary to the Marlatts, "you will be sorry to hear of Uncle Bill's death. That leaves Leonard [her adopted son] and I all alone again on the Island. We miss him everywhere we go."

In about the mid-1930s the Depression began to ease, though the signs were almost imperceptible at first. Bill and Bobbie Ballantyne were cleaning up after a dance at the Gorge Hall one day when they came across a tailor-made (store-bought) cigarette butt. "We officially declared that the Depression was over when we found that," recalled Bobbie. "We thought about framing it!"

Etta McKay and Clarence Byers were in the thick of the young social scene on Cortes. They married in 1938 and bought an aging floathouse for sixty-five dollars as their first home. They got it towed from Squirrel Cove to Seaford for another twenty-five dollars, redecorated it with fresh wallpaper and paint, and ordered a new stove from Marshall Wells, bringing their total cost for their first home to $125.

The Byers's floathouse had another advantage. In the late 1930s several branches of both of their families banded together to log in Von Donop Inlet from a floating camp. They hired the tug *Cheerful* to tow five houses strung out in a line, each on its own float, from Seaford to Von Donop Inlet, then called Von Donop Creek. Etta and Clarence's float was weighed down by the additional burden of a steam donkey and the first truck to be used for logging on the island. Both sets of their parents joined them in the inlet, along with Clarence's sister Amy and her husband Scotty McKenzie and Etta's sister Hazel and her husband Ken Hansen.

The skipper of the *Cheerful* agreed to tow the floats into Von Donop for free, hoping to get their log-towing business. All was ready, timed for the wind and tide, but Etta's brother-in-law Ken was nowhere to be seen. The tug set off anyway, as Etta recalls, and they were off Refuge Cove when he caught up with them in a speedboat loaded to the gunwales with island produce. "Ken had been out collecting sacks of spuds, carrots and farm vegetables from Uncle Johnny [Manson] and Bill Illman because he was sure we'd all starve without a garden in Von Donop Creek."

The loggers pulled their houses ashore at the head of the inlet with the donkey engine. The back ends were planted on shore and the front ends were jacked up and set on pilings. Etta and Clarence chose a sunny spot, as Etta recalled in a taped interview:

Clarence Byers (at the driver's door) logged in Von Donop Inlet in the 1940s with many other members of his own and his wife Etta's extended family. They were among the first to log with trucks on Cortes.
PHOTO COURTESY OF ETTA (McKAY) BYERS COLLECTION, MCR 9360.

When we were first in Von Donop, as Ken had feared, we were quite isolated from the rest of the world, but being young it all fitted into our daily living. Since we had no roads out, we went by boat to Redonda Bay, a Union Steamship port-of-call, for groceries and mail. We ordered enough groceries to last for several months, sent up from Malkins in Vancouver. Malkins would send the grocery bill to our log broker in Vancouver and it would be paid when the next boom sold. It was no small feat to manhandle 100-pound sacks of flour and sugar, 60-pound pails of shortening and cases of canned goods from the dock to the boat, enough to supply five families. There were 48 cans to the case of canned milk in those days. Fresh meat had to be canned. It was the only way we could keep it. Butter came in big squares; probably 50 pounds.

The men were busy building logging roads, the log dump and a massive bridge across the creek above the waterfall [at the head of the inlet]. Scotty was our high rigger. They all took turns doing all of the jobs. There were five men. Clarence drove the truck most of the time. My dad was chokerman. . . . Ken ran the donkey. Henry was on the rigging. That was before the days of having a whistle and a whistle punk. We just hollered. And we were real careful. We weren't in a big hurry, couldn't afford to be.

For all their thrift and hard work through the six years they stayed in Von Donop Inlet, none of these families earned more than their keep. "We just made a living off that timber sale, and that was all," recalls Clarence Byers. But they had weathered the tail end of the Depression and the start of World War II.

The Byerses followed the news of the war in Europe on the radio. As in World War I, men like Clarence—who worked in primary industries like logging, fishing and farming—were exempt. It was mainly young men without families who were conscripted.

R.M. (Dick) Andrews, a Canadian engineer and industrialist with investments in Denmark and Tokyo, foresaw the need to leave his expatriate home in Japan. He bought Twin Island just before the bombing of Pearl Harbor and built a palatial log house where the two parts of the islands join at a narrow neck. The Andrews family kept to themselves, leaving Cortesians to speculate about why a man would build a $250,000 home on a remote island.

Columns in city newspapers described lavish entertainments on Twin Island, adding to the intrigue. New Yorkers were said to be among their guests, accommodated in the sprawling L-shaped lodge that still stands. One arm of the building includes a vast dining room connected to a living room with a huge fireplace built from granite and fieldstone. In the Andrewses' day a mounted moose head hung on the wall and numerous bear rugs were scattered about the polished hardwood floor. Jim Spilsbury, who sold and serviced radios along the mid-coast by boat, installed a complex radio-telephone system and a radio in each of the lodge's eight bedrooms.

After the bombing of Pearl Harbor by the Japanese, the Canadian government rounded up all Japanese Canadian residents and interned them in camps in the Interior of the province. Mr. Nakasui of Cortes Island, a horse logger and farmer, was removed from the island with his shy wife, who came to Canada under an arranged marriage. The Nakasuis were close friends with their neighbours, the Mansons. "I recall him giving us Japanese treats at Christmas time—very, very small dried fish of different sizes, quite expensive to buy," wrote Rose (Manson) McKay. "It was a sad day for him when he was hustled out of his home without time to even pack. I hope he understood a little."

Mr. Nakasui corresponded with John Manson from the internment camp but his attempts to retain his property and horse logging gear were in vain. The government sold off their land, and not until four years after the war ended were Japanese Canadians once again allowed to return to the coast. Most, like the Nakasuis, chose to start their lives over again elsewhere.

By 1945, when the war ended, Cortes Island's population was estimated at between six hundred and a thousand people.[97] Seventy kids attended schools at Whaletown, Squirrel Cove and Mansons Landing. Cortesians voted to consolidate the management of their schools in 1946 by joining the newly formed School District 72 based in Campbell River. Their ultimate goal of bringing children together under one roof, a move that required improved roads for busing, wasn't achieved for some years.

Von Donop Inlet residents got their own school in 1946 with the arrival of more of the Byers's relatives. School was held in a settler's old log cabin for a few years and then in a shack dragged in by float in 1948. The first few teachers—including Violet Herrewig, whose family worked in the inlet—had local connections.

The kids bundled up in their mackinaws to stay warm as their teacher demonstrated sums on a tiny blackboard. When the school inspector arrived he was shocked, not so much by the condition of the drafty building as by the slippery boomstick he had to walk to reach shore from the float plane dock. "He was ready to condemn it as an unsafe place for children," recalled Violet Herrewig in an interview. "As he stood there screwing up his courage to navigate the boomstick, the children came running out on the sticks to meet him. One of the girls was carrying baby Connie on her hip. As dangerous as it seemed to him, he had to admit the children were in their element."

When Violet left in 1950, the School District sent in a young teacher named Bev Horrex (later Matthews). Bev was nineteen and fresh out of normal school (teachers' college). She had the vague idea Von Donop Inlet School was close to Victoria, but when the float plane stopped at the tiny dock she found herself far from civilization. The children watched from shore as she teetered along the boomstick in her tight skirt, high heels and feathered hat. Her city clothes and ways continued to entertain the kids, though Bev became a much loved teacher, as Doreen (Calwell) Guthrie recalls:

> I remember the whole class coming back to the school from Bev's house one time. She was walking ahead of us along the trail. I can still see her, slim as a stick, wearing a tight green skirt with a whole bunch of little pleats around the bottom that swung a bit as she baby-stepped along the trail. The skirt wouldn't allow for normal steps. Us kids all gaped at her, then began mincing along behind, baby-stepping and flipping our hands at our sides, single-file along the trail. We thought we were pretty funny, as long as she didn't turn around.

John Manson was among the resolute few who continued to farm in the postwar years. It was a way of life, however humble. The old man was living as a quiet bachelor when a niece and several friends visited from Powell River in 1945. The eccentricity of his lifestyle and the old-world charm of Sunny Brae Farm stuck in the memory of Marion Gallagher, who was quoted in the book *Chalkdust & Outhouses*:

> [There was] an ancient house surrounded by the most beautiful property I have ever seen. The orchard was in full bloom, behind was a sandy beach and blue, blue ocean. It could have been Hawaii, except there were no palm trees! Uncle John, an elderly, frail man was somewhat surprised to see us. First he offered us a bedroom in the old house. It smelled of mold and mildew—so, we turned it down in favour of the barn.
>
> The first action we took was to explore the ancient house. The living room was closed. The door was jammed and difficult to open. We pushed, and with a [mournful] creak, it revealed its secrets. First a brown needled Christmas tree (this was May!) decorated with ornaments and cobwebs. Unfinished drinks sat on the mantelpiece, with mold floating in the contents. On the table was a Christmas cake, with ants running over it. We froze in wonder and repulsion. It was a scene direct from "Great Expectations" by Dickens.

The girls never uncovered the story behind the abandoned Christmas party, and John rebuffed their attempt to give the house a big cleaning. He was happy with things just as they were. The next day the girls were picked up by a young man who escorted them to a picnic and dance at Mansons. "The only lighting in the hall was by coal oil lanterns swinging from the rafters. Three fiddlers made up the orchestra, and as they swung into their toe tapping music we were swung onto the dance floor by a trio of drunken loggers dressed in plaid shirts and hob nailed boots."

John Manson's niece Etta (McKay) Byers bought her produce at Sunny Brae Farm. As the old man dug a hill of potatoes in his rolling field that overlooked the sea, he told Etta if he could choose his own death, it would be here in his field, digging potatoes. Each new hill was a surprise, and as he dug he liked to look across to Hernando Island and remember his brother Mike.

To his northeast at Cortes Bay lived a man who had none of old John Manson's integrity. Herbert Wilson's real character, however, was unknown to most of his neighbours. He was, they thought, simply a bachelor who lived from the earnings of a small sawmill and his writing.

It wasn't until some time after Wilson moved away and his autobiography *I Stole $16,000,000* was published that islanders discovered he was the cunning Reverend Herbert Wilson, whose exploits as "the King of Safe Crackers" made him a North American legend. He'd lived as a Roaring Twenties gangster, complete with a flapper moll. He and his cronies, including his brother Lou the pickpocket, cracked sixty-five safes and stole an unbelievable sixteen million dollars.

Wilson's heists required a certain brilliance. He was a master of deception, it seems, and knew how to use oxyacetylene welding equipment and explosives to advantage. "In all my years on the prowl," he wrote, "I never got over the thrill of hearing the first boom and seeing what it did to the massive block of steel."

Wilson kept his life of crime from his wife, who was convinced her pious husband was simply a travelling Bible salesman with a genius for stock investments. It wasn't until 1923, when the Mafia closed in on Wilson and he wound up in San Quentin Penitentiary with a life sentence, that she learned the truth. Wilson got his sentence reduced by travelling the country to recover some of the stolen money, and in 1936 the US deported him home to Ontario. He wasn't there long before he was back at work. The inevitable happened, and he wound up in jail again to serve six years in Kingston Penitentiary for selling forged bonds. When he was released, he moved to the prairies, where he did time again shortly before his move to Cortes, a place recommended to him through a chance acquaintance.

Wilson lived in peace on Cortes, where he wrote his autobiography. He moved off the island just before his book came into print. After islanders saw his book, they connected some of his chance remarks, like the time he mentioned he'd been to San Quentin Penitentiary. When asked what he was doing there, he laughed and turned the subject, saying he'd done a lot of travelling and public speaking years ago.

Another writer of a more ethical stamp moved to Cortes Island after the war. Gilean Douglas bought John Poole's exceptional property at Uganda Pass off Marina Island, sight unseen, in 1949. Her new home had no road access, running water, electricity or telephone, but that's exactly as she wanted it. As the only child of a well-to-do Ontario lawyer, Gilean developed a vivid imagination and a passion for the wilderness that forged her future course as a nature writer. Gilean lived and worked in a variety of urban settings in the US and Canada until she found an ideal home in the mountains of the BC Interior, where she learned to live with and in nature. After fire razed her beloved mountain cabin, she searched for a new place to live. "When I advertised for a home—not realizing that I would get even more than that—I put in everything I wanted," wrote Douglas in her book *The Protected Place*. "I asked for a stream, timber, old orchard, barn, habitable house, separate cottage, waterfront, view and seclusion." John Poole's long abandoned property fit the bill:

It was after midnight when we made the port of Cortes Island where I had bought my home. I had three miles still to go, this time in a small boat with an inboard motor. We putt-putted into the silent dark. I was silent too. I was feeling so intensely that my nerve ends were like fingers, groping for, touching, exploring this strange country where I was to live. We ran in below a high, huge rock from which a house seemed to be growing, dim in the starlight. Struggling up the long, stony, slanting beach I found a path behind the boathouse and followed it to my back door. I could hardly wait to get there.

Lifting the latch I walked into a kitchen where none of the cupboards had doors and there was only a hole where a sink and perhaps a water tap had been. This room led into a much larger one, half-paneled in dark-stained wood, with a beamed ceiling, a medium-size window, two French doors and a window-seat fronting on the sea. By starlight and flashlight I could see that the room was bare except for a wall of built-in bookcases, a large, homemade table and what looked like a camp-bed frame of wood and chicken wire webbed with deer thongs. Paper and a few books littered the floor. One door had a broken pane of glass near the slide bolt. It should all have been chilly and desolate, but I felt strangely warmed and comforted. I slept deeply on the camp bed in the sleeping-bag I had brought with me. It seemed as though I had come home again.

The next day Gilean toured her property, with its pervasive sense of John Poole's personality and hard work in his stonework, cottage, barn and garden.

Douglas's sensitive observations of her surroundings provided the fodder for her columns in provincial newspapers and her books of prose and poetry. She also took an active role in the community. She joined the Women's Institute and shared islanders' pride in the building of a new church at Whaletown near the government dock and store.

"Whaletown was lucky for it had a small frame building," wrote Douglas in the *Vancouver Sun*, "which was used as both church and community hall. But the centre of occupation shifted and the church found itself more than a mile away from the rectory, store and the majority of homes." Douglas went on to describe the opening of the new church, fitted out with mementoes of island life. The prayer desk had port and starboard lights and an old anchor set into it. Halved log rounds formed the base of the lectern, and the handle of a logger's peavey formed its stem. The stained glass window came from a pioneer Anglican church in Victoria. "On Sunday the 13th if you had walked up the hill from the

Whaletown Store belonged to the Petrie family in 1946. The first Whaletown Store, opened in about 1894, was replaced by the Thompsons at the head of the dock in 1921. The store building still stands, though it was closed in 2007. PHOTO COURTESY OF CORTES ISLAND MUSEUM.

dock to the turn in the road, you would have come on one of the prettiest sights in all the countryside," wrote Douglas. "There, chalk-white shingled walls and red asphalt roof sharp against a blue sky, stood the new little church of St. John the Baptist surrounded by a wilderness of evergreens. Situated well above road level, its steeple surmounted by a white cross made a spiritual stop sign."

The new church was dedicated by the veteran minister of the Columbia Coast Mission, a respected friend to many islanders, the Reverend Alan Greene. Also on hand was the resident minister, prairie-born Rollo Boas with his wife Kay and their two daughters, who moved to Whaletown in 1944. Boas continued the work of the mission from this base, visiting far-flung communities in the *Rendezvous*.

As the closest clinics and hospitals to Cortes were in Campbell River or Powell River, requiring a lengthy commute by private boat, the Boas family opened their home as a medical clinic twice a month. Drs. Hall and Rose of Campbell River came to the island with Reverend Boas on the *Rendezvous* to attend a steady stream of patients in various rooms of the house until a

Mansons Landing in the 1950s was a dock and fuelling station for seaplanes when they became the dominant form of transport for logging camps. Their rise ended the Union Steamship Company's weekly freight and passenger service, which got islanders to Vancouver in about seven hours instead of today's full day. PHOTO COURTESY OF MCR 13,643.

separate clinic was built. Kay, formerly a nurse, assisted the doctors. (Over fifty years later, when Kay was well into her nineties, she and many other islanders posed in the buff for a calendar inspired by the film *Calendar Girls* as a fundraiser for a new health clinic at Mansons Landing.)

As Gilean Douglas noted in her article on the new Whaletown church and clinic, the cluster of services at the government wharf created a cohesive community centre. This worked well until postwar advances reoriented Whaletown yet again to the opposite shore.

A New Reality

The economy on the Discovery Islands fell flat after the war, though it was booming elsewhere. There were many factors involved. Fish stocks had dwindled, and regulations now favoured larger operators. When the government turned over much of the forest land throughout the Discovery Islands to large timber leases, it cut out small family operations like the Byers-Manson outfit in Von Donop Inlet. After the war it became increasingly difficult for these gyppo loggers to get a timber sale.

Island communities took another blow when the venerable Union Steamship Company announced the end of its service in the early 1950s. The company had lost much of its market to improved roads on the mainland and Vancouver Island. Seaplanes, now flying men and equipment into camps, also took business away from the Union Steamship boats. (A key fuelling dock was opened at Mansons for these seaplanes.) Many small inner coast communities became virtual ghost towns when the "USS Co." went out of business. A small private service picked up the slack for a time, but without a postal subsidy it soon quit. "The boat that calls Tuesdays with freight and mail will call no more after the 20th," wrote Peg Pyner in her 1953 Cortes column in the *Campbell River Courier*. "So we are back to one mail a week."

The island's school population remained surprisingly stable inspite of this decline. A logging-camp schoolhouse was barged across from Oyster Bay to Whaletown in 1950 to replace the old school at the junction of Coulter Bay and Carrington Bay roads. It was dragged into place on a hill that overlooks Whaletown Lagoon. Some of the other island

The second Whaletown School arrived by barge from Oyster Bay in 1950. Now a public art gallery, it remains on site on Carrington Bay Road. Seen here on Sports Day with teacher May Freeman are Louise Reedel, Marlene Guthrie, Betty-ann Hansen and Barbie McCoy (in front of Mrs. Freeman), Cindy Beaulieu, Frances Gurthrie (plaid skirt), Annette Beaulieu, Ricky Mathews in front of Janice MacLean, Sandi Brown, Marlene [?] Guthrie behind unknown, Sara Weiler behind Jan Hansen, Jeff O'Donnell, Jeanie Mathews behind unknown, David Cadwallader, Rod Hayes and Evan Hansen in front of three unknown people, Ronnie Block and Robert Gardner behind unknown, Johnny Brown. PHOTO COURTESY OF LOTTIE MCDEVITT COLLECTION, MCR 16,508.

schools were improved too. In 1949 the kids at Squirrel Cove got an ultra-modern Quonset hut school. The old Mansons Landing School was also expanded with a two-room addition.

Older non-Native islanders—whose memories stretched back to a time when Cortes's population steadily grew—watched with sadness as it slipped into a decline.

Tourism, though restricted by a short season, filled a small piece of the economic gap. Florence (Manson) and Ervin McKay sold their Gunflint Lake farm to a third generation of the Manson family, Hazel and her husband Ken Hansen, who maintained it as a dairy ranch and opened a children's camp that offered horseback riding and swimming.

The Hansens had seventeen Holstein cows. "'Hazie' was a really hard worker," recalls her sister Etta (McKay) Byers. "They seeded the top field in oats in the middle of the night to coincide with the start of a rainy spell. They butchered their own beef and had a big walk-in freezer to store the meat in. Her husband would often bring a crowd in to join them for dinner at the last minute, no warning, and she'd have to feed them. They had an acre in vegetables, but the dairy cows were the main income."

It was 1953 when the Hansens started the summer camp at Lakeview Farm (now Linnaea Farm), patronized mainly by Seattle and Vancouver yachters whose kids enjoyed a farm experience while their parents went cruising. There was a constant turnover of children, with new arrivals coming every Sunday night.

Another tourist facility that opened about a decade later was the Gorge Harbour Marina, built in 1968 by Doug and Jenny Morton on Charlie and Jennie Allen's old homestead. (Sarah Corneille's resort in the south end of the harbour was no longer in operation.)

The most prestigious tourists to ever visit the islands came to the "rustic" lodge on Twin Island, purchased by German nobility Margrave Maximilian von Baden and his wife Margravine Valerie von Baden in the 1950s. The Margrave and Margravine hosted their relatives Queen Elizabeth and Prince Philip of England for respite visits during their Canadian tours over the next few decades.

In 1960 Mansons and Whaletown were finally connected by land when MLA Dan Campbell opened the new Gorge Harbour Road. Though the road ended the isolation of the two communities, their history of mutual autonomy and rivalry continued. Each had its own attributes and personality.

Discussion of ferry service for Cortes began as early as 1963, sparked by a new car ferry from Campbell River to Quadra Island. Cortes Island's population of between 350 and four hundred people was too low to support a ferry, but Cortesians had a powerful ally in government. Dan Campbell of the Social Credit party was the second Cortes Islander to be elected to represent the provincial North Island riding.

In addition to lobbying for ferry service on Cortes, Dan Campbell ushered in regional government, making Cortes Island the province's Electoral Area I in 1965. It was the smallest regional area in the province, with teacher George Griffin as regional director.

On a stormy day in 1969 the *Cortes Queen* made its inaugural crossing from Heriot Bay to Whaletown. Elmer Ellingsen, a driving force behind the campaign for a car ferry, welcomed George Freeman's 1928 Ford, said to have been the first car on the island, as it came down the new ferry slip. MLA Dan Campbell's wife Jean cut the ceremonial ribbon, held by students, to officially open the ramp for a procession of cars and the Legion Pipe Band. A banquet followed at Mansons Hall.

In 1970 the island was hooked up to the electrical grid. "Electric power has finally arrived at this community," said the *Province*, "ending an era of cotton wicks, kerosene and hurricane lamps."

Ferry service and electricity were welcomed by the Klahoose Band, eager to find ways to keep younger members on the island. Billy Mitchell, who was interviewed in the *Daily Colonist* in 1968, talked about the issues his people faced and lamented the losses of the past decades. "Today our people just have to go to the corner store to buy a tin of fish," said Mitchell, "whereas at one time our people kept healthy and trim by

Barbecued salmon prepared by the Klahoose people in the traditional way, filleted down the back and roasted on splints, for the annual Oyster Festival. The village of Tork, in Squirrel Cove, is seen in the background. PHOTO BY JEANETTE TAYLOR.

fighting for what they got—and using it well. I can remember a time when the only part of a fish we threw away was the head and the tail."

It was a major blow to the aboriginal people's economy in the 1950s, when fish stocks began to be depleted in the inside waters and commercial fishing regulations were imposed. "Now there are no more fish," said Tom Hill of the Klahoose Band in a 1995 interview. "No more cod. No more salmon." When he was young, said Hill, his family barbecued and smoked salmon to last all winter.

Tom Hill was puzzled as oyster farming developed into the island's largest industry in the 1970s. In his view, the fat Pacific oysters introduced to the island from Japan in the 1930s weren't healthy to eat, unlike the delicate little native oysters his ancestors enjoyed. Harry and Teresa Daniels are credited with growing the first Pacific oysters on the beach in Von Donop Inlet in about 1938.

Cortes oyster farmers, working in a shellfish co-op, shipped tonnes of oysters to specialty markets in France and elsewhere in the 1970s. The

Kristen Scholfield-Sweet working her oyster lease in Gorge Harbour, Cortes Island.
PHOTO BY "THE OYSTER MAN."

Writer Gilean Douglas's former home at Channel Rock in Uganda Passage, Cortes Island.
JEANETTE TAYLOR PHOTO.

oysters mature on-site, producing a firm meat favoured in the gourmet marketplace. As the industry developed, farmers branched out into growing oysters on strings from rafts in Gorge Harbour and elsewhere. The industry appeals to younger residents. Islanders joke about the number of PhDs working the cold late-night tides of winter on Cortes beaches. Kristen Scholfield-Sweet, with her PhD in art education, is among them. She left her career as a prof at one of Canada's leading art schools to become an oyster farmer. It's hard work but it provides a lifestyle she believes in and the emotional and physical space to pursue her art practice.

Kristen and the other oyster farmers face many challenges. The drawbacks include the cyclical nature of their part-time work, the fluctuating market and the need to constantly maintain rafts and equipment that are battered by winter storms. And then there's the problem of the wealthy foreshore landowners, particularly in Gorge Harbour, where the work of oyster farming—a vital part of the island's economy—runs afoul of holiday residents' desire for a tranquil idyll. Though most part-time residents bought with the knowledge that their seascape included a key part of the island's economy, some want it gone.

After the New Democratic Party swept into power in 1972, and Dan Campbell lost his north Vancouver Island riding, several key parks were established on Cortes. Smelt Bay Park, with its long expanse of sandy beach, became a Class A Park in 1973. That same year Mansons Landing, with its sandy spit enclosing an expansive tidal lagoon, also became a park. To islanders' dismay, some years later the province removed Mike and Jane Manson's large home, a store and some cabins at the head of the wharf, leaving only the government dock on-site. The store, moved to Beasley Road, became a museum run by volunteers in a project sparked by Mike and Jane Manson's granddaughter Mae (Freeman) Ellingsen. One of the island's newest marine parks, added by an NDP government in the 1990s, is Ha'thayim, the Mainland Comox name for Von Donop Inlet.

Gilean Douglas took a lead role in progressive planning for the island when she was elected as a regional district director in 1973. During her term an official settlement plan was brought in to stave off a push by developers for small-lot subdivisions. She also championed the preservation of salmon habitat and wetlands.

A new wave of settlers arrived after the island got car ferry service. Among them were hippies, most of them urban dropouts wanting to live off the land. "New neighbours are all around me," Gilean Douglas is quoted as saying in her biography by Andrea Lebowitz and Gillian Milton, *Writing Nature, Finding Home*, "young couples—'long hairs and granny gowns'—as some describe them. I like these young people very much."

Dan Campbell continued to work for his party after its defeat in 1972, so when the Social Credit Party was re-elected some years later, he got an influential government posting. In 1979 his career went up in smoke, however, when it emerged that Campbell advised campaign workers to write phony letters to newspapers. Shortly thereafter NDP opposition leader Dave Barrett exposed improprieties in Campbell's disclosures of campaign spending, and he lost his government position.

The new ferry dock was built across the bay from the old Whaletown dock—with its store, church, post office, Louisa B. Tooker Library, manse and health clinic—so the village became a backwater. The stream of ferry traffic passes by the road that leads down to the quaint cluster of buildings. Only the post office, the smallest detached post office in Canada, remains in active use. Most people do their shopping at Mansons, which has a food co-op, community hall, library, school, restaurant, store, post office, museum, new health centre, bank and bookstore. But the old feeling of separateness between Mansons Landing and Whaletown remains. When an active Cortes Island Museum volunteer offered to help on a Mansons Landing research project, she paused to rethink her offer. "I wonder if it's okay for me to work on this? I'm from Whaletown," she added, half apologetically. She was quickly assured no one would hold that against her.

Tourism leaped to the fore as a dominant component of Cortes Island's economy after the advent of the ferry. The island offers peace and removal from the mainstream but with the convenience of hydro, telephone, internet and ferry service.

Tourism dollars also flow from the hundreds of yachters and sailors who converge on nearby Desolation Sound and stop in at Cortes Island. Some fall in love with the place and buy or build summer homes. Others return yearly for an annual boating holiday. Cortes's position as a base for cruisers strengthened in the 1990s when both the Seattle and Vancouver Yacht Clubs opened outstations in Cortes Bay.

The island's population nearly doubles in summer, with a steady stream of people heading for the Hollyhock retreat centre or returning to their seasonal homes. Some of their homes cost a million dollars or more to build, creating a rarified real estate market that soars far beyond the average Canadian's income, as is also the case elsewhere in the Discovery Islands. On the flip side, these lavish homes provide work for tradespeople, though many of them are hard pressed to find a place to live.

There are lots of holiday houses for rent in winter, but come spring there's a frenzied scramble to find places to live.

Is it worth it? Melissa Rickey has complex feelings about the demographic shift on the island and its cultural ramifications. An increasing number of permanent residents are forced to make way for off-island property owners in summer. "As a young family that could never afford to buy land, it's not a nice position to be in," says Melissa. But her situation is better than some. Her landlord allows Melissa and her two girls to leave many of their belongings in the house during their two-month sojourn in a tent in a friend's yard. There are others who have to make do for up to four months because their landlords turn their places into high-priced vacation rentals.

Melissa is a teaching assistant at the island's alternative school at Linnaea Farm on Gunflint Lake. Her work allows her two girls to attend Linnaea School, with its holistic approach to children's social and academic development.

Some young families have created their own employment. Mike and Samantha Moore treasure the fact that many islanders share their strongly held alternative social and environmental values. They bought property on the island while prices were still within reach, and within a decade built their own home, started a family and transformed their schooner-rigged motor-sailing vessel the *Misty Isles* into a kayaking mothership. In winter Mike works for a large tour company in the Antarctic.

A good portion of the *Misty*'s business comes from Hollyhock, started in 1982 by a group of friends with money to invest in an educational retreat, "a place that allows you access to what matters—a refuge for your soul," says their website.

Diane Redfern was so excited by the results of her experience at Hollyhock she wrote a rave review on a travel website. "I was leery about Hollyhock, too, at first. Curious, but leery," she said. "I was not at all sure what I was getting into with this holistic holiday idea." Diane took a sampler of the different programs on offer. There are dozens to choose from in health, healing, meditation, spiritual development and indigenous wisdom. Her skepticism quickly transformed into conversion.

"The experience in a word: euphoric. And most astonishing to me, the feeling lingered on for months."

There's a strong interest among many Cortesians in First Nations cultures, but the Klahoose people's reality is far removed from the experiences and sensibilities of non-Native residents. The band has many pressing issues that consume their attention. Their population is dropping as younger members go elsewhere to finish school and find jobs. There were 294 people registered in the band in 2007, but fewer than sixty lived on the reserve at Squirrel Cove. "Jobs are a key issue," says band councillor Kathy Francis. The band maintains oyster and clam leases to create jobs and is branching into tourism, but its key bid for jobs and revenue lies in a partnership with a private hydro company installing run-of-the-river generating stations in Toba Inlet.

Health care also concerns band leaders as they look for ways to mitigate the effects of a changed diet that's resulted in a high incidence of diabetes. Bringing back elements of their traditional culture is central to recapturing a sense of pride and uniqueness, says Kathy Francis. Some band members have begun to follow the old practices of mountain goat hunting and river bathing for purification.

Hollyhock's popularity and success spills into the community as a whole, providing about eighty-five seasonal jobs and colouring the island's social fabric. But some islanders chuckle in their beards as the expensive cars leave the island at the first hint of the driving southeast rains of winter. It's well and good to chop wood and carry water in summer, but it takes a deeper commitment to alternative living to stay on the island year-round. Those who do stay gather rich rewards in a place of shared values, where people pitch in and support each other in a dynamic working community loaded with eccentric charm and grace.

CHAPTER THREE

Desolation Sound, the Redonda Islands and Toba Inlet

ON REKSTEN PROMISED HIMSELF A TRIP TO DESOLATION SOUND to celebrate his sixty-fifth birthday. In 2006 he sailed solo from Victoria to Quadra Island, where he picked up his mate Leona for the final leg of his journey.

The weather was fair, though there wasn't enough wind for sailing, so they motored past Cortes Island and on to Refuge Cove on West Redonda Island, a few kilometres from Desolation Sound. The cove's rustic store, houses and dock are an essential part of the area's charm, but an old-fashioned Starbuck's coffee sign at a summer café gave them a hint they'd cruised into a wilderness of urban pleasures.

From Refuge Cove, Don and Leona headed for Prideaux Haven, where the charts showed a good anchorage. The jagged peaks of the Coast Range lent drama to their approach, but they found both Prideaux Haven and Melanie Cove jammed with yachts and cruisers. As they tied up alongside a raft of boats, they were assailed by conflicting strains of music and barbecue fumes. They had landed in the midst of a lively social scene frequented by boaters of every stripe, from movie stars and Seattle executives to weekend sailors and kayakers.

The relaxed party atmosphere of midsummer in Desolation Sound is part of the attraction, according to both Larry Seeley of Campbell River and Commodore Jack Sullivan of the Seattle Yacht Club. "There's an instant camaraderie among boaters," says Larry. "People invite you on board for a drink and that stretches into dinner. The next thing you know it's three days later."

If you want the place virtually to yourself, he adds, go anytime but July or August. Larry's goal is to spend Christmas in the Sound some year, based on a friend's account of a silence so deep he could hear the snowfall hit the water.

The attractions to Desolation Sound are many, says Commodore Sullivan. The water is extraordinarily warm, hitting the high twenties (seventies in Fahrenheit) in summer, and there are lots of great hikes to freshwater lakes. "Club members' kids remember their trips to Desolation Sound with stars in their eyes," says Sullivan. "It's not all built up with development," he adds, "and it's an easy destination for Seattle people with two or three weeks' holiday. Beyond there the cruising gets more challenging, at Seymour Narrows and Yuculta Rapids."

But a crowded marine park wasn't what Don was looking for on this birthday cruise. As an avid historian drawn to the romance of the Age of

Mount Denman in October, with a fresh dusting of snow, from Desolation Sound.
PHOTO BY JEANETTE TAYLOR.

Captain Vancouver anchored his ships in Teakerne Arm for nearly two weeks within view of Cassel Falls and its warm lake above, but described the landscape as desolate, gloomy and barren.
PHOTO BY JEANETTE TAYLOR.

Sail, he'd brought aboard Captain Vancouver's and Archibald Menzies's journals, chronicling British exploration of the area in 1792.

There was hardly a soul to be found anywhere from the Redondas to Toba Inlet in 1792. Steep mountains rise straight out of the sea, offering very few places to live. Mount Addenbroke on East Redonda Island makes an abrupt ascent to 1,591 metres (5,220 feet) to tower over narrow Homfray Channel, which has the second deepest sounding on the BC coast.

Menzies, a botanist and physician, was excited by the new plant specimens he added to his collection in Desolation Sound, but he described the region as inhospitable. Expedition leader Captain George Vancouver was more pointed in his disapproval. He anchored his two ships, the thirty-metre (hundred-foot) *Discovery* and the fifteen-metre (fifty-foot) *Chatham*, in Teakerne Arm on West Redonda Island for two weeks while he and his men explored and charted by small boat. "Our situation here," wrote Vancouver in his published journal, "presenting as gloomy and dismal an aspect as nature could well be supposed to exhibit, had she not been a little aided by vegetation; which though dull and uninteresting, screened from our sight the dreary rocks and precipices that compose these desolate shores. ... Our residence here was truly forlorn;

an awful silence pervaded the gloomy forests, whilst animated nature seemed to have deserted the neighbouring country."

Vancouver's pensive reflections were no doubt coloured by summer storms and his failing health. Historian Sir James Watt suggests Vancouver contracted malaria or yellow fever in Jamaica on an earlier expedition, destroying his health and leading to Addison's disease, which compromised his thyroid. He suffered periods of extreme lassitude and irascibility, and his moody outbursts cost him the respect and friendship of most of his men.

The rolling hillsides of Garry oaks on the Gulf Islands and Lower Mainland were more to Vancouver's liking. He and his crew met two Spanish ships, the *Sutil* and the *Mexicana*, in the southern waters. The Spanish ships under Captain Galiano were on a similar mission: to search for the fabled Northwest Passage—which was believed to lie beyond the entrance to Juan de Fuca Strait—and chart the northwest Pacific coast. Several years prior, Spain and Britain both claimed sovereignty over this coast without regard to First Nations ownership. The impetus was the lucrative sea otter trade, but after some war posturing, Spain and Britain agreed to find a diplomatic resolution. An investigation

Columbia III in Desolation Sound. The twenty-one-metre (seventy-foot) ship carries ten passengers and crew for cultural and eco-tours. Captain Vancouver charted the coast in 1792 aboard his thirty-metre (hundred-foot) *Discovery* with a crew of 101. His Spanish colleagues surveyed in the fifteen-metre (fifty-foot) *Sutil* and the *Mexicana* with crews of nineteen.
PHOTO BY JEANETTE TAYLOR.

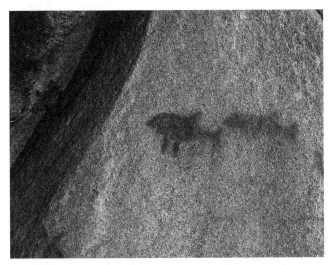

Pictographs at Walsh Cove Marine Park in Waddington Channel were created by First Nations people using red ochre (a naturally occurring iron oxide) with salmon roe as an oil base. The paintings can be anywhere from three hundred to a thousand years old.
PHOTO BY JEANETTE TAYLOR.

into their conflicting claims was a key part of Vancouver's commission, to be resolved through a meeting with Captain Bodega y Quadra at Nootka Sound.

The Europeans' method of surveying was laborious and slow. Several officers and crew were sent out for five days or more in small boats. According to historian John Frazier Henry, Vancouver's ships covered 100,000 kilometres (65,000 miles) in his four-and-a-half-year voyage, while the exploration teams covered 120,000 kilometres (75,000 miles), mainly under oar.

The surveyors rowed from what's now the city of Vancouver to Desolation Sound, and on their advice, the ships sailed north to use Redonda Island as their next base for charting. From Teakerne Arm, parties went in various directions. Archibald Menzies accompanied Peter Puget and Joseph Whidbey through what's now Desolation Sound Park. They encountered no Native people along their route, though they found empty fish-drying racks in Tenedos Bay and a deserted village that some historians suggest was located on the mainland adjacent to Roffey Island. "We came to a small Cove," wrote Menzies, "in the bottom of which the picturesque ruins of a deserted Village placed on the summit of an elevated projecting Rock excited our curiosity & induced us to land close to it to view its structure."

The defensive arrangements for this village were ingenious. Tightly packed house frames were crowded on top of a steep-sided rock promontory connected to land by a narrow neck. (The Native people moved their cladding boards with them to their seasonal villages.) Overhanging the three-sided outcrop was a boardwalk knee-braced into the rock walls, rendering all but a narrow set of steps at the land neck completely inaccessible. The maple trees that overhung these steps, speculated Menzies, served as a place for the occupants to defend their village against approaching enemies.

"We found the top...nearly level & wholly occupied with the skeletons of Houses," wrote Menzies. Cast-off bits of clothing and tools suggested the place had been recently deserted, as did the fact they were attacked by hoards of fleas, "in such incredible number that the whole party was obligd to quit the rock in great precipitation, leaving the remainder of these Assailants in full possession of their Garrison."

Coastal cruiser Francis Barrow recorded pictograph and archaeological sites in his journals of the 1930s and 1940s. He was convinced handloggers "Saulter and his chum Frank," of Roffey Island in Desolation Sound, lived atop the place Captain Vancouver's men called Flea Village in 1792.
PHOTO COURTESY OF EDNA MAE JOHN COLLECTION, MCR 14,142.

Another exploration party went as far as Toba Inlet, where they found extensive fish-drying racks and two recently abandoned canoes, in which the sailors left small gifts of nails and beads. Several other groups explored to the northwest through Discovery Passage. There they witnessed the meeting of the tides from the north and south and hastened back to the ships to let Vancouver know they were in a passage leading not to the Northwest Passage but back to the Pacific. From Desolation Sound the British and Spanish ships separated. The British continued north via Seymour Narrows, while the Spanish charted the mainland shore.

The British sailors continued their work along the northwest coast for several more summers, spending their winters in Hawaii. By the time they returned to Britain, Vancouver's health was in a ruinous state and so was his naval career. His punishment of a titled young officer related to the prime minister brought him disfavour, as did his poor relations with

Francis Barrow, who cruised the coast with his wife Amy, photographed the entrance to Toba Inlet from Pryce Channel in the 1930s.
PHOTO COURTESY OF EDNA MAE JOHN COLLECTION, MCR 14,153.

other influential officers. Vancouver died a few years after his return at the age of forty, leaving his brother and Whidbey to finalize the publication of his journals. Though Vancouver led the longest voyage of exploration of his era and created charts that remained in use for half a century, his name has been largely forgotten in British annals.

The abandoned village and fish-drying racks that Vancouver's men saw in Desolation Sound likely belonged to the Salishan-speaking Klahoose people, whose heartland is in Toba Inlet. Smallpox is thought to have struck the coast a decade before Vancouver's expedition. The resulting massive depopulation may account for the low numbers of people in the area, along with seasonal migrations and steep terrain.

The Klahoose people's population continued to fall over the next decades. When Hudson's Bay Company trader James Douglas visited in 1841, he estimated there were ninety adult males among the Klahoose, which suggests a possible total population of 360. By 1888, following a second smallpox epidemic in 1862–64, reserve commissioner Peter O'Reilly estimated their population at 122.

O'Reilly set aside a number of reserves for the Klahoose in Toba Inlet, but the flooding of the Brem and Toba rivers made it a difficult place to live. In the late 1890s, the church urged the Klahoose people to relocate their winter village to their reserve at Squirrel Cove on Cortes Island.

There were only a few non-Native residents in the Desolation Sound and Redonda Islands area in the 1890's, working in logging and an iron mine on West Redonda. The DeWolf brothers of Vancouver opened the Elsie mine in 1892.[98] It was about 180 metres (six hundred feet) above tidewater and could load ore directly into boats from an overhead chute. The company shipped 914 tonnes (nine hundred tons) of ore in 1893 to Oregon.

Klahoose men worked with some of the earliest logging companies in the region and began to log their reserves in Toba Inlet as early as the 1870s. They maintained their traditional lifestyle, moving seasonally throughout their extensive territory, from Toba to Squirrel Cove. Some combined trapping and fishing to earn a cash income. A few chose to

The 1892 headstone for Moses Lucey, two, and Marten Lucey, one, lies hidden in brush on the deserted coast south of Connis Point on West Redonda Island. Despite their unusual Irish name, the children's family remains untraced. Their father may have worked in an iron mine that opened there in 1892.
PHOTO BY JEANETTE TAYLOR.

maintain their principle residences on a reserve near the mouth of the Toba River even after the majority moved to Squirrel Cove. Among those who stayed was Annie Hill, a sister to hereditary Chief Julian. Annie, born in about 1871,[99] raised her family on her own for most of her adult life because her Lekwiltok husband served a life sentence for murder. Annie is said to have taken up with Read Island hotelier Edgar Wilmot Wylie, with whom she had a son. If this was the case, she didn't abandon her home or traditional lifestyle for the relationship.

This and other fragmented bits of information handed down about Annie Hill suggest she was a feisty and capable woman. Coastal cruiser Francis Barrow met Annie in the late 1930s and described her as a jolly, wizened-up old woman with a house in the slough of the Toba River.

Walter Tefler Barnes became part of Annie's extended family. Barnes's English parents immigrated initially to Quebec, where he was

Francis Barrow photographed Jim Stapleton in 1936 and noted in his diary that the homesteader lived in "a splendid little sheltered bay" in Toba Inlet. Stapleton was among the first non-Native settlers in the area. PHOTO COURTESY OF EDNA MAE JOHN COLLECTION, MCR 14,150.

born in 1886, and later to New Westminster. It may have been talk of a transcontinental railway terminus for the Toba River—planned but never built—that attracted young Walter Barnes to the area. Or it could have been the extensive delta land, perfect for farming, hunting and fishing. Barnes established a homestead a few kilometres upriver and in about 1906[100] settled there to raise a family with Annie Hill's daughter Lucie.

Peter Champion, on a visit from Vancouver, was likewise impressed by the riches of the Toba River valley. According to historian and novelist Maud Emery, Champion declared the valley a homesteader's paradise and returned to Vancouver to assemble a group of friends to form a settlement. The river was navigable for about thirty-two kilometres (twenty miles), and the whole reach offered choice farmland. About thirty families made their way upcoast in small boats or by Union Steamship boats in 1910–11. The sandy loam of their homesteads grew massive cabbages and thirty-five-centimetre (fourteen-inch) potatoes and carrots.

One of the new settlers arrived with a scow load of dry goods and groceries and a horse and cart, planning to open a store, but he wasn't there long before the settlement began to fail. Discouraged by isolation and the high cost of freight to distant markets, all but Peter Champion and his family gave up and left.

Amy and Francis Barrow visited the Champions in the 1930s. Their homestead was about nineteen kilometres (twelve miles) up the river. "They have few visitors," wrote Francis Barrow in his diary of 1936, "the last about four years ago." Sometimes, they told the Barrows, they were frozen in for three to four months of the year.

The Champion and Barnes families maintained their isolated farms for several generations, but it was logging and a bit of fishing that kept them. The handful of logging shows listed in the region at the time of the 1911 census included Arthur Pleas's twenty-five-man camp at Sarah Point at the entrance to Okeover Arm and two camps run by French Canadian families at Tenedos Bay and Unwin Lake. There were several more on West Redonda and in Okeover Arm, but logging in the Desolation Sound area was marginal and employed few men compared to that in the Okisollo region to the north. The total population from Okeover Arm to Redonda Bay was 238, plus sixty-three Klahoose Band members mainly living at Squirrel Cove on Cortes Island.[101] Clarence Byers, whose father logged in Teakerne Arm, says that while the steep mountainsides of the Redondas were ideal for handlogging, the timber tended to be "conky" (infested with fungus).

The loggers lived in primitive conditions. Cecil Harlow Edmond worked in a logging camp near the junction of Toba Inlet and Pryce Channel in 1903. A red-haired Irishman named Frank Gallagher ran the five-man camp, logging hemlock for the bark to supply a tannery in New Westminster.

The crew shared a log bunkhouse with a shake roof and a dirt floor, wrote Edmond in his memoirs. Their bunks were made from sapling poles, and they had fir boughs for mattresses. "There was one window at one end, where somebody had chopped a hole in some of the logs about a foot square and through which no one could see for grime." The mess hall was an open-sided structure with shiplap roofing. On rainy days they ate in the bunkhouse, huddled around the pot-bellied stove.

The head faller in Gallagher's camp earned $2.50 for a ten-hour day, but young Cecil's pay was two dollars a day less board. "Board was really worth about $1 a month but we paid two bits a day for it. Provisions would come up every week or so. The meat would sometimes nearly walk off the ship but by long boiling could usually be eaten. We had hardtack mostly but sometimes bread and butter."

Two Desolation Sound bachelors made famous in M. Wylie Blanchet's book *The Curve of Time* were living in logging camps at the time of the 1911 census. Andrew Shuttler or Logger Mike, as "Capi" Blanchet called him, was in Anthony MacGuire's camp in Desolation Sound, along with eight other men. Blanchet and her five children made regular stops at Shuttler's homestead at the head of Melanie Cove on their summer cruises. "Almost out of sight up the bank, stood a little

Fascinated by the rugged lifestyle of the men and women who lived on this part of the coast, Francis Barrow pasted their photographs in his cruising journals. These loggers worked on a Powell River Company boom in Teakerne Arm in 1939. PHOTO COURTESY OF EDNA MAE JOHN COLLECTION, MCR 20110-12.

cabin—covered with honeysuckle and surrounded by flowers and apple trees," wrote Blanchet. "We walked with him along the paths, underneath the overhanging apple-branches."

Shuttler was in his sixties when Blanchet met him in the late 1920s. He had immigrated to Canada in 1887[102] and worked as a logger. A fight with another logger, who left him for dead with a jagged cut running up his nose, caused him to seek isolation "to think it out." Shuttler devoted the rest of his life to study, supporting himself by handlogging. The numerous books that lined the walls of his cabin included Marcus Aurelius, Epictetus, Plato and Emerson. He delighted in his philosophical conversations with Blanchet and some of the other summer cruisers who visited him.

Shuttler's nearest neighbour was Phil Lavigne of Laura Cove, a French Canadian who was forty-eight at the time of the 1911 census. He was working on a farm, likely his own homestead, but lived in a logging

Francis Barrow photographed Phil Lavigne outside his Laura Cove homestead in 1938. When Lavigne's neighbour Andrew Shuttler died in 1931, a "city-man" took over Shuttler's place in Prideaux Haven and lost his sanity, holding Lavigne at gunpoint in his cabin for most of a day.
PHOTO COURTESY OF EDNA MAE JOHN COLLECTION, MCR 20110-37.

camp in Homfray Channel with eleven other men. Lavigne listed himself as literate, but Francis Barrow wrote letters for him on his summer visits. Capi Blanchet noted that Lavigne could neither read nor write, but when Andrew Shuttler died in 1931, Lavigne took all his books. "All dem words," said Phil, "and 'e 'ad to die like all de rest of us!"

The settlers and loggers of the region had a choice of places to pick up their mail and supplies. Some went south to Lund, and some went to Squirrel Cove on Cortes Island. There were also stores and post offices at Refuge Cove and Deceit Bay (now Redonda Bay) on West Redonda Island.

Refuge Cove—an ideal place to lay over a tug, boom logs or get fresh water—became a small settlement sometime before World War I. Heather Harbord notes in her engaging book *Desolation Sound, A History* that it was also the social hub of the region. There were enough people living in the cove in 1914 to open a school,[103] and Robert Donley opened a store during the war years, adding a post office in 1922.

School children at Refuge
Cove in 1924.
IMAGE H-04053 COURTESY
OF ROYAL BC MUSEUM, BC ARCHIVES.

McGuffie's homestead at Refuge Cove in 1924.
IMAGE H-04053 COURTESY OF ROYAL BC MUSEUM, BC ARCHIVES.

The Refuge Cove General Store, with a few brief interruptions, has been in business for nearly a century. It has remained in the same approximate location, though it has had numerous owners and suffered two major fires. Donley went bankrupt in the deep recession that followed World War I. His creditors leased the store out for several years until a young man named Jack Tindall showed up on the scene. Historian Maud Emery said Tindall arrived with a lease for the store, the keys, his suitcase and eleven dollars in his pocket. Within a few years he built the business up into a thriving small store. A dance hall behind the store attracted people from as far away as Owen Bay in Okisollo Channel. When Tindall sold the store in about 1945,[104] he joined Jim Spilsbury's radio business, conducted along the coast by boat.

The largest settlement in this region was at Redonda Bay, which in the 1920s had a railway logging camp,[105] a sawmill and a cannery. The Redonda Bay Cannery and Cold Storage Plant opened in about 1916,[106] processing salmon, herring, clams and dogfish at different points in its history. Salmon from the Toba, Bute and Loughborough Inlet runs were the primary source of fish, and the crew included Native people from Church House, a few Japanese Canadian families and Euro-Canadians.

A 1923 fire insurance survey gave production numbers starting in 1918, when the cannery packed sixteen thousand cases of pink, blueback, spring and chum salmon. The output dropped to 2,600 cases in 1919 and to 2,200 in 1920, after which the cannery closed for a few years.[107]

An interesting feature of the cannery's operating plant was an old Fraser River sternwheeler ferry used to generate power. The SS *Transfer* was kept on pilings, wedged between the cannery buildings and the shore, where it also served as a bunkhouse. The cannery itself was built entirely on pilings on the north side of Lillian Russell Creek (no doubt named for the glamorous Victorian musician and actress). A First Nations village and the J.P. Russell Shingle Mill were across the creek.

There were a store and post office attached to the cannery, managed by Norman Dillabough in 1921. Syd Vicary, a bookkeeper, took over the management of the cannery and store the next year with the help of his daughter. The cannery and shingle mill closed during the Depression, in about 1931,[108] but when the economy picked up again in 1939, the Millerd family of Vancouver brought the cannery back into production. Syd Vicary and his daughter remained in charge of the store and post office.

Gerry Olmstead, with his wife and four sons, took over the logging operation in the southern part of Redonda Bay about the same time the Millerds bought the cannery. Olmstead converted the old railway camp into a truck-logging operation and added family quarters to attract and maintain a skilled crew. By 1940 there were about 115[109] people living at Redonda Bay and enough children to open a school in the Olmsteads' home. A year later the Olmsteads built a school that remained in use until 1948.[110]

Among the residents of Redonda Bay were two Japanese Canadian families that fished commercially. When the little community got wind that Japanese Canadians were to be interned and their possessions impounded, the loggers dragged their boats ashore and hid them in the forest. And when government officials came in search of the Japanese Canadian families, the loggers said they had left some time earlier in their boats.

The Redonda Bay Cannery, seen here in the 1940s, opened in about 1916 and operated until the late 1950s. The cannery and a nearby logging camp were the nucleus for a busy centre. Children who grew up there still have fond memories of deep friendships formed at Redonda Bay.
PHOTO COURTESY OF FRANK MILLERD COLLECTION, MCR 19,263.

Redonda Bay Cannery workers in 1942: Mary Harry, Nora Wilson, Eva Wilson and Louise Henshall.
PHOTO COURTESY OF HAINES-HENSHALL COLLECTION, MCR 8386.

Redonda Bay remained a viable community for another decade. The Olmsteads sold their logging company in 1949 to Giroday Sawmills, a large company with the heavy equipment needed to reach the steeper grades of the site. In 1954 the Millerds added a dogfish reduction plant to their cannery for a few years, but it was a marginal part of their operation. In the late 1950s, when salmon stocks began to dwindle, they shut down the cannery. For the next two decades only the net house—used by a fishing camp—and the store remained in use.

There were also changes in Refuge Cove during the 1940s and 1950s, but the little community managed to survive. The Hope family took over the store and post office in about 1945, remaining in charge until they sold their extensive property and store to the Refuge Cove Land and Housing Co-op in 1972.[111] Norman and Doris Hope, the "Duke and Duchess of West Redonda," as co-op member and author Judith Williams dubbed them in her book *Dynamite Stories*, remained at the cove. An interesting mix of young city folk joined them. A few made Refuge Cove their permanent home, but most maintained their city jobs and spent summers on Redonda. A few, like Judith Williams, now alternate between homes at Refuge Cove and on Cortes Island.

The co-op members have managed to keep the store at Refuge Cove operating through all the economic shifts of the past four decades by catering to coastal cruisers. Larry Seeley of Campbell River always makes a stop at Refuge Cove when he's boating in the area, even if it's just to buy a book from the store's excellent stock. He enjoys watching all the action in the quaint little community. "Everyone's so relaxed when they're on the water," says Seeley. "The same pressured businessman who'll pass you on the highway with a dirty look will be quietly waiting his turn to pump gas at Refuge Cove. You're as likely to see someone like Goldie Hawn in shorts pumping gas into her boat as you are weekenders from Campbell River."

A new development for the region is a controversial run-of-the-river project installed by Plutonic Power Corporation of Vancouver on the East Toba River and Montrose Creek. The Klahoose Band signed an agreement with Plutonic Power in 2007 to sell water rights in their traditional lands

Colin Robertson and Bonnie MacDonald are longstanding partners in the Refuge Cove Store on West Redonda Island. It is one of the few remote island stores to survive population decline by catering to summer yachters. PHOTO BY JEANETTE TAYLOR.

in exchange for jobs and compensation. The chief at that time, Duane Hanson, was quoted in the Powell River *Peak*. He told a packed audience in the Klahoose community hall at Squirrel Cove that the agreement "will let us find out what self-sufficiency and self-determination is." For his part, Plutonic Power president Don McInnes said their first cheque was simply a down payment. "There will be more of these and also, for you, training, apprenticeships and ongoing employment."

The deal has clear benefits for the Klahoose people and is expected to generate up to 196 megawatts of power for a province that has begun to max out its current power supplies. Environmentalists are concerned, however. They say the 145-kilometre (ninety-mile) transmission line and the generating stations will be a blot on a wilderness landscape. The BC Creek Protection Society worries about the environmental impact on wildlife and fish stocks, saying run-of-the river projects may not be as green as they are touted to be and require further study. The New Democratic Party has also expressed concern, saying such projects should be managed by BC Hydro to maintain the province's power sources in public hands.

On a warm long weekend in July 2008, when we paddled our kayaks from Cortes Bay to Desolation Sound, our experience was quite different from Don Reksten's and Leona Taylor's. With fuel prices hitting record highs and the US economy in a recession, we saw no more than ten sailboats and cruisers in the park in early July. This may reflect just another cyclical downturn in the economy of the Discovery Islands region, but it may also signal a shift in tourism. Added to the loss of early fishing, logging and milling, it will shape a new reality—yet to be determined.

CHAPTER FOUR

Sonora and Maurelle Islands, Okisollo Channel

Shooting the Rapids

W E PICKED DAFFODILS IN THE LUSH GRASS OF THE WILDE FAMILY'S long abandoned orchard on north Quadra Island and then headed across Okisollo Channel in Miray Campbell's fast boat. We were off to see Crazy Dave at Owen Bay on Sonora Island.

Our visit to Okisollo, the passage that separates Quadra from Sonora and Maurelle islands, was timed to avoid the boil of rapids racing through at ten to twelve knots on a flood tide. On such a tide, a standing wave off Cooper Point climbs as high as two to three metres (about six to ten feet). Adventuresome types like Miray's husband Luke Hyatt shoot through this rush of water in kayaks, just as local kids did in their rowboat sixty years ago. Across the way is another tricky piece of water. The south entrance to Hole-in-the-Wall, the narrow passage that separates Sonora and Maurelle, sounds like a waterfall when the tide rushes through.

Dave Sayers lives in a cabin on a rock bluff that overlooks Hole-in-the-Wall and Okisollo. He came to Owen Bay in 1978, leaving a career in forestry to live off the land. His first home had a tarpaulin roof stretched over a cluster of three hollow stumps. "You could catch rock cod right off the shore then," recalls Dave. His soft English accent seems slightly at odds with his wild halo of greying hair and makeshift clothing. There was plenty to eat back then, Dave says, but you had to work for it. He harvested an abundant crop of apples in the old Schibler orchard at the Owen Bay dock and hunted deer, ducks and raccoons.

Ralph Keller of Coast Mountain Expeditions, with lodges on northern Quadra and Read Islands, photographed his son Albert surfing in a kayak on the standing wave off Cooper Point. The tide rips through Okisollo Passage at ten to twelve knots.
PHOTO COURTESY OF RALPH KELLER.

"Why did you choose this place?" I asked. Dave talked about the climate, this being the northernmost reach of the arbutus belt, and then waved an arm toward the ocean. "You couldn't ask for a better moat than that," he said with a wry smile. His point is well taken. His property is part of a multi-lot subdivision developed more than thirty years ago, but the tides, currents and rapids keep people at bay, so the lots sold slowly until recent years.

It's harder to live off the land and sea now, with fish stocks dwindling. "I had the fish back then but not the chips," says Dave of those years before he had a productive garden. "Now I've got the chips and no fish."

Miray and Luke live to the south of Dave's place at Diamond Bay, where they watch the tide rip through Okisollo from their cabin windows. Miray's parents Fern Kornelsen and Ross Campbell and her siblings Farlyn and Tavish live nearby. In fact Diamond Bay is a busy hub of activity, a mini-revival of an old way of life otherwise largely gone from this part of the coast. Tied to their float is the twenty-one-metre (seventy-foot) *Columbia III*, a heritage vessel the family uses as a mothership for kayaking trips and eco-cultural tours. Next to them is retired fisherman Dennis Mattson, who lives aboard his classic troller. In Dennis's yard is Jody Eriksson's sawmill, fabricated from materials at hand and parts he ordered in. The young man, raised at Owen Bay, earns his living cutting lumber for housing projects throughout the Okisollo.

No more than about thirty people live in the general area now, but a century ago there were nearly five hundred people on Sonora, Maurelle, the Rendezvous Islands and the northern end of Quadra. Not many were Native people, as only a few had survived of a century of diseases introduced by Europeans.

The first wave of smallpox struck a decade prior to the arrival of European explorers in 1792. It swept up North America from Mexico, taking as much as ninety percent of the aboriginal population. Three Salish groups occupied this region: the Island Comox of Discovery Passage and Johnstone Straits, the Xwemalhkwu (Homalco) of the Bute Inlet area and the Klahoose of Toba Inlet and Cortes Island. They had major village sites in Waiatt Bay on northern Quadra, in Whiterock Passage on Maurelle, at Cameleon Harbour on Sonora and in Kanish Bay on northwestern Quadra.

Spanish and British expeditions, each with two ships, surveyed this area in 1792. They anchored near Desolation Sound, and small parties rowed through the area to chart the coast. They missed the passages that separate Read, Sonora, Maurelle and Quadra and mistook the clustered islands for one, which they named Valdez after one of the Spanish captains. When the British Navy updated these maps in the early 1860s,

The Campbell-Kornelsen-Hyatt property in Diamond Bay on Okisollo Channel revives a century-old way of life. The extended family supports itself with eco-cultural tours in the restored Columbia Coast Mission vessel *Columbia III*. Dennis Mattson lives aboard his fishing boat nearby and neighbour Jody Eriksson operates a sawmill. PHOTO COURTESY OF MIRAY CAMPBELL.

they discovered Read was a separate island. They failed to find Okisollo Channel, however, so the charts still showed Sonora, Maurelle and Quadra as one landmass.

In 1872 Canadian surveyors visited the area. This time their mission was to find the best route across the supposed Valdez Island for a proposed transcontinental railway link from Bute Inlet to Vancouver Island. Surveyor Joseph Hunter was surprised by what he found, as he wrote to an associate:

> I had great hopes up to last week that the CPR could be carried to Victoria without a break, but since then we have made some discoveries, fatal, I am afraid to the continuity of the Railway, and I believe recourse must be had to a ferry for the purpose of reaching VI.
>
> What is known as Valdez Island is intersected by two passages cutting it into three parts. One of these passages, neither of which is marked on the chart, must be crossed in order to reach Seymour Narrows. The narrowest crossing cannot be less than 2000 feet, in deep water, rather a wide span I should think for a Suspension Bridge. And then this is only one of four such bridges which would be required between the mouth of Bute Inlet and Vancouver Island. The country here is good for nothing. Twenty miles on each side would hardly pay for Railway spikes.

After Hunter's "fatal" discovery, Burrard Inlet was selected as the terminus for the national railway, giving birth to the city of Vancouver.

Hunter gave the three islands new names, but they didn't stick. Instead people referred to Quadra Island as Big Valdez or Lower Valdez. Maurelle they called Little Valdez, and Sonora was Middle Valdez. Or people simply used Valdez for all three. (The current names weren't assigned until 1903.) In the absence of government-assigned names, the ancient Salish and Kwakwala names became official. Okisollo translates to "passage," Waiatt Bay means "place that has herring," Chonat Bay means "place that has coho" and Kanish Bay describes a shape like a pinched waist.

First Nations use of this area had shifted by the time Hunter's party came across Okisollo Channel. Whiterock Passage was under the control of the Lekwiltok, a group with ties to the Kwakwala speakers of northern Vancouver Island.

A thick bank of clamshells runs along the eastern shore of Maurelle

Island at Whiterock Passage for about a kilometre, suggesting a major village in use for thousands of years. The Xwemalhkwu claim Tatapowis ("place that becomes dry") as their ancient territory, but its ownership is the subject of ongoing debate. Tatapowis overlooks a boulder-strewn passage that, as the name suggests, went dry at low tide before it was dredged. Whiterock Passage still takes concerted skill to navigate, requiring skippers to line up the stern and bow of their boats with shore markers to avoid a minefield of boulders. Such a place, with its restricted access, offered protection. To add to its defences, the houses were surrounded by palisades.[112] These protective measures didn't stop the Lekwiltok from taking over Tatapowis in about 1830.[113] One particular Lekwiltok group, the We-Wai-Kum (now of Campbell River),[114] remained at Tatapowis for over fifty years. "Surge Narrows was a very, very large settlement," wrote the late James Smith of the We-Wai-Kum. "My Dad lived there for a short time when he was small, but it was a very ancient town then. Here, at its greatest, people were so numerous they didn't know each other."[115] In the 1870s the place was provisionally allocated—but not confirmed—to the We-Wai-Kum as a reserve. Just eight houses remained at Tatapowis when a surveyor visited in 1885. About a year later these houses burned, after which the We-Wai-Kai moved farther south.

By 1894, when Indian Agent Pidcock visited Tatapowis, Old Harry (Harry Good) and his family were in residence. Harry's wife told Pidcock her husband was with the Klahoose Band of Cortes Island and Toba Inlet. On a subsequent visit in 1899, Pidcock noted there were about ten people living at Tatapowis, all of them members of Harry's family.[116]

Harry Good, the Xwemalhkwu claim, originally belonged to their band, but following a dispute he transferred to the Klahoose. As a result Tatapowis was officially designated as a Klahoose reserve in 1900. Harry Good's sons, Chief George Harry Good and Peter Good, remained with the Xwemalhkwu Band. They protested this allocation and put their case before Royal Commission hearings on land tenure in 1915.[117] According to them, Tatapowis belonged to the Xwemalhkwu. Members of the Harry family continued to live there until the 1970s.

Another significant site was at Waiatt Bay near the Octopus Islands on northeastern Quadra Island. This protected enclave, flushed by the nutrients and oxygenation of the surrounding rapids, is loaded with archaeological sites, some of which are nearly two metres (six feet) deep.

Historian Judith Williams examined the tidal beaches of Waiatt Bay on the advice of her Klahoose informant Keekus, who said her people tended and seeded clam beds there. Just as Keekus suggested, Williams found vast clam beds with piled rock borders that can be seen along the shoreline at the lowest tides of the year. The site is a fine example of what Williams dubbed "clam gardens" to describe these managed sites. Williams discussed her discovery with archaeologists but some were skeptical until the publication of her book *Clam Gardens*, when the theory became widely accepted. Clam gardens can be found throughout the inner coast where choice butter clams grow on the lower edge of tidal beaches.

When Indian Commissioner Vowell laid out the reserve at Tatapowis in 1900, he noted Harry Good and his family earned their cash income by selling game and fish to area logging camps. The twentieth-century history of Sonora and Maurelle is almost exclusively tied to logging. The steep islands, with limited agricultural land, attracted very few homesteaders compared to some of the other islands.

There appear to have been only two settlers prior to 1900. A. Hagen, who had a place near Hole-in-the-Wall (perhaps at Diamond Bay) in 1894, got a brief mention in the *Nanaimo Free Press*, when Mike Manson of Cortes was sent to investigate a charge by the First Nations people that Hagen abandoned his Native wife to marry "an eastern lady." Nothing further is known of Hagen. Across from him, on the Quadra Island shore, was John William Mogg who pre-empted land in 1891.[118] Mogg, an Englishman, seems to have moved back and forth between Vancouver and northern Quadra Island throughout the 1890s, working as an engineer and logger. He was the Justice of the Peace for this area but resigned in 1903, when he married and made a permanent move to Vancouver.

Aside from Hagen and Mogg, the rest of the land bought or pre-empted by non-Native people was claimed for logging. The earliest known logging in the area was in 1883, when Burrard Inlet logger Alex Russell bought a huge tract of land on southern Maurelle Island near Antonio Point. Leamy and Kyle, who had a sawmill in False Creek in Vancouver, bought land in the southern part of Cameleon Harbour on the west coast of Sonora in 1888–89. Moses Cross Ireland, who logged throughout the southern Discovery Islands, purchased 136 hectares (338 acres) in Waiatt Bay in 1884. The first outfit in Owen Bay on Sonora appears to have been the Vancouver Lumber and Manufacturing Company. A decade later the dominant companies were the Victoria Lumber Company, with an 1893 claim on the southwestern tip of Sonora, and Laidlaw and Rithet at Chonat Lake on northern Quadra Island.

The camps of the 1880s used ox teams to haul logs to tidewater along corduroy roads made of logs. Some switched to horse teams in the 1890s, and in about 1905 companies started to use steam donkeys for hauling. This new technology made it possible to haul logs from farther inland and resulted in a proliferation of camps throughout the Discovery Islands.

Reverend John Antle, founder of the Columbia Coast Mission, a seagoing medical and religious service, passed through Okisollo regularly en route to the mission's hospital at Rock Bay on Vancouver Island. Antle described the various camps and loggers he met in his magazine, *The Log of the Columbia*. He cited Tomlinson's camp near the rapids in Okisollo Channel in 1906 as a model:

> Snow fall. Visited Tomlinson's camp, Okis Hollow [Okisollo]. The boom logs were covered with five inches of snow. Perhaps a small amount of excitement goes a long way with me, at any rate, I found crossing those logs, to reach the camp at night, enough excitement to last for several days.
>
> This camp, owned by J.A. Tomlinson of Vancouver, and managed by J. Graham, is in many respects a model camp. The bunkhouse, cookhouse and office are the Hastings Mill Co's patent sectional houses, all neatly painted. The "tin cow" is not needed and salt junk is unknown in this Utopian Camp, for real, live cows supply the milk, and livestock, such as oxen, pigs, chickens, keep the larder supplied with fresh meat, and when you add to that two white cooks to exercise their culinary art upon those good things, who would not live at Tomlinson's Camp?

Here, too, I met a new class of logger, no less than five Russians, fresh from the battlefields of Manchuria. They are rather handicapped by their ignorance of the English tongue, but judging from their good physique and open faces, they will make good men.

The soldiers were survivors of the two-year Russo-Japanese war that claimed ninety thousand Russian lives. The failure of this ill-advised war sparked a revolution in Russia, so when their soldiers were released from prisoner-of-war camps in Japan, they couldn't go home. The *Daily Colonist* reported on January 1, 1906:

The 21 Russians, who were delayed here because of eye trouble, have been released and go to Vancouver to join those who preceded them. Nearly all who came here from Japan on the last steamer have found work in logging camps up the coast. Some of the members of the party hold farms in Russia, but they have no desire to return while the present state of affairs exists. They are a hardy, intelligent looking lot of men, who are likely to be good woodsmen, as many of them have had previous experience in Russia.

Reverend Antle met another Russian soldier in a camp at Granite Point on northwestern Quadra. Mike Lobrinsky had "several scars as souvenirs of the Russo-Japanese war." Nothing further is known of these men.

Very few logging camp operators before the mid-twentieth century allowed women and children in camp, believing men worked better without the distraction of family life. An exception was the Vanstone and Hughes tent camp at an unspecified site in Okisollo Channel in 1907. William Hughes of Quadra Island had his wife Eliza with him, and Ed Callow also had his wife in camp. David Vanstone brought his pretty English bride to camp when he married in 1907. Napolean LeClair had his wife with him, and many members of her family as well, including her siblings and her mother Annie Assu.[119]

While Vanstone and Hughes had progressive views about family life, they were not leaders when in came to running a dry (alcohol-free) camp. Alcohol abuse was a fixed pattern in the lives of many loggers, sometimes with disastrous results. In fall 1907 a group of men and women from the Vanstone and Hughes camp attended a masquerade ball at the Heriot

Bay Hotel on Quadra Island. Crew member Tom Drapeau got thoroughly drunk on the night of the ball. The next day he stocked up on whiskey before heading back to camp, where he continued to drink in Napolean LeClair's busy household. Though it was illegal to sell or give alcohol to Native people, Drapeau and LeClair served Annie Assu a few drinks.

Annie's family later testified she was only slightly drunk when she followed Drapeau to his cabin. LeClair left at the same time as Annie, and though he was drunk, he said he went to his saw-filer's shack to sharpen his saw for work and stopped at Drapeau's cabin on his return. "I saw Mrs. Annie Assu in bed with him and I told him, 'Now you ought to have more sense than that.' I didn't say any more but walked out and went home and told my wife all about it."

Annie Assu's daughter Eliza Wallace and some of the younger children went to see what was happening. They were followed by Eliza's husband Jimmie:

> Myself and my little brother and sister were the three who went over. When I went in the house I saw Mr. Drapeau with his hands on her [Annie's] throat and [he] was straddled over her. Blankets were scattered all over the floor. I knew that my mother was dead. He just had his drawers on. Drapeau said get out of the house or he would throw [us] out. Drapeau had his hands on her throat when Jimmie got there. As soon as Drapeau saw Jimmie Wallace he let go and began to curse. I said to Jimmie, 'don't listen to him.' I was going to arrest Drapeau. Jimmie took Mrs. Assu down from the bed. Drapeau felt her pulse after Jimmie laid her down on the floor.

The family took Annie's body to Cape Mudge Village, where the resident missionary examined her. It was clear Annie Assu was murdered. Her neck was broken and she had a bite mark on her arm and bruises around her neck and elsewhere, said the minister. Despite the missionary's testimony and the fact that Eliza and several others saw Drapeau choking Annie, he managed to get off the charge of manslaughter. Annie's body was too decomposed by the time it was examined by a coroner to bear witness to her cause of death. The coroner wrote on Annie's death certificate that she died of "natural causes, from excessive use of whiskey furnished by Napolean LeClair and Tom Drapeau." Drapeau was charged with serving alcohol to a Native person and got the full penalty of six months' incarceration. His friend LeClair, who was also charged with the liquor offence, got off with a fine.

Though the Columbia Coast Mission only made passing mention of this tragedy, they constantly urged sobriety. Some loggers were persuaded to amend their ways, but most just humoured the CCM's fussy interference. The dangers of their work made them appreciate the mission's excellent medical services. Some of the patients the mission cared for were easily treated on board ship, as when T. Tame sat down hard "on the business end of an axe" in 1907 and needed stitches.

Many times the CCM came to the rescue and saved lives, but Engineer Jesse William Angle was beyond their help. He took the East and West Lumber Company's locomotive, at their Maurelle Island camp, down a steep grade, though he was warned the brakes needed to be adjusted. The train went out of control and the engineer was killed. "Angle was still living when taken from the wreck, but died while being conveyed to the Rock Bay hospital," said the *Daily Colonist*.

Of the 488 people living on northern Quadra Island and on Sonora, Maurelle and the Rendezvous islands at the time of the 1911 census, only sixteen were women and children.[120] There were 363 loggers, ten farmers and two fishermen living at "the rapids." Only one of the women was listed with a profession. Japanese immigrant Sin Saigo was a logging camp cook, living with her husband and two toddlers.

A number of the men listed in the census were handloggers working on their own or in small groups. A few had settled down on pre-emptions, cheap government land grants intended to encourage farming. With the proliferation of camps and homesteads, Charles Stelfox opened a post office (and possibly a store) in 1913 on his homestead on the northernmost Octopus Island, facing into Okisollo Channel. By 1919, according to the British Columbia Directory, thirty to forty permanent residents throughout Okisollo got their mail at Waiatt Bay. Most said their occupations were a combination of ranching and logging, but there was also a boat builder named Ferdinand T. Clarke and "gasoline expert"

Thomas Clarke. John T. Cook managed the Wyatt Bay Fish Oil and Fertilizer Company, and Mrs. E.A. McWhirter was caretaker. Nothing further is known of this company, which likely extracted fish oil for lubricants and lamp oil.

William Kilpatrick and Thomas Keefer and their families lived as squatters at Antonio Point on Maurelle Island before World War I. Though land pre-emptions were cheap, there was a fee for filing and surveying a claim. When William Kilpatrick enlisted for war service, he left his family on Lot 1040 with its "good house and garden." Their neighbours Thomas Keefer and family had a house and garden, too, and ran sixteen head of cattle on Lot 1041, where an old logging skid road served as a community trail.

After the war the Kilpatrick and Keefer families were informed the properties running along the curve of bay from Antonio Point to the reserve at Whiterock Passage were being "thrown open" for a soldiers' settlement. Public notices were circulated. To be eligible to get title to the land they had to be at the Land Office in Vancouver at 9:00 a.m. on July 29, 1919. The land was assigned on a first-come, first-served basis. Presumably both families secured title to their properties, as they continued to live in the area for many years. Other veterans claimed the adjoining sixteen-hectare (forty-acre) land grants. Ellsworth Le-Roy Barber and W. Hollyer asked for more land at Antonio Point to be removed from expired timber leases and allocated to returned soldiers:

> The land I have mentioned is flat and very good soil and the clearing is not difficult. There are only four or five lots there that are any good, and there is a returned man waiting to go to work on each lot as soon as they are assured that they can get it. Some of them have even built houses, but are getting discouraged by the delay. It seems as if the department does not intend to let us have it. I am prepared to go right to work and spend money in clearing up Lot 1030 as soon as I can get a record on the place.

The vets and their families collected their mail at the Waiatt Bay post office, which Herbert and Rolla Bentley took over in 1919. They in turn sold the property and store to George and Harriet Dusenbury in

1928. The Dusenburys operated the store out of a room in their home. There were a counter and weigh scales at one end of the room, where they sold incidentals like canned milk, potatoes and candy. The latter was not a popular item after someone spotted the Dunsburys' little dog peeing in the floor-mounted candy bin.

Most islanders ordered their supplies in bulk through Vancouver merchants, who shipped goods on the Union Steamship boat from Vancouver. The *Chelohsin* stopped at the Dusenburys' wharf, when weather and tide permitted, to drop off mail, freight and passengers.

Across from the Dusenburys, on the Quadra Island shore, lived the Blanche and William Wilde family. Lukin Johnston, a reporter with the *Province*, paid an early morning visit to the Wildes in the fall of 1925. Their apple trees, near the house, were loaded with fruit:

> Mrs. Wilde, the mistress of the farm while her husband was away working at a logging camp across the channel greeted us with the warmth one grows accustomed to expect among these islands. It is never too late or too early to call.

Harriet and George Dusenbury, photographed by Francis Barrow in 1929, ran a store and post office in their home on the Octopus Islands that served most of the Okisollo region. The childless Dusenburys, with their English accents and particular ways, awed the Okisollo children.
PHOTO COURTESY OF EDNA MAE JOHN COLLECTION, MCR 20,110-7.

It would amaze many city women to see what one of their sex can do when put to it as are these brave women of the coast. Here was Mrs. Wilde, with her three children, cut off from all the world, except for their little rowboat, working the farm, feeding horses and cows and minding the family—all without thought that this was really a hardship.

The children, the eldest of whom was 13, helped her, but all of them must be taught by the government correspondence course, and this meant giving up several hours a day. Incidentally, the house, though some might think it was bare, was spotlessly clean and neat.

With justifiable pride she showed us the clearing they had accomplished—fields literally carved out of the thickest kind of slashed land. Gradually they were making a farm—which those that come after may enjoy.

A family who would have a tremendous impact upon the Okisollo area moved to Raza Island, to the northeast of Whiterock Passage, in 1921.[121] Logan Schibler got a timber lease on the steep and otherwise uninhabited island after his fish-buying business and store on the Columbia River in the US went bankrupt because of a swindling partner. "He was doing all right, but he was a terrible businessman," says his daughter Helen (Schibler) Clements. "He never kept books and if someone wanted $100 he'd give it to them—without a receipt."

Logan's family followed him in about 1922, though the best he could provide was a pole shack and homemade furnishings. Logan's wife Gunhild arrived in her silk dress and hat—remnants of a better life—to live with shelves and chairs made from boxes, a stove made from an upturned wash tub and fir boughs for mattresses. This was not the life Gunhild had hoped for when she immigrated from Norway at the age of sixteen. She never did adjust to coastal life.

Logan may have been an impractical man, but he was a hard worker. As his eldest daughter Helen (Schibler) Clements recalls, he logged by himself on Raza. He tied one end of his crosscut saw to a small tree with some bend to it so he could pull his saw back and forth. He jacked the felled timber down the slope or dragged it over greased skid roads to the sea. "Then he'd have to walk all the way down the hill, get in his rowboat to retrieve the log, tie it up and head back up the hill again," recalls

Gunhild Schibler, standing, emigrated in her teens from Norway to the US, where she met Logan Schibler. When his business on the Columbia River failed, they moved to the Okisollo area. Homesteading on the coast left Gunhild with disappointed dreams of a better life.
PHOTO COURTESY OF ADELE TURNER COLLECTION, MCR.

Helen. He augmented his handlogging with stints as a gillnetter in Smiths and Rivers inlets in summer and quickly replaced their pole shack with a timber-frame floathouse built on skids. The new house had a large living room and an attic bedroom for the children.

Helen recalls eating all the wild food they could find, from new salmonberry shoots and nettles to goose grass that grows on the seashore. She played house in the forest, dressing in hemlock-bow skirts and tops to sashay about "like a grand lady." Helen also made dolls from kelp bulbs, with carved faces, and houses on the beach for stick people with salal-berry heads.

When it was time for school in 1923, Helen boarded with the Johncox family on the west coast of Middle Rendezvous Island to attend school in the upper room of a house. Teacher Alex Rose Housley and Helen both stayed with Victor and Francis Johncox in the comfortable manager's house attached to a defunct reduction plant. "They had many luxuries, compared to our house," recalled Helen at the age of ninety-four, "including a piano."

The Johncoxes' home was part of a small settlement centred around the reduction plant. Victor Johncox worked at the plant, which processed dogfish for oil and fertilizer during World War I, and when it closed he stayed on as the caretaker. The Johncoxes maintained the post office from 1921 to 1923 and may have had a store, too, in the cluster of buildings at the dock where Union Steamship boats from Vancouver called. There were a few other families living on the three Rendezvous Islands, enough to maintain a school with a minimum enrollment of ten.

Miss Housley delighted young Helen by playing the Johncoxes' piano. When the school inspector came, he too played for the family, with Helen at his side. "You like the piano?" he asked her. "Oh yes," Helen replied, "but Miss Housley plays much better than you." Her childish frankness didn't keep her mother from scrimping to pay a woman living at the southern end of the island ten cents per lesson to teach Helen to play.

Like many other island communities reliant upon a small transient population, the South Rendezvous School didn't last more than a few years. It closed after 1928 for lack of enrollment and didn't reopen.

The Schiblers were among those who left. Henrik R. "Whiskey Harry" Williamsen offered them his land at Owen Bay at a reasonable rate[122] in exchange for their care through his senior years. Whiskey Harry, a Norwegian immigrant, came to the area to log sometime before 1911. He cleared land and planted an orchard at Owen Bay, where he also had

Helen Schibler (Clements), right, with her brother Jack, has fond memories of her simple childhood games and toys. Her family lived in a primitive shack on Raza Island until her parents saved enough money to build a large floathouse they moved to Owen Bay on Sonora Island.
PHOTO COURTESY OF ADELE TURNER COLLECTION, MCR.

a barn and a frame house with two bedrooms and a dining room. A combination of alcoholism and bad legs plagued Harry as he aged. He struck an excellent bargain when Logan and Gunhild Schibler became his caretakers. They were a steady, sober couple with three young children. Some recall the property was signed over to Gunhild because Logan's business affairs were still entangled by his bankruptcy.

Alcoholism claimed Whiskey Harry's life not long after the Schiblers moved their floathouse onto his land, north of the current government dock. He was presumed to have fallen from his rowboat after a night of drinking with a neighbour, since his boat was found adrift with his canes inside. His body was never found.

After the Schiblers' move to Owen Bay in about 1925, Logan continued to support the family by gillnetting in summer. He also built a sawmill from equipment he salvaged in Loughborough Inlet, on what came to be known as Mill Point, to the northeast of the current government dock. With his own lumber, Logan built a dock that curved from their house south to the slough, and the place became a favourite layover for fishermen waiting out a tide or stormy weather.

"Anyone who arrived in Owen Bay would automatically be invited to join the family for a meal," recalled Logan's son-in-law Bob Turner. With such a welcome, their home became the social hub for the district, as much for their generosity as their good-natured welcome. "They were never ones to gossip," recalls their granddaughter Adele Turner. "Everyone, of every nationality, was accepted and welcome."

Logan's strongly held socialist values sparked this hospitality and open attitude. His values coloured the whole community, making Owen Bay a memorable place to live. Logan's former neighbours describe him fondly as the heart of their community. He shared whatever he had. If someone was in need, and through those years many were impoverished, Logan found a way to help. Gunhild and the children sometimes paid for his generosity, scrimping on their own meals to make the food go around for extra settings. At Christmas, Logan gave a goose or a pork roast to every neighbour and everyone pooled resources. Alma Van der Est supplied bullets, and the Schiblers did her hunting. Others traded salmon or deer for potatoes.

Whiskey Harry on the porch of his home at Owen Bay on Sonora Island. His house, later a school, lay just behind what's now the government dock. He persuaded the Schiblers to buy his farm in 1925 at a reasonable price in exchange for a home and care in his senior years.
PHOTO COURTESY OF ADELE TURNER COLLECTION, MCR.

Gunhild and Logan Schibler's granddaughter Adele Turner and Betty Garbutt watch Chris Struck repair a fishing net in about 1949 on the network of docks that Logan built in front of their Owen Bay home.
PHOTO COURTESY OF RUTH (VAN DER EST) OPPEL COLLECTION, MCR.

Homesteads dotted the deep recess of Owen Bay. Mr. Walter, a veteran who married the Dusenburys' English housekeeper, lived next to the Van der Ests at the head of the bay. Justin Door, another vet, and his family lived at the far end of Hyacinthe Lake at the head of the inlet. "He'd bring his horses and a stoneboat down to the lake shore and then row across the lake to get out to Owen Bay to go for supplies," recalls Ruth (Van der Est) Oppel. "He couldn't figure out why his wife didn't want to stay there!"

Everyone grew a big garden. Gunhild was the gardener of the Schibler family. Logan cleared about 2.4 hectares (six acres) for a kitchen garden. He dug and raked it each spring, ready for Gunhild to plant and tend. The Schiblers also added to Whiskey Harry's orchard, bringing it up to about a hundred fruit trees. Their livestock included geese and pigs, and they had about thirty goats for milking at one point, until the ever-present cougars killed them off. In fall Gunhild canned about five hundred quarts of fruit, meat and fish.

A picnic at the Walters's homestead at the head of Owen Bay in 1939. From left to right are John Van der Est, Mr. and Mrs. Dalgeish, Billie Walters (rear, with suspenders), Gunhild Schibler and Louise Walters. Seated in front are Miss McCrae (right) and Minnie Case.
PHOTO COURTESY OF RUTH (VAN DER EST) OPPEL COLLECTION, MCR.

Owen Bay's first school class in 1926 posed with their teacher Miss Procter (back left). The children are (left to right) a Goss girl, Marilyn Donnelly, Dean Donnelly, curly-haired Helen Schibler (Clements) and Jack Schibler. In the front row are two Goss children and Jean Schibler (Turner). PHOTO COURTESY OF JEAN TURNER COLLECTION, MCR 19,996-13.

What Owen Bay lacked was a school. Helen (Schibler) Clements went to live with relatives in California the year the Schiblers moved to Owen Bay. Meanwhile Logan advertised in newspapers and magazines for school-aged families, promising to find them homes. There were numerous responses, and eventually two families came to stay. One took over an abandoned shack on an island in front of the Schiblers' place, and another moved into an empty house across the bay on the western shore.

The Wilde girls from Waiatt Bay also enrolled, and the Owen Bay School opened with twenty pupils in September 1927[123] in the kitchen of Whiskey Harry's former home. Teacher Edith Proctor and the Wilde girls boarded in the remainder of Harry's old house.

Teachers rarely stayed in small rural communities for longer than a year, but Miss Proctor remained at Owen Bay until the enrollment dropped and the school closed in 1932. Logan once again placed an ad offering to locate homes for families in Owen Bay. He also offered part-time work in his sawmill.

John and Alma Van der Est saw Logan's ad in the *Family Herald Magazine*. They were the perfect candidates. They had six children, and

Alma was an experienced schoolteacher. Part-time work was ideal for John, who suffered from malaria he contracted when he went to sea as a youth. The family packed up their belongings and travelled by train from Rossland to Vancouver, where they caught the Union Steamship boat. They were dropped off at Chonat Bay, at the west end of Okisollo, and lowered from the boat on a platform suspended from guy wires.

Alma liked the homestead Logan recommended at the head of Owen Bay and bought the twenty-one hectare (fifty-two-acre) place for $250 from a man named Morissette. John and the boys winched together Morissette's two small cabins to create one T-shaped structure, part of which remains on-site.

Alma's life was demanding. She had a busy household to manage, five energetic boys and a toddler to raise and her new job as the Owen Bay schoolteacher. The trail that ran around the eastern part of the bay to the school at Schiblers' place wasn't safe, because there were too many cougars on the island. Alma and the boys kicked off their shoes to drag their rowboat across the tidal flats in front of their home in preference to an encounter with a cougar.

Alma was a kind and motherly woman, her daughter Ruth recalls, but she kept strict rule in the classroom, especially when it came to her own children. She wanted to show no hint of favouritism. Alma's monthly wage, in those Depression years, was sixty-eight dollars. In the summer she was forced, like many of her friends and neighbours, to rely on a fifty-eight dollar relief cheque every month from the provincial mothers' assistance program. The police came in once a month by boat to check that recipients like the Van der Ests had no other source of income.

School was relocated to an old fish processing plant on floats in 1933. It was a large building, but that was its only redeeming attribute. Its massive skids, firmly planted on the beach, were so waterlogged that it didn't float, and seawater sloshed around the children's feet on extreme high tides.

Another family Logan encouraged to move to Owen Bay was that of August and Zaida Schnarr of Bute Inlet. August Schnarr was already something of a legend in the area, a loner with a bitter edge bruised into his soul by an alcoholic father and poverty. He was equal to anything Bute Inlet had to offer, from glaciers and fast rivers to freak winds, but he found it hard to work with others. "When I work I wanna get something done!" said August in a taped interview. Sometimes his strong views got him into fights. "I wouldn't back down for anybody! Why should I?"

One of the Schnarrs' daughters, Pearl (Schnarr) Macklin, wonders if part of the reason for her family's move was their mother's declining health. Owen Bay was much closer to Zaida's family, the Lansalls of Cameleon Harbour, and at least one of her siblings lived in Owen Bay. Zaida passed away from cancer about a year after the Schnarrs' move. Her daughters Pansy, Pearl and Marion were not allowed to attend the funeral in Cameleon Harbour. As a result, young Pearl never fully accepted the fact her mother was gone.

After Zaida's death, August went back up to Bute Inlet to tow their floathouse to Owen Bay. He had nearly reached the mouth of the inlet when a wind came up and swamped the floathouse, sinking it and taking all their possessions, including their winter's supply of potatoes. "He couldn't do anything about it," recalled Pansy (Schnarr) Eddington, "it

When classes got cramped in Whiskey Harry's farmhouse kitchen, Logan Schibler towed an old fish-camp float into Owen Bay and anchored it in the slough to the south of the government dock. On high tides the school's water-logged skids sank and sea-water came through the floorboards.
PHOTO COURTESY OF ADELE TURNER COLLECTION, MCR.

just broke the float up and the house went down to the bottom." After this, Logan Schibler helped August salvage wood from an old logging camp in Bute Inlet to build a cabin at Schiblers' place in a slough, where August cleared about 0.4 hectares (an acre) for a garden.

Given his own tough upbringing, August did the best he could with his three daughters. "August was a hard man but he was soft when you came right down to it," recalls Ruth (Van der Est) Oppel. "He was severe with the girls but if something hard or emotional happened he was there for the girls."

"August never stopped working," recalled Pansy (Schnarr) Eddington. And he expected his girls to do the same. "When he wasn't around," said Pansy in a taped interview, "we'd play a little bit. He didn't believe in play. If we didn't have anything to do then we had to go chuck rocks [from the garden]. In summer, when August went gillnetting farther upcoast, he took the girls back up to Bute Inlet to live on his homestead. They picked hundreds of kilograms of wild berries and strawberries from his huge garden to can outside on a propane stove along with quarts of fish.

Zaida Schnarr with her daughters Pansy, Pearl and Marion. The Schnarrs raised their daughters at their isolated homestead in Bute Inlet until Zaida's failing health and the girls' need to attend school forced a temporary relocation to Owen Bay on Sonora Island.
PHOTO COURTESY OF AUGUST SCHNARR COLLECTION, MCR 14,409.

Marion, Pansy and Pearl Schnarr's father—a cougar bounty hunter—once brought orphaned cougar kits home as pets for the girls. Girlie and Leo lived for about six years. Pansy (Schnarr) Eddington recalled, "They were nice pets, we could pet them and they'd purr just like a cat." PHOTO COURTESY OF MCR 15,624.

Schnarr earned part of his income as a cougar bounty hunter. While they were living at Owen Bay, he shot a female and brought home her four newborn kits for his girls to raise. Two of the cougars lived to adulthood, bound by heavy chain to keep them from straying. They loved the Schnarr girls, who fed them on cooked mash and fish. "We never gave them anything alive," recalled Pansy, "never allowed them to kill anything. They would break their chains, then hide in the bush and jump out at us when we walked home from school. It would startle us for a minute. Then we'd just take them by the chain and hook them up again. When that was enough of that my dad put heavy anchor chain on them."

For the first few years after their mother died, one of Zaida's sisters stayed with the girls at Owen Bay while August worked his traplines in Bute Inlet for parts of the winter. After their aunt married, the girls sometimes stayed with the Van der Ests. When Pansy hit her teen years, August took the girls back up to Bute Inlet for good. "He didn't think girls needed much education," recalled Pansy.

As logging began a slow transition to larger, more expensive operations, the number of people living and working in the Okisollo region decreased, except for the little enclave in Owen Bay. It would eventually be abandoned, too, as fishing tapered off and logging switched to fly-in crews, but many families hung on at Owen Bay, bonded to a community with heart.

A Return to the Backwaters

The Columbia Coast Mission's Christmas gatherings during the Depression years were exciting occasions. Word was spread throughout the surrounding area about where the parties would be held and everyone congregated to welcome Reverend Alan Greene.

"It was honest-to-goodness winter weather," Greene wrote in *The Log* about a Maurelle Island gathering. "The snow lay deep in the woods. And the boom-sticks to which I tied the ship were so deeply covered with snow, that one's only guide was the long arrow of undisturbed snow that suggested a log underneath." Greene and his assistant carried Christmas gifts, the portable organ, a "moving picture machine" and the heavy battery that operated it, crates of Japanese oranges, gas lanterns, flashlights, Christmas records—and Greene's Santa costume—along the boomstick. An elderly woman they took onboard somewhere near Antonio Point, "who couldn't walk a step," was carried ashore from the ship's tender. Once all the gear was stowed in the schoolhouse, Bill Heinbokel served a feast of roasted venison, cabbages, carrots, potatoes with gravy and Oregon grape jelly in his little cabin.

After dinner the party moved up to the schoolhouse, including Greene's elderly guest, who was pulled over the snow in a makeshift sleigh. "About eight o'clock we carefully checked on those present and the party began." Greene showed Charlie Chaplin's *The Gold Rush*, speeding it up and slowing it down for the "thrilling scenes," to add to the suspense. Carol singing and Bible stories followed, after which Greene disappeared to deck himself in his Santa gear. "Fitz helped me don my Santa costume, by the inadequate light of a flashlight. [He] rouged my face, straightened my beard, and stuffed my mid-ship section with air-balloons. I staggered toward the school to be welcomed by a mob of happy children as they threw open the door and dragged me in." After gifts were circulated, "Santa" disappeared again, replaced by Greene just in time for a supper of sandwiches, cakes and coffee made in a huge wash-boiler. A dance followed. "The babies had long since fallen asleep, laid out wherever space permitted on piles of soggy overcoats," wrote Greene, as they danced the night away to his phonograph player.

This same complicated celebration was repeated in every little community throughout Greene's widespread parish.

In 1929 the soldiers' settlement on Maurelle Island opened a school in Bill Heinbokel's old cabin, with Elizabeth Mrus as the teacher. The families with children were the Armstrongs (where the teacher boarded), Pattersons, Nelsons and Morrises. A year later an official schoolhouse was built, and the McIntyres moved across to Sonora from Waiatt Bay to enroll.

As Reverend Greene looked back on the Maurelle Island settlement, he puzzled over what kept the few families on the "rocky, almost soilless" land. It was their fierce need for independence, he decided. They were willing to live in want and isolation for their freedom, but by 1933

Reverend Alan Greene of the Columbia Coast Mission had a wry sense of humour and a full-hearted commitment to his parishioners that made him welcome throughout the Discovery Islands.
PHOTO COURTESY OF ALAN GREENE JR. COLLECTION, MCR 17,922.

most of them gave up on their eastern Maurelle homesteads and moved on. The school was closed and never reopened.

Another little enclave of non-Native residents sprang up on the western shore of Sonora Island, at the Thurston Bay forestry station. Enough people lived there to create a small village where housing, a school and other services were provided for the men and their families. The men patrolled the logging camps of the inner coast between Vancouver Island and the mainland and issued logging permits. They also took responsibility for fire watch and suppression and experimented with reforestation.

Among the scattered settlers in the region was the Ishii family of North Rendezvous Island. Arthur and his sister Joy were grade-school children when the Canadian government decided to remove all Japanese Canadian residents from the coast. Joy (Ishii) Nebres was just seven years old at the time, but she remembers the day the big grey ship arrived to take them away after the bombing of Pearl Harbor in 1942. "I said, 'Hurry! Hurry! We're leaving the island," recalled Joy in a newspaper interview many years later. "I think we had two hours to pack. But they said we'd be coming back." The Ishiis were interned in a camp in the interior of BC, and their beautiful homestead was sold cheaply, along with all their belongings, for a song. They didn't return to the island for fifty-six years, when the family gathered at Rendezvous Lodge to revisit the past.

By 1943 about twenty-four people lived along Okisollo Channel between Waiatt Bay, Owen Bay and Chonat Bay, according to the provincial directory. Most were loggers, and a few were fishermen. Though the post office and store remained at Waiatt Bay, Owen Bay was the community hub.

The younger set throughout the Okisollo area looked forward to dances and would travel many kilometres by rowboat or gas boat to go to a dance at Stuart Island, Cortes Island or Refuge Cove on Redonda Island. They came and went with the tide, using it to speed their travel. Ruth (Van der Est) Oppel's mother made over clothes sent by her mother. "Blouses and petticoats were made out of flour sacks," recalls Ruth. "You bleached the flour sack to get rid of the 'Robin Hood' emblem." Ruth's mother made her a fancy dress when she was fourteen from green organdy drapes she got from the Alert Bay Hospital.

Gunhild Schibler in about 1935 at the Owen Bay Dock. The Schibler home is in the background, at the head of what's now the government dock.
PHOTO COURTESY OF JEAN TURNER COLLECTION, MCR 19996-2.

Logan Schibler of Owen Bay constantly improved his family's living circumstances. Ruth (Van der Est) Oppel recalls the Schiblers had the most comfortable home of anyone in the region, with their electrical plant, running water and flush toilet.

Helen (Schibler) Clements was a good student, so her parents sent her to Vancouver and then to California to stay with family friends while she finished high school. She returned to the coast, married in 1932 and wound up back in Owen Bay during World War II. As she had completed high school, Helen was granted special permission to take over as the teacher at Owen Bay. "It was heated by a 45-gallon drum and [had] only the windows for light," wrote Helen in her memoirs. "The door didn't fit very well and one inspector's comment was, 'No worry about ventilation!' We chopped our own wood to feed the stove." When the tide came up through the floorboards of the old float camp shack, Helen got her pupils to wear their gumboots to school and scrub the floor with lye and seawater, using worn brooms. "One Christmas we couldn't have the concert in the school as the really high tide that brought the water into the building occurred on the same night." They crammed into an even older building on shore to enjoy their pageant. "That year the community got together and built a new school on dry land!"

Helen and her husband Gus Clements took over a store and opened a post office on a log raft north of her parents' property in 1945–46. At Logan's urging, they made it a co-op store serving twenty-seven families in the immediate area. Shortly thereafter they built a frame structure on shore at the head of the wharf. A few years later the Clementses moved

The Schibler family was the heart and soul of the little community at Owen Bay on Sonora Island. Seated on the dock are Jean Schibler (Turner), Helen Schibler (Clements), Gunhild Schibler, Logan Schibler and Jack Schibler. PHOTO COURTESY OF JEAN TURNER COLLECTION, MCR 19,996-11.

to Quadra Island and eventually to Campbell River, where Helen got her teaching certificate and taught school for many years.

Ruth (Van der Est) Oppel was standing on a small island at the entrance to Owen Bay, jigging for cod, when Neil Oppel entered the bay in his fishing boat—wanting to know where Owen Bay was. They wound up getting married in 1951 and raised three of their daughters at Owen Bay while Neil ran a logging outfit based there. Ruth's father-in-law took over the Clements' store, and in 1957–58 Ruth became the postmistress for a short while.

Many small communities throughout the Discovery Islands fell apart after the Union Steamship Company's freight and passenger service went out of business in the 1950s, replaced by seaplanes.

Owen Bay weathered these changes until Logan Schibler's health declined. He underwent a hernia operation and beachcombed through his convalesence to earn enough money to take Gunhild to Norway. It was kindly meant, but a lifetime of unfulfilled dreams made her hard to please. "It would have been better if he hadn't made it a surprise," said their daughter Helen (Schibler) Clements, expressing her mother's disappointment at not having the opportunity to anticipate the trip. As with the time Logan bought a sewing machine for Gunhild but chose the wrong model. It was hard to please someone whose long-held wish for urban life had not been realized.

Logan returned from Norway after two weeks, but Gunhild stayed on. As she returned across Canada by train, Logan suffered a heart attack at Owen Bay. His son and daughter-in-law had no means of getting Logan out to hospital until the next morning. By then it was too late. After Logan's death Gunhild went to Vancouver, where she became a housekeeper.

By 1960 Owen Bay was virtually a ghost town, like many other settlements in the region. A new wave of residents, with the same hardihood and determination to live an independent life, arrived in the 1970s. Some found the isolation difficult and left. Others, like Rob and Laurie Wood of southern Maurelle, became permanent residents. The newcomers banded together to build a new school at Surge Narrows on Read Island that served Okisollo, Read and northern Quadra islands.

Rob and Laurie Wood bought their property at Port Maurelle in the 1970s as part of a co-op with twenty undivided shares. For the first decade the Okisollo region buzzed with activity, but gradually people began to leave. Some moved to keep their families together when it was time for their kids to enroll in high school. By 2007 Rob and Laurie Wood and one other fellow were the only co-op members living on the property full-time.

You have to take the tides and weather in your stride to live in a place like this, says Laurie Wood. People who visit from Eastern Canada or abroad, adds her husband Rob, recognize a distinct difference in the culture of the BC coast. "It's laid-back," says Rob, who hastens to add this gets misconstrued as laziness. "It's not. It's a lesson taught by wind, tides, currents and rapids. You don't buck the tide. You go with it. You go with the flow. If you listen to old-timers, the tug boat drivers, the fishermen, the loggers, the people who work in the bush, they're all like that." People have a wait-and-see attitude, says Wood, because they never know what's coming. "When they do get a window of opportunity, they go for it with all their heart and accept the consequences."

A friend of Bob Turner's wanted to borrow his boat to go to Owen Bay to meet Jean Schibler, but Bob didn't want to loan his boat, so he took him there and in the end it was he who married Jean. She's seen here reading one of Bob's letters from his logging camp just days before they were married in 1940.
PHOTO COURTESY OF THE JEAN TURNER COLLECTION, MCR 19996-3

CHAPTER FIVE

Bute Inlet, Stuart Island
and Church House

THE TWISTY DIRT ROAD TO THE SURGE NARROWS DOCK ON QUADRA Island was littered with tree trunks and branches from recent storms. The trees had been cut away and shoved aside by passing motorists. Rob and Laurie suggested I pack a chainsaw in the trunk, and now I could see why.

We'd been without electricity on Quadra and in parts of Campbell River for more than twenty-four hours. Even the Elk Falls pulp mill was down, but Rob Wood assured me on the phone that morning it was business as usual on Maurelle Island to the north of Quadra. He and Laurie would be waiting to pick me up in their skiff so we could talk about Bute Inlet.

Like others among the handful of Maurelle Islanders, the Woods have their own electrical system. They've been off the grid for more than thirty years, but they're not out of the loop. Rob's and Laurie's neighbour was engineering structural designs on a computer when I arrived, and the kitchen light blazed over a huge map of Bute Inlet spread across the kitchen table.

Rob ran a finger along the Homathko River at the head of the inlet. Old August Schnarr, a trapper who raised a family there in the 1930s, once told Rob and Laurie not to worry about Bute's grizzlies. "They never hurt anybody. You watch those side rivers!" he said, referring to the glacier-fed streams that race into the Homathko River.

Schnarr was an authority on the inlet. He elaborated on the dangers there to historian and novelist Maud Emery. "In that country, where mountains, canyons, valleys, lakes, rivers and river-jams all hold traps for the unwary and inexperienced, if you make a mistake, it's your last." And he was right. Scores of adventurers and trappers have died on the Homathko River and its tributaries over the past century.

I had come to hear about the Woods' Bute Inlet mountaineering experiences. I knew from Rob's book *Towards the Unknown Mountain* that the place has a grip on his and Laurie's souls, just as it did on the Mundays'. The famous mountaineering couple tried for two decades in the 1920s and 1930s to reach the top of Mount Waddington. At 4,019 metres (13,186 feet) it's the highest peak wholly within BC. They came near to the final spire but never made it. Many others before and after them have also been obsessed by the mountains and rivers of Bute. I wanted to know why.

Eco-cultural tour boat *Misty Isles* at the head of Bute Inlet, with the entrance to the Homathko River in the background. Fall can be the best time to visit the inlet. At other times the infamous bute winds funnel down the inlet. PHOTO BY JEANETTE TAYLOR.

Rob, who has a gift for words, described the huge satisfaction that self-reliance brings and his compulsion to live within the rhythms and dynamic forces of nature. It's this above all else that draws Rob and Laurie to the mountains.

Mount Waddington began to tug at Rob's imagination when he was a young man in Britain. Though he knew nothing about British Columbia, the hushed tones of awe and respect among climbing friends as they described Mount Waddington caught his attention. "It's one of the top twenty great mountains in the world," said Rob as we sipped tea. "Most mountains have an easy route up them, but Waddington does not have an easy route." From any angle you choose, says Wood, Waddington demands skilled mountaineering.

Mount Waddington is the most dramatic feature of the seventy-five-kilometre (forty-seven-mile) long inlet, but it's a place full of intensity and contradictions. "You've got 2,800-metre (9,200-foot) peaks that rise straight out of the water in Bute Inlet," says Rob. "That's extreme mountain fjord geography. I find myself sounding like I'm exaggerating when I talk about the inlet, but you can't talk about it to someone who doesn't know the place without sounding like you're exaggerating. It's so wild. There is nowhere, anywhere, as wild as this—certainly not in Canada. This is way wilder, way tougher country than the Rockies. And there's no river in the Rockies to compare with this."

The freakish weather in the inlet also poses challenges. The infamous Bute winds that funnel down the long inlet sometimes blow for weeks on end. And the depth of snowfall on Bute's mountains, where coastal and cold interior climates mingle, can be phenomenal.

Rob and Laurie led groups up Mount Waddington for several years until government red tape overwhelmed them and their focus shifted toward grandchildren. Nowadays they climb for their own pleasure and explore the coast in their catamaran. Sailing in these waters also requires steely nerves and a complex knowledge of the tides, as Spanish explorers discovered when they sailed into the maw of Bute Inlet in 1792.

The anonymous author of the journal for this Spanish expedition described a near shipwreck in the Arran Rapids off Stuart Island. It was the most harrowing misadventure of their voyage.

Native people near Arran Rapids warned the men in the *Sutil* and *Mexicana* not to approach the rapids until the sun reached a certain mountain peak, so they watched "the waters flow as if they were falling from a cascade" from a safe vantage point. "The time passed quickly" wrote the Spanish "with the entertainment afforded by watching the rush of waters."

In spite of the Native people's precautions the sailors mistimed their departure and got caught in a boil of whirlpools, one of which snatched the *Sutil* and spun her like a top in three tight circles. "Finally at half-past nine at night we succeeded in finding an anchorage," said the anonymous chronicler of the Spanish voyage, "both vessels lying under the shelter of a point. Much later the wind increased in strength, so that we heard it whistling through the trees on the mountain. At the same time the violent flow of the waters in the channel caused a horrible roaring, producing an awe-inspiring situation. We had so far met with nothing so terrible."

The Native people who assisted the Spanish explorers may have been the Xwemalhkwu (Homalco), Salishan speakers who had hunting and fishing stations along the length of Bute Inlet. A few decades later, when Hudson's Bay Company traders arrived, several groups were using the inlet, including the Xwemalhkwu and Klahoose of Toba Inlet (both Salishan-speaking), the Tsilhqot'in at a camp forty-eight

Alfred Waddington's hand-drawn map of his failed plan for a wagon road up the Homathko River to the Chilcotin goldfields in the early 1860s. COURTESY OF BC LAND TRANSFER AND LAND AUTHORITY.

kilometres (thirty miles) up the Homathko and the Lekwiltok.

The Lekwiltok, who have ties to the Kwakwala speakers[124] of northern Vancouver Island, acquired guns through trading connections at Nootka Sound much earlier than the others. As Hudson's Bay Company fur trader John McLoughlin noted when he visited the inlet in 1839, the "You-cult-taws" were "the terror of the surrounding tribes." Their highly trained warriors took slaves as far south as Puget Sound. The women and children they captured were released for ransom or traded with Native groups far to the north for European goods.

When Alfred Waddington steamed up the inlet in the *Henrietta* in the late summer of 1861,[125] he brought irreversible change. He came to assess the inlet's potential as a route to the Cariboo goldfields, several hundred kilometres to the east on the mainland. For a man like Waddington—with a glib tongue, ambition and influential connections—there was money to made from gold miners anxious to reach the Cariboo. Some of his Victoria business associates regarded him as a good citizen, though perhaps a bit eccentric and irritable. At sixty, Waddington had no time to lose in his race for wealth and fame.

The idea for building a wagon road through the Homathko Valley came to Waddington earlier that year, when he was housebound in Victoria with a nasty flare-up of gout. As he studied his map of BC, he noticed that Bute Inlet pierced deep into the interior mountains. This, he speculated, was the shortest route into the goldfields and a vast improvement upon the arduous trail up the Fraser River. Such a route would retain business in Victoria, where he was a merchant, rather than let it slip away to the mainland. Miners could outfit in Victoria, sail up the Strait of Georgia to Bute Inlet, hike from there to Alexandria and journey on to Barkerville. It looked entirely feasible on paper.

From his first look at the map of Bute Inlet, Alfred Waddington began to promote it as the ideal route. In the spring of 1861 he wrote a detailed description of this and several other wagon road options in his friend's newspaper, the *Daily British Colonist*. Publisher Amor de Cosmos ("lover of the universe"), was a key wagon-road investor. Profit was to come from a toll on the trail and land speculation in a townsite.

Waddington had not yet seen the place, but he rated Bute Inlet as the most feasible route to the goldfields. "The country is not mountainous," he said, "and there are frequent openings with fine tracts of land. In short this route appears far superior to all others, in every respect."[126]

When Waddington finally visited Bute Inlet that summer he was thrilled. It was just as he'd imagined. There was a large natural harbour at its head, and the first sixteen kilometres (ten miles) of the Homathko River delta was an alluvial plain, the perfect place for a townsite. To his delight, the Native people confirmed rumours of a foot trail through the mountains to the Cariboo. Waddington was so excited he turned back, while his party was still in the open delta, to return to Victoria with the good news. He left his surveyor, Captain Pryce, with several canoe men and Chief Telloot of the Tsilhqot'in to continue up the Homathko River along the Native people's pack trail to the Cariboo.

Just beyond the expansive delta, Waddington's men soon discovered, the river became a raging torrent full of log jams and steep-sided canyons. Pryce, who found himself at the helm of a difficult expedition, was no outdoorsman. His porters had to carry a huge cask of ale for his daily pleasure, and his days didn't begin until 9:00 a.m., at the call of Hudson's Bay Company voyageur Francois Côté.[127] When they finally reached the difficult five-hundred-metre (1,650-foot)[128] Homathko Canyon, with its vertical rock walls, Pryce decided to turn back. This was far more than he'd bargained for.

Some of the more experienced men such as Francois Côté and Henry McNeil offered to go on alone, but Pryce couldn't manage without them. Instead the party climbed to a viewpoint from which, as Pryce reported to Waddington, they saw the trail cross over into bunchgrass plains. A few months later another of Waddington's surveyors, Hermann Tiedemann, climbed the same hill and was taken aback. What lay before him was a sea of interlocking mountains "thousands of feet in height and clad in perpetual snow." Tiedemann made a tongue-in-cheek comment in his report that perhaps Mr. Pryce mistook the snowy peaks for bunchgrass in his dreams.

When the party reached the harbour again, Pryce scribbled a commendation for Telloot. The Tsilhqot'in chief wrapped it into multiple folds of cloth and tucked it away.[129] Language barriers likely kept him from

Mount Waddington, shown in this 1933 photograph, is the highest peak wholly within BC and one of the world's most challenging climbs. The Xwemalhkwu (Homalco) people said a man with wanderlust was transformed into the mountain to become the keeper of the north wind. Skilled First Nations men climbed the mountain on goat-hunting expeditions.
IMAGE I-51584 COURTESY OF ROYAL BC MUSEUM, BC ARCHIVES.

fully understanding Waddington's wagon-road plans. What would have been clear was that he now had access to European goods, including guns, which put him on an equal footing with his old enemies, the Lekwiltok.

Had language not been a barrier, Telloot could have told Pryce the Tsilhqot'in trail was about a seven-day journey for an experienced packer. It was a deer track that crossed dense bush, swamps and waist-deep, frigid streams. In other places it climbed up high mountain slopes and over the 1.6-kilometre-wide (mile-wide) Tiedemann Glacier that stretched up the mountain—sparkling in blues, greens and golds—as far as the eye could see. Throughout its vast expanse lay hidden crevasses, traps for the unwary.

Waddington and Pryce didn't know that Major William Downie, a veteran prospector and explorer, had hiked up the Homathko River just weeks earlier. Downie and his companions, like Pryce, were surprised by the rugged terrain, but persevered on foot after a canoe swamped and their Native guides refused to go on. At Tiedemann's Glacier, Downie saw only snowfields extending to the horizon and, with no pass in sight, finally made the dangerous journey back down the Homathko's rushing tributaries. Downie wrote in his autobiography, "It was one of the most trying journeys I ever undertook, which is saying a good deal."

When Downie returned to Victoria he was surprised to learn some leading businessmen had bought land at the head of Bute Inlet on Waddington's advice. When he rented a hall to present his findings, an angry crowd hurled garbage and shouted him down.

James Douglas, colonial governor of Vancouver Island and former chief factor for the Hudson's Bay Company, respected Downie's word and continued with development of the Fraser River wagon road. His government was not averse, however, to seeing an alternative route at Bute Inlet developed as a private enterprise.

In late October, with winter quickly approaching, Waddington sent a second canoe expedition of seven men into this wild country. The intrepid voyageurs Francois Côté and Henry McNeil agreed to accompany Waddington's engineer-surveyor Robert Homfray. Côté was a memorable character, with shoulder-length black curls, steely nerves and a propensity for flamboyant French Canadian curses. He had been with the Hudson's

Bay Company for many years and knew how to navigate a canoe under any conditions, including the stormy seas of early winter.

Somewhere near Desolation Sound, the expedition encountered a group of Native people going south in four canoes rafted together, moving their household to their winter quarters. The Natives rushed their women and children to shore and made for the survey party with their guns levelled, but when suitable gifts were offered, they allowed the men to pass.

Yet farther north, at what's now Homfray Channel, another Native group took offence at their approach and boarded the surveyors' canoe. They ordered Côté and his men to paddle for shore, and as the survey party had few guns, they did as directed. Côté and the others were lined up on the beach, prepared for the worst, when a war cry rang out from a far shore. At the helm of a canoe that shot across the water toward them stood a tall, proud-looking man who proved to be a chief of the Klahoose. At the sight of this man, the survey party's attackers fled.

The Klahoose chief took Côté, Homfray and the others to his fall camp, where he shared the bounty of a good season in a feast of mountain goat, bear and beaver. He was amazed to learn that his guests planned to cross the mountains of Bute Inlet to the Chilcotin. People used that trail only in spring and summer, he told them. It wasn't just the deep snow they must fear, but avalanches, grizzlies and Lekwiltok warriors.

The surveyors continued, however, and persuaded the chief to guide them up the Homathko River, where they dragged laden canoes over snow-covered log jams until they were forced to abandon their boat and gear. When the men refused to turn back at the Klahoose chief's urging, he left them. It was only by their chance discovery of a Tsilhquot'in camp a few kilometers further upriver that they survived. With some food from the Tsilquot'ins, the surveyors headed back down the river in a hollowed log. From the inlet they went in search of the Klahoose, who fed them and took them to Victoria by canoe.

Waddington glossed over Homfray's failed mission, forbidding him to pubish an account of his harrowing experiences. The only information that mattered to him was the confirmation of reports of a trail. In the spring of 1862, with hundreds of miners again heading for the Cariboo,

From 1862–64, Tsilhqot'in people worked as packers for Waddington's crew, building a wagon road up the Homathko River to the Cariboo goldfields. When one of Waddington's men threatened to infect the Natives with smallpox, it sparked a war. Klatsassin led the warriors and, with other leaders, was hanged for murder. *KLATSASSIN AND OTHER REMINISCENCES OF MISSIONARY LIFE IN BC, 1873* BY ROBERT CHRISTOPHER LUNDIN BROWN, COURTESY OF THE ROYAL BRITISH COLUMBIA MUSEUM LIBRARY.

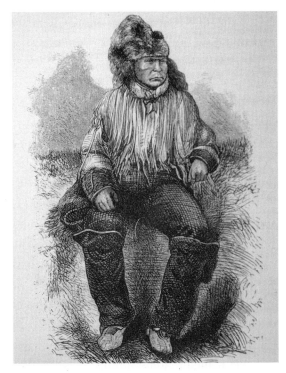

Waddington sent work crews to Bute Inlet to start his wagon road and build the townsite of Waddington.

Disaster followed. Work dragged on for two years and Waddington's crew, living on tight rations, refused to feed Native packers. When the Tsilhqot'ins railed against this, one of Waddington's men threatened them with smallpox. The disease had reached an epidemic among Native people so the Tsilhqot'in took up arms and killed nearly twenty men in an act of war. Their leaders were captured through a ruse and hanged. In 1993 a Cariboo-Chilcotin Justice Inquiry found the warriors were unfairly sentenced and the province gave a formal apology. Some Discovery Islanders feel the name of Mount Waddington should be changed to Klatsassin, to honour one of the lead warriors.

Railway Promises

Waddington's initial reaction to the death of his road crew was to lament the loss of a season's work, but he failed to find new investors for his wagon road. He badgered the colonial government for compensation for his losses with no success.

In 1868 Waddington developed a new scheme. Today he is sometimes credited as the first to push for a transcontinental railway as one of the terms of Canadian Confederation. His vision, of course, was for Bute Inlet to be the Pacific terminus.

Waddington promoted his idea in Britain and then moved to Ottawa to seek supporters, using a detailed report he prepared of the potential routes across BC to Bute Inlet. From there the trains were to cross a series of suspension bridges over "Valdez Island"—actually Sonora, Quadra and Maurelle islands—to Vancouver Island and on to Victoria.

A transcontinental railway deal, as Waddington hoped, did become a promise of Confederation. In 1871 methodical surveys of more than ten possible BC routes began. As the work proceeded, intense rivalry arose between Lower Mainland and Victoria interests over the siting of the terminus.

The Bute Inlet survey was led by a passionate and strong-willed engineer named Marcus Smith. He had three crews at work in Bute Inlet in 1872, two on the river and one between the inlet and Vancouver Island. Initially he hired Klahoose people to assist with river navigation and packing, but when they demanded adequate rest time, he replaced them with twenty Lekwiltok men. The Lekwiltok didn't possess the river canoes or white water experience of the Klahoose but they were willing to work for a dollar per day plus grub. The Tsilhqot'in people, who had the most experience on the river, flatly refused to work for the whites.[130]

The crew's rodman, Edgar Fawcett, calculated altitudes and marked them every 0.8 kilometre (half a mile) along a potential rail grade. His camp, as he wrote, was on the spot where Waddington's road crew was killed nearly a decade prior, at what was now called Murderers Bar. When they arrived, the old tent poles were still in place and the men's shovels were stacked as they'd been left, ready for the next day's work. The surveyors found some of the crew's books stashed in the storehouse near the ferry landing a few kilometres up the river, including *A History of Scotland* and *Arabian Nights*. Near Waddington townsite, they found three feral mules whisking their tails in the sunshine as they beat off the incessant flies.

Fawcett and his workmates surveyed upriver, while another party surveyed below. Their journals describe the rigours of the terrain and the difficulty of working for Marcus Smith. "On July 4 we got up at a quarter to six o'clock, and had to work amidst the roar of waterfalls, and after a hard day of 13 1/2 hours, got back to camp and to dinner. Smith had done nothing but growl and swear at us all the time the last four days." The third crew explored the waterways and islands for a suitable crossing under the direction of Joseph Hunter, the MLA for the region. That fall he wrote to tell a Victoria colleague of his shocking discovery that "Valdez Island" was actually three islands (see chapter 4), beyond the span of any suspension bridge.

An 1862 painting by J.R. Mackey shows the Waddington townsite on the Homathko River delta. Waddington hoped to make his fortune from the townsite and a toll on a wagon road to the Chilcotin goldfields, but he didn't reckon on the intensity of Bute's weather systems, mountains and glaciers.
IMAGE PDP00083 COURTESY OF ROYAL BC MUSEUM, BC ARCHIVES.

Alfred Waddington was spared this troublesome news. He contracted smallpox in Ottawa and died on February 26, 1872. That he should die of the disease was a supreme irony. It was his associate who touched off the Chilcotin War, and the many deaths that followed, with his threat to infect Waddington's Tsilhqot'in crew with smallpox.

The surveys of various routes continued for nearly a decade, and the merits of each were hotly debated among politicians and the surveyors themselves. Each had a stake in his own preferred route. As Pierre Berton wrote in his book *The Railway Pathfinders*, there were many strong egos at work.

Marcus Smith believed Bute Inlet to be the best choice, so when Bute Inlet's lack of deep water anchorage gave the edge to Burrard Inlet (Vancouver) in 1875, he was outraged. He used his temporary posting as federal engineer-in-chief to push the merits of Bute Inlet. His abrasive personality, says Berton, turned many against him and became a factor in a final decision in favour of Burrard Inlet.

Throughout this time of surveys and national debate, the Xwemalhkwu people of the Bute Inlet and Stuart Island area continued to live as they had done for centuries. They fished, hunted and gathered berries at the Homathko and Orford rivers, where reserves were allocated to them in 1888. A large reserve on the Homathko encompassed much of Waddington's townsite. According to ethnographers Dorothy Kennedy and Randy Bouchard in their book *Sliammon Life, Sliammon Lands*, houses stood on stilts along the river to withstand flooding.

The Xwemalhkwu were also granted a reserve across from the mouth of Bute Inlet at Mushkin on Maurelle Island and another at Aupe (Church House), where they had ten houses at the south entrance to Bute. Numerous other important fishing and hunting sites were requested but refused. Each extended family had ties to specific places.

Some other bands that figured in the tragic end of Waddington's Bute Inlet road project continued to use the inlet toward the end of the nineteenth century. A small fishing station at Vancouver Bay in Arran Rapids, where the Spanish were spun about in the turbulent waters, was allocated as a reserve to the Lekwiltok people. And the small Tsilhqot'in

The Xwemalhkwu people left their isolated village at Church House and relocated to a new reserve south of Campbell River. The Catholic church, built in the 1890s, toppled over in the winter of 2007. PHOTO COURTESY OF MARSHALL FRANCIS COLLECTION, MCR 7141.

band that lived up the Homathko in Waddington's time still came down the river to fish.

In 1888 the Xwemalhkwu people's population was seventy-four.[131] Many had converted to Catholicism, but it was hard to minster to a group that ranged over a vast territory, so in the early 1890s the Oblate Mission encouraged them to make Mushkin on Maurelle Island their winter village. They selected the place for its good soil; both the church and the Department of Indian Affairs were keen to convert the coastal Natives into farmers. Mushkin was also on the Union Steamship freight and passenger route from Vancouver, which made it easier for the missionaries to visit.

The band built houses at Mushkin as requested, and the Oblates erected a church, right in the teeth of the powerful outflow winds that race out of Bute Inlet. They weren't there[132] many years before a fierce Bute wind completely flattened the village. Thereafter the Xwemalhkwu relocated to their more protected 5.7-hectare (fourteen-acre) reserve on the mainland shore near the south entrance to Bute Inlet. The name

Church House was adopted for this second village, and another church was built there in about 1896. "We come over here in the winter time to meet the Priest and for church," said Chief Harry of the Xwemalhkwu to government officials in 1914. "It is too cold up at the head of Bute Inlet and there is lots of snow there, and that is why we come down here. In the summer time we go to Homathko River and places like that."

When reserve boundaries were set in the late 1880s, several logging camps were at work in the inlet. J. Elgeson was handlogging to the north of Amor Point, in the lower part of the inlet, in 1888. After two months of work he shipped a boom containing 76,000 metres (250,000 feet) of logs to a Nanaimo sawmill. One impressive log was forty metres (130 feet) long and 1.7 metres (5.5 feet) in diameter at the butt.[133]

Elgeson was still at work when two canneries opened at the head of the inlet in about 1890. One was operated by C.S. Windsor and George

View from the Homathko River toward the mountains on the southeast shore beyond the Southgate River.
PHOTO BY JEANETTE TAYLOR.

Hobson and the other by Laidlaw and Henderson. According to records collected by canner Henry Doyle, the Windsor and Hobson output was 2,627 cases[134] in 1890, but the next year was a bust. By 1892, when some Chicago railway men came to check out the inlet's potential as a terminus for yet another railway scheme, both canneries were closed. The *Daily Colonist* reporter who accompanied the railway men said the problems were lack of a ready market and a scant supply of fish. (At least one of the canneries reopened. John B. Henderson's cannery was listed in the British Columbia Directory for Bute Inlet in 1897.[135])

This new push for a transcontinental railway was a corporate initiative. Bute was one of several sites considered for a terminus. Stanley Smith, a mountaineer with a keen interest in geology and botany, went up the Southgate and Homathko rivers in 1895 on a government exploration contract. An experienced climber at forty, Smith had traversed numerous mountains and river valleys on the south coast over the previous decade.

Smith travelled on the Union Steamship boat up to Bute Inlet. "His pack, when leaving, weighed 114 pounds," said an observer,[136] "which surprised us old packers." Smith reached the Chilcotin country via the Southgate River within fourteen days and then headed back down via the Homathko. When he was not heard from again

Florence and William Walker moved their family of eight children from England to a small settlement at the head of Bute Inlet in the early 1890s. The Walkers pinned their hopes on the promise of a transcontinental railway terminus planned for the inlet.
PHOTO COURTESY OF BOB AND FAY LOGAN COLLECTION, MCR.

for many weeks, the government sent Chief Mitchell of the Xwemalhkwu in search of him. He found Smith's body floating in a quiet pool thirty-two kilometres (twenty miles) up the Homathko River. His canoe was stuck in a log jam a few kilometres farther up, at a portage over a particularly rough stretch of water.

Sixteen families, for a total of sixty people, lived at the head of Bute Inlet in 1895.[137] They'd hoped Smith would return with favourable news of the route's potential for a railway.

The Walker family from Berkshire, England, were among the first to arrive. In 1893 William and his wife Florence came halfway around the globe with their eight children to settle at Bute Inlet on the strength of railway promises publicized in Britain. Florence and the children stayed in Vancouver for a few months while William went upcoast to assess the inlet. Three trappers—Ben Franklin, Tony Bernhardt and Mart Blanchfield—were pleased to show the newcomer around.

Ben Franklin was the only married man in this group. He and his common-law wife Augustine Forest, a Métis woman from northern Ontario, travelled across the northern US from Wisconsin to Oregon on horseback with a wagon train. They settled on a ranch in the Chilcotin at Tatla Lake just before the birth of their second son in the mid-1880s. They both worked as prospectors and ranchers and eventually expanded their holdings to include ranch land at Bute Inlet.

Augustine's descendants remember her as a gregarious, self-determined woman who was as comfortable in the forest and fields as she was in her home. She claimed to be the first prospector to take a team and wagon from the Gang Ranch to Tatla Lake in 1889. Some years later, when she lived at Bella Coola, she wrote to the government calling for a cleanup of the Lunaas Trail and offered to carry out the work for a grant of five hundred dollars. "I'm not a woman who wants to take anything from the men but I feel capable to handle this little job," said Augustine. "I think I am the best one to ask to open this trail."[138]

Ben and the other two trappers helped Walker locate a forty-nine-hectare (120-acre) homestead on the Southgate River across the harbour from the Homathko. Walker also bought an eight-hectare (twenty-acre) property from one of the men at the head of the inlet, where a small townsite later formed around the Walker family.

Walker chartered the Union Steamship Company's tug *Skidegate* to move his family and furniture to Bute Inlet. Dennis, one of his sons, wrote about their early experiences at Bute Inlet. It was a blustery day in March when they finally arrived at the head of the inlet. Franklin, Bernhardt and Blanchfield helped move some of their possessions into temporary quarters in the upper floor of one of their cabins, where the family stayed for two weeks while they built their own cabin at the head of the inlet. The whole family pitched in, rushed by the fact that most of their worldly goods had only a covering of cedar boughs to protect them from the spring rain.

"How we ever managed," wrote Dennis Walker, "is beyond me as we knew absolutely nothing of backwoods life. After many months of hardship and shortage of food we had to go by canoe to Mansons Landing [on Cortes Island], a journey of about sixty miles and then get John Manson to go to Comox in his steamboat to get supplies."

It was about a year before more settlers arrived, some in response to articles that William Walker and Martin Blanchfield submitted to provincial newspapers. First to join them was the Carbutt family with five children, followed by the extended Hicklenton-Leyland family with eight children.

By 1896 there were enough children at Bute Inlet to warrant a school, and when weather permitted, Mike Manson brought the *Stella* up from Cortes Island to deliver passengers, mail and supplies. The Blanchfield brothers and Harry Carbutt, a one-legged man, opened a store selling "Dry Goods, Millinery, Hats and Caps, Boots and Shoes, Rubbers, Groceries, Drugs, Books, Stationery and Fancy Goods, Prospector's and Miners' Supplies, Sporting Goods, Ammunition and Gunpowder, Hardware, Furniture, Sewing Machines, etc.," as their letterhead proclaimed.

The soil in the wide deltas of the Homathko and Southgate rivers is so deep and rich it goes down beyond reckoning, say the few inlet residents of today. The choicest farmland was on the reserve at the mouth of the Homathko River, and a "Syndicate"[139] had appropriated land on the Southgate. As a result, settlers like the Walkers pre-empted land farther up in the river deltas. "Our potatoes were the finest grown in BC," recalled Dennis Walker, "and our strawberries were as large as plums." What was lacking to make these farms a success was transportation.

"Among the principal requirements," wrote storekeeper Blanchfield, "are roads to connect the ranchers on the Southgate River, with the salt-water. This would be very easily constructed, one bridge only being needed, and would run directly through four or five miles of syndicate land. Meantime we are making this road at our own expense in hopes that the government will help to improve it."

The government sent surveyor H.P. Bell to the inlet in 1895 to assess the possibility of building a wagon road from the Southgate River to Tatla Lake. "The summit over which this trail passes is too high for use except for a limited time during summer," wrote Bell. Another surveyor, Mr. F.A. Devereaux, was sympathetic to the homesteaders' need for roads along the rivers, but estimated it would cost about thirteen thousand dollars to reopen the old Waddington trail.

Shipping to and from the inlet was also a continuing challenge. When Manson dropped his unprofitable Bute Inlet run in 1895, the settlers petitioned for subsidized boat service from the Union Steamship Company's *Comox*. They received service every six weeks.[140]

Even with steamer service, it was hard to make farms pay through the deep recession of the early 1890s. The rapidly growing new city of Vancouver was a good market, but prices were so low that one of the Walkers' 15,240-tonne (fifteen-thousand-ton) shipments of exceptionally fine potatoes didn't even sell for enough to cover the freight costs.

Every six months the Walkers ordered their staples from Vancouver, including forty-five-kilogram (hundred-pound) sacks of brown beans, flour, sugar and dried apricots, along with slabs of sourbelly (salt pork). If they ran short between times, it was a long paddle with overnight stops to Cortes Island to restock. Dennis Walker made such a trip in a five-metre (sixteen-foot) canoe one Christmas, when he and his brother rowed pelts from their trapline to the trading post on Cortes. The trip took twelve days, including a three-day layover to wait out a storm. They filled their mother's grocery order, bought a few Christmas gifts and wound up with a bit of extra cash as well.

With the promise of the second transcontinental railway still on the horizon, more families arrived at Bute Inlet through the mid-1890s. The Grahams brought one child, and divorcée Elizabeth Miles had four grown children. One-armed Hiram Spaulding and his wife cleared a ranch on the Homathko delta.

When a group of men came to check on the inlets' fishing prospects in 1895, the settlers showed them a good time, described in Vancouver's *Daily News Advertiser*. "On the evening of the 19th, they called at our little town, put up at the Manor House, to which all the settlers were invited, and, after having some pleasing conversation in the drawing-room, adjourned to the hall, where all enjoyed themselves thoroughly with dancing, singing, recitations, etc, lunch being served at 2:00 a.m."

Eight children were born at the inlet in the 1890s, said Dennis Walker, five boys and three girls, including his sister Bessie. "I am the happy mother of a dear little daughter," wrote Florence Walker to her sister in Britain, "who is today just 12 days old! She is a pretty little thing, everyone allows that, so it must be true, eh? [She has] lots of dark hair, nearly black, and dark eyes. She is the first white baby here up the Inlet and everyone says she ought to be specially noticed—by having a piece of land or something given her!"

Many of the Bute Inlet settlers persevered to the end of the 1890s, though the railway still hadn't materialized. Some endured extreme hardship. The Walkers lost three daughters in their six years at Bute Inlet, the victims of infrequent steamship service and distant medical care, as their father noted on their death certificates.

The first to die was twelve-year-old Lily. She contracted scarlet fever the day after the Union Steamship boat came in October 1894. She was dead and buried before the boat returned. "Father had to make the coffin," remembered Dennis Walker, "and mother read the burial service." A few years later, sixteen-year-old Minnie Rose died after thirteen days with a "brain fever" and was buried beside her sister. Within months baby Bessie was also dead.

Their graves, once marked by wooden crosses, stood side by side at the head of the inlet. During World War I a logger's wife, Mrs. Bernard, tended them. Later, around the 1930s, a Bute Inlet handlogger named Parker built a fence around them. There's no trace of these graves today, though the memory of the girls and their isolated grave has haunted succeeding generations of the Walker family.

The lack of a market for their produce and the rigours of isolation spelled the end of the Waddington Harbour settlement in 1897–98, when the government relocated the residents.[141] The Walkers moved to Vancouver, followed by the Carbutts and Blanchfields, who ran a grocery store in Vancouver for a few years. Though some scattered far afield, the Bute Inlet settlers stayed in contact, and a few of their children intermarried.

The short-lived settlement had some unique elements. There were many families in the inlet, compared to other fledgling communities, and many of the women had a remarkable degree of autonomy. Elizabeth Miles, who left her first husband before she came to Bute, formed a new relationship with fellow settler Tony Bernhardt, but left him to marry

Minnie Walker was one of three girls who died during their family's attempt to establish a settlement at the head of Bute Inlet in the 1890s. Later residents tended their graves, but the markers have long since disappeared. The memory of these graves still haunts Walker descendents.
PHOTO COURTESY OF BOB AND FAY LOGAN COLLECTION, MCR.

Union Steamship skipper Captain John Gosse. Trapper-rancher Augustine Franklin left her common-law husband Benjamin in the 1890s to work in the Britannia Mines, where she married Frank Walker, also formerly of Bute Inlet. Last to leave the inlet were the Grahams, after their son drowned. They moved to Vancouver, where Mrs. Graham became one the city's first police matrons.

Still waiting for the promised railway, Ed Blanchfield and Tony Bernhardt hung onto their properties in the inlet for years, though they no longer lived there. In 1909 railway talk started up again, and there were more surveys until Prince Rupert became the terminus for the Grand Trunk Pacific Railway in 1914, silencing six decades of railway speculation at Bute Inlet.

John Hackett (left) and Albert Georgeson at work on the Xwemalhkwu (Homalco) Band's racing canoe at Church House, south of the entrance to Bute Inlet.
PHOTO COURTESY OF MARSHALL FRANCIS COLLECTION, MCR 7140 (A).

Church House and Stuart Island

French Canadian trapper and handlogger Anderson Secord was the only permanent non-Native settler in Bute Inlet when he pre-empted land at Amor Point in about 1898. He lived on his own near the entrance to the inlet. "Strikingly grand and magnificent," wrote Secord in the Columbia Coast Mission magazine *The Log* in 1906, "stupendous and sublime as is the landscape, there is a solemnity and silence in the utter desolation which prevails during the long months of winter. No human voice, no living creature, disturbs the monotony of this awful solitude. In summer a few lonely Indians may be met with. These alone, except for the reverberating echo of a hundred waterfalls, disturb that serene silence."

The mission ship visited a large logging camp at the head of the inlet in 1906. Reverend Antle, founder of the marine medical and religious service, made the eight-hour run up the inlet and tied up to a maze of pilings connected by boomsticks at the river mouth:

> In the morning I rowed to the camp in the dinghy, but found only a few men about, the majority of the crew being at work in the woods. At high tide the *Columbia* was admitted through the gap into the log trap, and proceeded up the river, and after some difficulty with the bar arrived at the camp. Being late in the evening the men had finished work and lined the bank to see the largest boat that had ever come up the river. A very cordial reception awaited me on shore. Mr. Pallen was absent, but the foreman, James Spilman, very kindly accompanied me to the various bunk-houses and shacks and introduced me to the men.

The Xwemalhkwu people had a fishing camp at the head of the inlet during these years. By 1911 their population was on the rise, and their general health and economic success were lauded in Department of Indian Affairs (DIA) annual reports. The 1911 census listed 105 Xwemalhkwu Band members: thirty-two loggers, twenty-two fishermen, one deckhand and one farmer. All the Native fishermen were handliners, because until 1922 it was illegal for Native people to work on mechanized boats. They sold their catch to buyers who ran packer boats through the area, including representatives of a cannery to the south of Bute Inlet at Redonda Bay.

Three unidentified young Xwemalhkwu men from Church House.
PHOTO COURTESY OF DICK COLLECTION, MCR 4428.

Church House, near the mouth of the inlet, remained the Xwemalhkwu people's principal village. In 1907 the band applied to the Department of Indian Affairs for additional lands to the north of their reserve. They required the land because their gardens and cemetery were there and they needed the additional firewood the site would provide. They were refused, though some of the land in question had been carved off their original reserve allotment in error.

When the band's priest and the DIA urged the Xwemalhkwu to send their kids away to residential school, they pooled four thousand dollars and built their own school on the contested land, as their DIA agent reported, "without consulting anyone." The two-storey building had living quarters to accommodate teachers and kids whose parents had to be away for work. In the face of such determination, their priest recommended sixty-nine-year-old William Thompson and his wife Emma as teachers, and the school opened in 1909. The Thompsons were assisted by a female servant who helped care for the kids living in residence. Twenty-five children, none of whom spoke English, enrolled the first year.

The Thompsons were an ambitious couple. Within months of their arrival, they opened a post office and store in the Xwemalhkwu people's school "as a convenience to the Native people." They also served the settlers, fishermen and loggers of the region, including a nearby camp with about twenty-nine men and a few settlers on Stuart Island. The next year the Thompsons filed for a pre-emption on land that included the band's school and cemetery, despite the clearly stated pre-emption proviso that land applied for must not be occupied. They planned to meet the grant's three-year residency requirement while living at the school.

If the Thompsons hoped to push their land grant through without opposition from the Xwemalhkwu people, they were in for a surprise. In 1910 the band hired a Vancouver law firm to contest the application. As a result, the province called the Thompsons to task for applying for occupied land, and the process became enmeshed in bureaucratic waffling between the federal and provincial governments.

With relations tense between the Thompsons and band members, school enrollment dropped to less than half, and the Thompsons were dismissed from their teaching position. When Miss Kathleen Richards and her sister were appointed, attendance shot back up to twenty-seven. "The [children's] reading, spelling and geography were very good," reported the DIA agent. "They are now all able to speak some English." A year later the school burned to the ground because of a faulty chimney, and the DIA replaced it on the contested site.

When a Royal Commission touring the province met with the Xwemalhkwu, the commission recommended a twelve-hectare (thirty-acre) tract be carved off the Thompsons' pre-emption application. Vehement letters from the Thompsons and their refusal to surrender their application forms, however, continued to stall the process. In the midst of the debate, William Thompson passed away in 1915, but Emma continued the fight. She refused to give up any portion of the land in question, so it was another decade before the matter was finally

Bertha (left) and her husband Frank Asman moved to Stuart Island sometime before 1909 with their grown son Ickes and his wife Mary Jane. Ickes and Mary Jane's son Charles, left, was the first non-Native child born on the island.
PHOTO COURTESY OF FRAN (ASMAN) SMITH.

settled in 1924. The Xwemalhkwu got eight hectares (twenty acres) including the school and cemetery, and Emma Thompson got the remainder of the quarter section for $180.20. (The Xwemalhkwu Band never forgot this inequity, and when the land came up for sale in 1993, they bought it for $250,000.) Emma Thompson and her adopted son Arthur Prendergast continued for many years to run their store and post office from the large home she built on her pre-emption.

Ickes and Mary Jane Asman and Ickes's parents Frank and Bertha were the first non-Native settlers on Stuart Island. They arrived some time before 1909, when Mary Jane gave birth to Charles, the first non-Native child born on the island. Their homestead and large home was at Asman Point, to the north of Big Bay, called Asman Bay for a few decades. Both families lived by a combination of fishing, farming and logging.

The Asmans sold most of their produce and fish to the nearby logging camps. One of the largest operations in the area was run by Traford Bernard, president of the Homalco Logging Company, which had camps on both the Southgate and Orford rivers in 1918.[142]

About a hundred fisherman worked the tides off the mouth of Bute Inlet during the war years. Nick Stevens, a fish buyer with a Washington state cannery, worked at Stuart Island in the summer of 1918. The competition was stiff. There were four other buyers in the area, including BC Packers, the Royal Fish Company, the New England Fish Company and an independent named Theo Malahias. Stevens called upon his old acquaintance Chief Harry, who agreed the band would sell all their fish to him, provided he bought their grub and promised to stay through the season.

"I sent down to Vancouver for 700 loaves of bread," wrote Stevens many years later, "400 of them raisin bread and 100 bottles of syrup." He also bought a hundred raisin pies for twenty dollars from the cook of the Union Steamship Company's *Chelohsin*. There was no haggling over fish prices in those war years, said Stevens. He bought forty-five thousand fish from the Xwemalhkwu people at the government's fixed rate of fifty cents each for coho and thirty-five cents for chum.

The Muehle home at Big Bay on Stuart Island was a gathering place for the Stuart Island community. Bertha and her first husband Frank Asman were among the earliest non-Native settlers on the island, where a mountain is named for Bertha and her second husband William Muehle.
PHOTO COURTESY OF STUART ISLAND REUNION COLLECTION, MCR 16,653.

American writer Stewart Edward White was among the growing number of sports fishers who came to Stuart Island. They mixed in with the commercial fishers, who fished not with rods but with green cuttyhunk (braided or twisted linen) lines tied to their legs. White described the scene at Big Bay in his 1925 novel *Skookum Chuck*:

> The occupants were as various as their craft. There were half-a-dozen white men. Three had skiffs, one a lapstreak double-ender, and the other two well-shaped dugout canoes fitted with oars. Two bare-headed white women pulled what looked like pleasure boats. Two Indians, one old and one young, handled dugouts. A fat squaw, dressed in four different primary colours, had come to sea with a baby, two small children, some chickens, and a dog.
>
> Inside the eddy the water was like glass. Back and forth, crossing and recrossing, the boats drifted slowly. Occasionally, two of the whites exchanged a brief remark in a low tone. The Indians said nothing.

There seemed to be not even an atmosphere of expectation to disturb the peaceful somnolence. Imperceptibly the twilight was infusing the air. This became especially noticeable when one of the fishermen lit his pipe: the flare of the match shone bright and yellow in the dusk. More boats arrived, shooting down the current or craftily edging along the eddies.

"Where do they all come from?" speculated Marshall.

"The people? A few live here. Most are camped along in various small coves. They are here for the fish."

Almost simultaneously, three men snatched at the lines tied to their legs and arose to their feet. Their thin green lines were cutting through the water; their boats were surging erratically here and there. They knew their business, however; and first one, then another, lifted his fish over the rail to the accompaniment of a chorus of 'Up high!' Once in the boat the salmon seemed to take a new lease of life and thrashed about with powerful strokes of their tails until hit over the head with a club. Against the hollow structure of the boats the blows sounded loud and staccato, like the quick excited beating of a drum.

The spell that had held the little gathering of people in a silence of expectation now broke. They chattered and shouted at each other. Jokes flew, rough sarcasm, joshing. One or more salmon were always being landed, and the other boats were crowding in as near the spot as they dared in order to connect with the school.

The 1918 provincial directory estimated the Stuart Island area's population at 150 people. Of the thirty-five people listed, ten were loggers, six were fishermen, seven worked at a combination of ranching, logging and fishing, three were trappers and three were machine repairmen or engineers.

George Bruce took over a homestead at Big Bay in 1918 and in 1919 transformed it into a commercial hub, called Bruce's Landing, with a store and post office. He also served as a fur and fish buyer. Henry Ives, who followed the fleet through the fishing grounds, operated a competing store on a float.

Electrician Matt Gerrard gave up the bustle of the city to follow his passion as a Stuart Island fisherman in about 1920. Later he became a fish buyer and built a store, house and gas dock on floats. He was a staunch supporter of the Pacific Coast Fishermen's Union and only bought fish from union men, as a huge sign on the roof of his ice house proclaimed.[143]

Kellsey Moore, who lived to the south of Big Bay, arrived in about 1913, leaving his career as a Montreal acrobat. He had toured the country as an "eccentric acrobatic juggler, peerless and alone." One of his playbills said he offered "the cleverest animal impersonations and most up-to-date comedy wire acts before the public, seen at many of the leading Fairs and Expositions."

Like many others of his day, Kellsey likely moved to Stuart Island for the exceptional fishing. He supported himself and his mother Rosanna through a combination of fishing, ranching and logging. Those who didn't know Kellsey were surprised by his acrobatic feats on the fishing grounds. It was his custom to leap from the wharf to the bow of his fishboat in one swift movement, and he liked to turn cartwheels along the narrow gunwale of his boat.

Trappers came from various points along the mainland coast to sell their furs to the Bruces on Stuart Island. Among them were three lads from Washington state. August and Johnny Schnarr and a childhood friend arrived in about 1911[144] to log and stayed on to trap in Bute Inlet for a winter. The drama and intensity of the inlet were a fit with August Schnarr's tough-minded individualism. He left behind a difficult childhood of beatings from an alcoholic father and made a new life far from civilization.

In 1922 Schnarr married nineteen-year-old Zaida Lansall, a single mother with an infant daughter, who lived with her parents on their homestead in Cameleon Harbour on Sonora Island. The couple went on to have two more daughters, Marion and Pearl.

August towed their floathouse around to the various logging claims where he worked for the first few years and then took it up Bute Inlet to Schnarr's Landing below Purcell Point. "It blew like heck up there all the time, summer and winter," recalled Zaida's daughter Pansy many years later. "I don't know what he liked that awful place for, but that's what he chose."

The Schnarrs grew much of their own food and were almost entirely self-sufficient. Mountaineer Don Munday wrote about them in his 1948 book *The Unknown Mountain:*

August Schnarr made his living by trapping up the Southgate and Homathko rivers, gillnet fishing in Smith's Inlet, handlogging and working other jobs. He's seen here acting as a guide for surveyors on the Homathko River.
IMAGE I-52517 COURTESY OF ROYAL BC MUSEUM, BC ARCHIVES.

We found Mr. and Mrs. Schnarr interesting hosts. We knew something of wilderness life from our own experience, so could appreciate their simple stories of difficulties faced and overcome by courage and perseverance.

In later years we came to realize August Schnarr was a half-legendary figure along the coast and in fact throughout the Coast Range for his strength, hardihood and skill as hunter, trapper and woodsman.

The Schnarr girls were raised to work hard, recalls Pansy. Their father taught them to fish, hunt and trap. When they reached school age, they boarded out. Pansy started school at Shoal Bay, to the north of Bute Inlet, and later the three girls lived with Bertha Muehle (formerly Asman) at Big Bay on Stuart Island, where a school opened in 1927. Little Pearl chewed on her pencil, so the teacher made her take the dunce's seat on a corner stool and chew on kindling as a humiliating punishment.

Around 1931 the Schnarrs moved to Owen Bay on Sonora Island so the family could stay together while the children went to school. They weren't there more than a year when Zaida died of cancer.

After their comfortable little floathouse sank on the trip to Owen Bay (see chapter 4), all that remained on their Bute Inlet property was August's boat shed. This became the Schnarr girls' home in summer while August fished far to the north at Rivers Inlet. The girls tended the garden, canned their produce and managed one of August's sixty-four-kilometre (forty-mile) traplines.

There were a number of bachelors in the area. The most remarkable of them were the Leask brothers, eccentric Orkney Islanders who were in their seventies when Vancouver journalist Lukin Johnston visited them at Amor Point in 1925. Their isolated lifestyle was a decided switch from their professional lives in Scotland. One had been a banker, another an accountant and a third a retired New Zealand sea captain who had begun to lose his eyesight. Their house was full of hundreds of ancient books, classics like Ruskin and Shakespeare, but they also had a keen interest in the outdoors. Their homestead was a model of its kind. They had a

The Leask brothers from the Orkney Islands led demanding professional careers in Scotland and Australia before retiring to their Bute Inlet homestead.
PHOTO COURTESY OF RON GREENE, *FROM BEYOND THE ROCKIES*, BY LUKIN JOHNSON.

well-stocked root cellar and generated electricity from a waterwheel to power a saw for cutting firewood. One of the brothers was building a telescope, using a complex fusing chamber to melt glass and heat metal. Another had a rowboat under construction.

Some bachelors would have liked to marry, but their options were limited in such a remote spot. One man became deranged in his loneliness and said a voice directed him to take seven wives. He entered the home of a married woman on Stuart Island and insisted she become his first. Her husband came to her rescue, and the demented man took up an axe and wounded both the woman's husband and her mother-in-law.[145] Fisherman Henry Maurin stepped in and overpowered the man with a pike pole.

A French Canadian, probably Anderson Secord, took a more passive approach. He posted a sign on a tree by his cabin that read "Wife Wanted."

The Bernard Timber Logging Company at Orford Bay in about 1926, photographed by H.W. Roozeboom, had at least three Climax locies and a shay at work in their six hundred-man camp. The pilings from their log dump are still visible in Orford Bay.
IMAGE D-05050 COURTESY OF ROYAL BC MUSEUM, BC ARCHIVES.

Logging was the dominant industry in the Bute Inlet–Stuart Island area by the 1920s when the Bernard family opened a large railway camp at the Orford River. They used about three locomotives and had a six-hundred-man crew, according to mountaineer Don Munday, who stopped there in 1926. The camp was big enough to include its own doctor and clinic. Munday noted the high accident rate in this and other logging camps. "The tradition of loggers being 'tough' still persists," wrote Munday, "with machinery setting the pace nowadays instead of horse or ox."

By the 1930s the area's resident population was about 255 people. The Bernards' big railway show at Orford River was still in operation, as were several other camps. The ones hit the hardest by the Depression were fishermen. Alan Greene of the Columbia Coast Mission said cod-fish prices dropped to one and a half to two cents per pound, so some fishermen worked on government relief building a trail to the school at Asman Point.

Jack Parrish, a Stuart Island machinist, never ran short of work. He and his wife Margaret moved to the Stuart Island area shortly after they were married in 1927. Jack had lots of experience working with gas engines, so when he opened his own shop on Stuart Island sometime before 1931,[146] he had a steady clientele among local people, sport fishers and coastal cruisers. His shop was on floats at The Landing, where the Willcock family had a store. Later Jack and Margaret bought their own property farther north at what's known locally as Parrish's Bay. The new operation included a boat ways, built from lumber Jack cut with his own mill. "We would work in the sawmill on the weekend when the machine shop was closed," reminisced Stan Larson, who worked for Parrish. There were regularly three or four boats tied up at the Stuart Island machine shop to wait for Jack's expert attention.

Though Stuart Island was a sport fishing mecca for many years, it didn't get its first official resort until the 1950s, when Bert and Mary Brimacombe rented a room in a beach shack to a fisherman. The next summer the Brimacombes squeezed a few more fishermen into their shack and that winter they built a cottage attached to their new home. From then on their resort was always full. The Brimacombes' guest book

Coastal cruisers Amy and Francis Barrow (back left) pose with Margaret Parrish, holding Ron, beside Roy and Jack Parrish in about 1936. A string of boats always waited at Jack Parrish's Stuart Island machine shop for his skilful repairs. His descendants still own property on the island.
PHOTO COURTESY OF RON PARRISH COLLECTION, MCR 19,354.

included names like Roy Rogers, Ethel and Robert Kennedy, Governor Albert Rosellini and Senator Jackson.

The Willcocks, who took over the post office on Stuart Island in 1940, wrote an article about the store at Big Bay in the 1950s. As in most coastal communities, it was the focal point for news and social activity. Boat days, when the Union Steamship boat called with mail and supplies, were special events. Mr. and Mrs. Dickie ran the store. "A fisherman stands at the counter," wrote Willcock. "Piled on it are groceries, rope, fishing gear, paint and oh yes, a dress for his wife. The storekeeper knows the wife, so knew the size. These stores carry a varied assortment of practically everything one needs. In fact, it's a hardware, grocery, drug, dry goods and ship chandler rolled into one." Willcock described a sport fishing client, a woman who dashed into the store in need of a bedpan for her ailing husband. To everyone's amazement Dickie had one, tucked in a dusty corner. "I better order another one," he told Willcock. "Somebody might need it!"

Mountaineers also discovered Bute Inlet in these years, bent on climbing one of the world's most difficult peaks, Mount Waddington. Nothing much was known about the peaks at the head of Bute Inlet until Vancouver-based writer and mountaineer Don Munday published his book *The Unknown Mountain*. At first no one, including the province's surveyor general, would accept Munday's assertion that Waddington was the highest peak wholly within BC.

The first recorded ascent of Mount Waddington was by Weissner and House, but perhaps the most remarkable ascent was by the Beckley brothers in 1942. Fred was eighteen, and his brother Heimy was just sixteen. The two crossed the Franklin Glacier to climb the south face.

"To climb the south face of Waddington is a long and fairly difficult rock climb," says contemporary mountaineer Rob Wood, who marvels over the feat of these young men. "It involves some fairly steep technical

Mountaineers Don and Phyllis Munday spent years trying to reach the summit of Mount Waddington but never made the final spire. In 1926 Phyllis photographed her husband on the Franklin Glacier on the southwest flank of Waddington Massif.
IMAGE E-05004 COURTESY OF ROYAL BC MUSEUM, BC ARCHIVES.

rock climbing. At that time you'd have to be a world class rock climber to be able to get up there."

Phyl and Don Munday made many attempts to reach the top of Waddington after their first sight of the mountain from a peak on Vancouver Island in the mid-1920s. "Phyl's eyes shone as she handed me the binoculars and pointed to a tall mountain nearly due north through a new cloud-rift," wrote Don Munday in *The Unknown Mountain*. "The compass showed the alluring peak stood along a line passing a little east of the head of Bute Inlet. Clouds refused to reveal its neighbours. It was the far-off finger of destiny beckoning. It was a marker along the trail of adventure, a torch to set the imagination on fire." The Mundays never reached the summit, but Phyl was taken there by airplane toward the end of her life.

Gisele Uzzell joined her brother Claude and school friends Keith Liseth, Brian Giles and Mark Burch to spend the summer alpine climbing in Bute Inlet in 1973. They chartered a plane to fly in with their gear and set up a base camp on the Bear River, around the corner from handloggers Len and Laurette Parker. "I don't know what the Parkers thought of a bunch of hippie kids camped out across from them," Gisele said in a taped interview.

Though Gisele and her friends had at least one tough experience that summer, when Mark Burch fell from a tree and broke his pelvis while setting up a pulley system, they were "Bute-struck." Gisele has lived there intermittently ever since.

"It's very majestic," says Gisele. "It's a powerful place. It can be the most unbelievably beautiful place, with this crystal clear, glass smooth water and massive mountains coming out of the inlet, on a beautiful summer day—or a screaming, horrible place." But even that notorious wind has its beauty, says Gisele. "It can be spectacular if there's a Bute wind blowing and there's a full moon and the snow's on the mountains. In the middle of the night you wake up and there's so much moonlight reflecting on the snow it's [like daylight]. You can actually see colour. It's not just black and white and grey."

The young people left at summer's end, but Keith Liseth spent that winter with Len Parker handlogging and log salvaging. Gisele and several of her brothers and friends followed the next season to work on their own handlogging claim, where they built a large shared house from salvaged lumber.

Gisele's Halloween parties were an annual event for inlet residents, who arrived early for one such gathering. They were up late and noticed the weather had turned mild, with lots of rainfall on a "pineapple express" wind. The water in the ravine beside their house was running hard, but they didn't give it much thought.

When Gisele got up early the next morning to feed her toddler, she could see huge fir trees falling on the hillside behind the house and woke everyone up. The mud, debris and trees had fanned out as a landslide spread down the hillside, knocking over trees in its path. "Every time a big wave of mud and rock came down it would knock over more trees, huge trees. I'm talking about couple of hundred year old fir trees!"

"We all ran to the boat, hastily getting dressed," recalls Gisele. They untied their tug and watched from the inlet. "There was a lot of noise and a lot of serious mountain coming down. I wasn't even afraid. I was too awestruck. Eventually it hit the water and then things started to get dramatic." The mud and trees displaced enough water to send huge "dead" waves that jostled their tug with giant swells. The waves built up into a mini-tsunami that hit the opposite shore and smashed out part of the Parkers' dock.

"Your senses were completely heightened. I remember the smell of ground up dirt and mud, and the smell of ground up tree pitch. It was so strong. And the noise was deafening. It was really, really loud. And every once in a while we'd see this huge chunk of tree shoot up out of the water."

Finally they gave up their vigil and motored up the inlet to a friend's place. The next day, when they returned to survey the damage, they found their house was still intact, but the mud had knocked out part of its foundation, leaving it in a precarious state.

The group built individual homes on a new site after the slide and continued to log in the inlet for a number of years. Gisele and her husband Danny Uzzell now own the former Parker place across from the mud slide site at Bear Bay, where they have a fishing lodge.

There weren't many commercial fishers in Bute Inlet when Gisele and her family lived there. In 1969, when the Department of Fisheries downsized the fishing fleet, many Xwemalhkwu fishers at Church House gave up. "That was when they lost their licences," says elected chief Darren Blaney. "And not too long after that, forestry started to slow down. Once a certain number of people had moved out of Church House, the school was no longer feasible. When it closed in the early to mid-80s, the whole community declined."

The school at Church House only went to grade six when Darren was a student in the 1970s, so he had to go to residential school in Sechelt for a few years. He was in Vancouver, pursuing a career as an artist, when he realized he was drinking far too much and quit at the age of twenty-three. He turned his life around and went to university, where both he and his sister Fay Blaney attained degrees.

By the time Darren became an elected chief, the band was set on a new path. Under the previous chief, Richard Harry, the band acquired a quarter section near Campbell River Airport and sold logging concessions in Bute Inlet that allowed them to build on their new reserve. Only three or four Xwemalhkwu families remained at Church House in the late 1980s, but now there are about five hundred registered members. They returned from all over the province, says Blaney. "In another five years or so we'll be back up to the pre-1860s smallpox epidemic population levels."

Among Blaney's central causes is a push to create jobs for band members and achieve better health and education standards. The band is considering a variety of different schemes to add to their popular grizzly-bear-watching tours on the Orford River. A major resort is under discussion, to be powered through a run-of-the-river hydro scheme, as are heli-skiing trips.

There's a strong precedent for tourism in the area. Most of the old homesteads and handliners' properties on the west coast of Stuart Island have been converted to luxury residences for sport fishers. There are a number of fishing lodges to choose from. To the north of Big Bay, billionaire Dennis Washington has transformed an isolated piece of coast into an urban landscape, complete with a golf course and airstrip.

The Xwemalhkwu Band Council will create more jobs in tourism and others sectors, based upon environmentally sustainable practices that help band members regain an economy and self-pride. They also want to address land claim settlements and help the youth to regain their culture and independence. "I call them the McDonald's generation," says Blaney, gazing out the window of his large boardroom to the rows of houses on the new reserve. "Because they were largely raised in institutions, they lack parenting skills and they don't know the basics of nutrition." The incidence of diabetes on the reserve is high, and as a consequence not many elderly people are among them. There is a lot of work to be done, said Blaney, but his people have made tremendous strides. "You have to have hopes and dreams to succeed," says Blaney.

In the spring of 2008, Plutonic Power examined the Homathko River for a potential run-of-the-river hydro generation project to extract power from the force of the running water. Company executives are excited by the tremendous potential of the river and feel optimistic that it will not be difficult to run power lines through the mountains and valleys of Bute Inlet.

CHAPTER SIX

The Thurlow Islands and Hardwicke Island, Phillips Arm, Blind Channel, Shoal Bay, Port Neville, Loughborough Inlet and Frederick Arm

The First People

THE RAIN SOAKED THROUGH MY WATERPROOF JACKET BEFORE I GOT halfway down the Shoal Bay dock, but the ruined store at the end beckoned. It's not all that old, a relic of the 1950s, but it's the only thing left that hints at Shoal Bay's past as a thriving gold rush town. The rain was driving in against the ripped-open side of the building and water ran in rivulets across the tideflat at the head of the bay.

A century ago hotels, bath houses, barber shops and cottages lined this waterfront. Now there's just a modern bungalow plunked among the remnants of foundations and chunks of twisted metal. My sister and I poked along the beach for bits of china, glass and metal, reluctant to leave because we could feel the presence of ghosts. They have stories to tell of prospectors, trappers, loggers, newlyweds, prostitutes and barroom brawls.

We faced the same unpopulated landscape throughout the Thurlow Islands on this history cruise aboard the eco-cultural tour vessel *Columbia III*. The restored ship, one of the last of the Columbia Coast Mission's fleet, provided medical and religious service to hundreds of people in days gone by. The mission's log from the early twentieth century describes a very different place to what we see now. These mountains, valleys, forests and streams supported a permanent population for thousands of years.

The Native people of the Thurlows region had food-gathering sites, fishing camps and winter villages scattered throughout these islands and in the inlets that pierce the mainland shore like a row of fingers. Port Neville, Topaze Harbour, Loughborough Inlet, Phillips Arm and Frederick Arm had phenomenal salmon runs. In summer the fish were trapped in weirs and smoked for later use. In winter the hunters followed game up the long watersheds that empty into the inlets. The younger men, the expert climbers, took their bows strung with stinging nettle up these rocky slopes in search of mountain goats, prized for their rich meat and fine white fleece.

It requires a discerning eye to find traces of these village sites today. Matlaten,[147] near Green Point Rapids, was an important winter village with a row of big houses that straddled the beach. Now it's a mound of clamshells, cut open by an old logging road and overgrown in stinging nettles. There were huge gatherings here, potlatches where hundreds of people were feasted and presented with gifts to witness the greatness of the leading families. The famous canoe maker O-wat-tee lived here, as did a cagey old man white people called Loughborough Bill, and carver Thomas Wallace, whose totems still grace the entrance to Lewis Park in Courtenay.

Farther to the north at Jackson Bay is another impressive mound of crushed clamshell stacked three metres (about ten feet) high and topped by a few straggling daffodils and bluebells from a white settler's ranch. Farther north at Kakum, on the Fullmore River at the head of Port Neville, the jagged stumps of fish-weir stakes trace the meandering course of a tidal stream. A fourteen-year-old Kwakwala-speaking girl named Kuin-qua-lar-o-ba fished with her family on this river. In her day the months were called by names of the food-gathering cycles and a girl became a woman with her first menses.

Kuin-qua-lar-o-ba's people were relative newcomers to Kakum, as this old Salishan place name attests. Until the eighteenth century, Port Neville belonged to Salish people who were absorbed through intermarriage, or forced out, by a federation of groups from northern Vancouver Island called the Lekwiltok.

Two Lekwiltok bands—the We-Wai-Kum and the We-Wai-Kai—established their winter base to the south of Port Neville at Topaze Harbour on the mainland. The Walas clan, anthropologist Edward Curtis wrote in his 1913 book *The North American Indian*, came here in a distant time when magic ancestors could transform between animal and human:

> Yakayalitnulhth was walking near Tekya, when he saw sitting on a rock a very large bird covered with soft down of dazzling whiteness. The tip of its hooked beak could just be seen in the midst of the thick down. He cried out, 'Whatever you are, I tlugwala you,' [claim your special powers]. The bird threw back the feathers and skin from its head, revealing the head of a man, and spoke: 'I am kolus, yet I am a man. My name is Toqatlasaqiaq [born to be admired].' His face was steaming with heat, because of the thick covering of feathers. Soon the entire coat fell away and he stood forth with the full figure of a man.
>
> The bird man accompanied Yakayalitnuhl to his home, and told him: 'Give a winter dance, and you shall have these dances from me: thunderbird, hokhok, nu'nalalhl, ha'maa, hamasilah and kolus. All these dances came from creatures of the sky.
>
> Yakayalitnulhth founded the Walas clan, this word being another name of the bird kolus. It is believed that members of this clan are easily thrown into perspiration, as was the bird man by his feather garment.

From Topaze Harbour, the Lekwiltok spread throughout the Thurlow Islands and adjacent inlets. Each group had its specific traditions and territories. The Tlaaluis ("angry ones") and the Kweeha ("murderers") fished and hunted in Frederick Arm and Phillips Arm.[148] The Komenox ("rich people"), a group thought to have had Salish roots, fished in Loughborough Inlet. The combined population of the Lekwiltok may have been as high as four thousand people.[149] With so many to support, they expanded southward into Discovery Passage through periods of warfare or through intermarriage with the Salish.

Sometimes the Lekwiltok suffered retaliatory attacks from Salish groups to the south and at other times they had to fend off rival groups from the north. One particularly aggressive attack wiped out the Komenox as a distinct group. The late James Smith of Campbell River, who claimed Komenox ancestry, recounted one of their important legends. After many wars, only four brothers and their families remained, wrote Smith. They hid in the mountains on the south side of Loughborough Inlet and seldom went to the seashore, but as time passed they began to hunt mountain goats once again.

One day the eldest brother, Maqualahgulees, was hunting above Heydon Bay when he spotted an exceptionally fine mountain goat. The magnificent creature turned to face Maqualahgulees, and he noticed it had just one horn in the centre of its forehead. Maqualahgulees, who was a skilled marksman, shot the animal, and though a patch of blood appeared on its side, it climbed to a cave far above Maqualahgulees.

The hunter followed the goat to the cave and when he stepped inside he was mesmerized by a light deep within. He followed it and soon found himself in the home of a tall, regal man who stood with his arms outstretched in a chiefly welcome. The man invited Maqualahgulees to stay for a meal, and as he sat he noticed several mountain goats lay about him. There were haunches of dried mountain goat meat hanging from the ceiling and strips of dried fat and bales of wool and skins tied to the walls. This was a place of great riches.

Maqualahgulees turned to observe his host more closely. The man wore an unusually fine goatskin robe, but its brilliant whiteness was stained on one side by blood. When Maqualahgulees noticed the head on this robe had just one great horn at its centre, he realized he had been lured into the home of the One-Horned Mountain Goat, a great spiritual being.

When asked what food he wanted, Maqualahgulees told the truth. It was futile to lie to one with such powers. "The mountain meat," he said. After his meal Maqualahgulees lay before the fire as directed and was soon fast asleep. There was little he could do to protect himself in such a place, but he clutched his bow and arrow at his side. It was a bow Maqualahgulees made himself, using finely twisted stinging nettle fibre as his bowstring. When he awoke the next morning, the bowstring was bright green and it had begun to sprout buds.

All that day the One-Horned Goat and his attendants hurried to and fro from the cave. He placed food before Maqualahgulees occasionally, but otherwise no words were spoken. The second and third days passed much the same way, and each day his bowstring grew more buds.

On the fourth day Maqualahgulees's host asked when he planned to leave. His tone and bearing reassured Maqualahgulees of his safety, so he told him that as it was the fourth day he would be on his way. "I have been preparing for you," said the Goat. "All these bales and bundles are ready. They are tightly packed, full of wool, skins, dried meat and dried fat. We will roll them out of the cave where they will fall down the mountain side. All you have to do then is call your brothers to help you remove all this wealth to your homes."

Then, instructed the Mountain Goat, Maqualahgulees must call all the tribes to a great feast and perform a dance and song, wearing the cape of the Mountain Goat. And he must henceforth include a One-Horned Goat in his heraldry. "You and your people shall be known as the Glu'glagwala [those who are blessed]," said the goat.

Maqualahgulees left the cave, and the song of the One-Horned Mountain Goat welled up inside him as he climbed with the ease of a goat down the narrow crevices of the mountain and back to his home on the south side of Loughborough Inlet. His relatives ran to meet him. They had long given him up for dead, as he had been gone four years and not four days. Maqualahgulees and his brothers Za'ga-use, Za-kul-lath' and Zak-ate' went back to the foot of the mountain they now called Glu'gwalus to bring home the treasures from the cave. And shortly thereafter they gave a big potlatch, as instructed by the One-Horned Goat. They no longer had to live in fear.[150]

It may have been Maqualahgulees's descendants who came out to meet a small party of Spanish surveyors exploring Loughborough Inlet in their ship's cutter in the summer of 1792. The sailors returned to their ships some time later to report their findings to Captains Valdez and Galiano.

Loughborough Inlet, they said, was not easy to explore. Nor could they make contact with a Native group there because the wind was against them. When they tried to proceed farther up in the inlet, where there were two rivers "of considerable importance," they were also blocked by a fishing weir "excellently made with stakes and planks":

> The Natives of the settlement there had observed our launch, and when they saw that it did not come nearer they came out in two canoes, with eight or ten men in each, shouting and showing otter skins. Our men could not wait for them as the launch was in a critical position, and orders were given to make sail for the coast to the east in order to avoid the waves which dashed upon the shore. This action would seem to have excited the suspicion of the Indians and have caused them to think that our men were hostile, for they returned to their settlement, put on their war dress, re-embarked and, joining a canoe in which was a [chief], followed the launch, in which Salamanca at once prepared to make use of such feeble means of defence as were at the disposal of our men. The braves landed and followed the launch on shore, displaying alternately otter skins and arrows, until they could follow no farther, when they returned to their settlement. As it was

The Apple River delta in Loughborough Inlet.
PHOTO BY ÉTIENNE CÔTÉ.

This Cortes Island petroglyph, south of Mansons Landing, is one of the few with a known story. It is said to have been carved by a young Mainland Comox man whose year-long spirit quest brought him power from a star. He became such a successful hunter he was called Tl'umnachm, because he filled his canoe so full of fish and game there was only room for him in his boat. PHOTO BY JEANETTE TAYLOR.

growing dark, our men found a small creek to which they made their way in order to pass the night, a time which was very unpleasant as it rained heavily.

Massive depopulation followed these Europeans, who introduced virulent diseases. The worst of these was a smallpox epidemic in 1862 brought by an infected gold seeker. The epidemic claimed thousands of lives. Measles, mumps, influenza and TB also raged among the Native people, who had no immunity.

And so, in spite of the good fortune predicted for the people of the One-Horned Mountain Goat, the Komenox declined to so few that they joined with the We-Wai-Kum. The Tlaaluis of Phillips Arm and Frederick Arm suffered a similar fate and also joined with the We-Wai-Kum and the Kweeha. By 1881 the Lekwiltok population, once at four thousand or more people, was down to 374. Only the Kweeha remained in the Thurlows area; the other groups had been either wiped out or had moved to the southern part of the Discovery Islands.

Only sixty-one people remained among the Kweeha, who maintained fishing stations in Loughborough Inlet and Phillips Arm. In winter they moved to Matlaten, at Green Point Rapids, where there were five big houses in 1881.[151] The data in the census of the Kweeha shows the destructive forces at work among them. There was only one elderly person in the band. Tlel-poo-eet, at the age of seventy, was the head of her family, which may have descended from Maqualahgulees, the man who met the One-Horned Mountain Goat. They lived in the big house of fifty-five-year-old Ah-mah-kullis and his wife Ko-kwaht-ke-luk. Of the twelve people in this household, only two were children. In fact, among the whole group, there were only twelve children. Many couples in their twenties were childless, indicating a decreased fertility rate among the survivors of smallpox. Other than Tlel-poo-eet, the eldest were widowers in their fifties.

In the next decade, when a sudden rush of non-Native residents descended upon the Thurlows in search of gold, the Kweeha would endure yet another trial. There would be many new opportunities for them in work and trade, and an end to their ancient way of life.

The Gold Rush

Port Neville made provincial news in 1863 when an aggressive English sea captain named Edward Stamp announced his plans for a sawmill there. Stamp was an experienced sawyer, having opened one of the first sawmills in the province on the Alberni Canal in the 1850s. He selected Port Neville on the advice of his timber cruiser Jeremiah Rogers, whom historian Ken Drushka called BC's first professional logger.

Port Neville, 320 kilometres (two hundred miles) north of the main centres in the Lower Mainland, was very remote in those days of sailing ships, but its tremendous stands of trees impressed Rogers. Stamp negotiated for a large timber lease at Port Neville and then set off for Britain to secure financing.

Rogers began work at Port Neville in June 1864, as reported in New Westminster's *British Columbian*:

> The schooner *Meg Merilees* carrying eleven lumbermen, eight work oxen, a cargo of provisions and feed will sail today for Port Neville, where Captain Stamp intends to erect sawmills on a most extensive scale. The captain is now in England completing arrange-

ments, but is expected here early next month when he will at once proceed to active operations. Meanwhile a logging camp will be formed at once, and a quantity of spars got out for shipment.

In April 1865 Rogers sent a boom of two hundred ship spars to the settlement of Burrard Inlet, now Vancouver. The difficulties of a long tow through tricky waters may have caused Stamp to look elsewhere for a mill site. That summer he negotiated a deal with Colonial officials, brokered on the strength of his British financing, and secured a logging concession of six thousand hectares (fifteen thousand acres) in Burrard Inlet and a twenty-one-year lease of four hundred hectares (one thousand acres) in Port Neville. Shortly thereafter Hastings Saw Mill went into production at what's now Vancouver. Nothing further seems to have transpired at Port Neville.

Stamp's competitor in Burrard Inlet, Sewell Moody, also expanded, having profited by the increased business Stamp brought to the inlet. He brought in his old partner Moses Ireland, who had started the Moodyville Sawmill with him a few years prior. "I was sent to find a site and open up a mill," said Ireland years later, "and I was given a credit of $100,000. I was tending to this business when a telegram came saying that Moody had fallen off a ship and was drowned."

Though Stamp also died prematurely in the 1870s, these rival sawmills remained thriving businesses. By the 1880s, with the Lower Mainland logged out by the reckoning and methods of that day, the mills began to log in the Thurlow Islands region.

Big Billy Dineen was among the first to run camps in the Thurlows. Another famous timber cruiser of the next generation, Eustace Smith, considered Dineen the quintessential logger. "Those were men—and they were real men—proud of their strength and of their woodcraft," wrote Smith in his chronicles of the industry. "Dineen was a mighty man with the axe, and what he could do with it was almost unbelievable. On one occasion he accepted a challenge to cut 40,000 feet in a single day, using only an axe. He selected four big trees, each scaling a minimum of 10,000 feet, and in eight hours he had felled them all!"

By the late 1880s there were three camps in the Thurlows area, at Bickley Bay on East Thurlow, in Nodales Channel and north of Green

Fallers in one of the Bendicksons' logging camps, Thurlow Islands region.
PHOTO COURTESY OF THE BENDICKSON COLLECTION, MCR 12,345.

Point Rapids, where Cameron and McCrae had a camp on the main-land[152] that played a minor role in a murder case.

Police constable Flewin was called in to investigate the rumour of a murder reported by Campbell River trader James McNerhanie. Three men were said to have been killed aboard the schooner *Seabird* in the summer of 1886 in Blenkinsop Bay on the mainland.

The *Seabird* was en route from Vancouver to Juneau that summer, loaded deep with trade goods of all sorts, including kegs of whiskey. On board were Captain G.G. Wells, who was missing half of his left hand, pilot Henry Moore, a young man who'd recently lost one arm, and their German mate Henry Boldt. Henry Moore's father, a famous sea captain and explorer, sailed to Alaska several times looking for the *Seabird* with no luck, so Flewin was dispatched to search Blenkinsop Bay.

Henry Moore was a reluctant participant in this trading venture, as he implied in a letter to his wife sent from one of the *Seabird*'s last ports of call. His options were limited, given his handicap. "But a faint heart never won a fair lady," wrote Henry, "as I done you My Dear. I will close in sending you the fondest love of a true husband and many kisses for my babies."

What Flewin and his men found at Blenkinsop Bay confirmed the worst. While they didn't find the schooner, they found plenty of pieces from her stashed in the nearby forest. There was also a trunk full of personal belongings, including a one-armed shirt.

Flewin arrested the men rumoured to be responsible—Mahk-moo-iss (Macamoose) of the Salmon River Band and Klah-kwas-qum—at Cameron's and McCrae's logging camp near Green Point Rapids. Flewin also took key witnesses Nar-lar-cum-arlas and his fourteen-year-old daughter Kuin-qua-lar-o-ba into custody.

It was nearly a year before the case went to trial in Nanaimo, in which time Klah-kwas-qum died of consumption, so Mahk-moo-iss faced the charge of murder on his own. "The Jurors for our Lady the Queen," read the court documents, "upon their oath present that Mahk-moo-iss on the twenty-ninth day of June in the year of our Lord one thousand eight hundred and eighty six feloniously, wilfully and of his malice aforethought did kill and murder one Henry Moore against the peace of our Lady the Queen, her crown and dignity." Each charge was translated into Kwakwala by a Native woman who was married to an Alert Bay merchant.

Nar-lar-cum-arlas, the chief witness, told a packed courtroom that he and his daughter were deer hunting on a summer morning when they happened upon Mahk-moo-iss and Klah-kwas-qum chopping up a schooner at Blenkinsop Bay. Near the ruined vessel one of the Native men's wives waited with her baby in her arms. The witness and his daughter slipped out of view and watched for a short while. Some time later, when they met the men again, they asked what they had been up to in Blenkinsop Bay and were offered a fifty-dollar bribe for their silence. The two men then told the witnesses that two of the three traders were drunk when they came upon them, and an altercation ensued. "They said they killed the men through jealousy," reported Nar-lar-cum-arlas. His daughter corroborated these details, including the fact that a bribe was offered for their silence. When they saw the accused again at Matlaten that winter, Mahk-moo-iss and Klah-kwas-qum had a stack of paper money, whiskey and guns, but refused to pay the offered bribe.

"Mr. Mills made an eloquent and stirring address on behalf of the prisoner," reported the *Nanaimo Free Press* on July 11, 1888, "using strong arguments in favor of reducing the crime from murder to manslaughter." The jury hotly debated the case, loaded as it was with hearsay and ambiguity, before they arrived at a verdict of manslaughter "with a strong recommendation for mercy." A motive was never established. It may have been robbery or vengeance for ill-treatment from this or some other trader, or the white men—as suggested by the comment about jealousy—may have made advances to the Native woman with the accused murderers. Mahk-moo-iss served a seven-year sentence and then lived out his days with his wife Jenny in Phillips Arm.

Apart from the detailed coverage of the *Seabird* Massacre, the Thurlows were seldom mentioned in provincial news. When they were, it was usually in connection with loggers killed on the job or dying from alcohol-related causes. In 1887 Mike King brought the body of a twenty-two-year-old man—killed on the job at one of Moodyville Sawmill's camps on Thurlow

Island— to Nanaimo along with a boom of logs. "Mr. King heard the man's name but had forgotten it," reported the *Nanaimo Free Press*. Four years later the Thurlows were again in the news when logger Charles Sisson committed suicide by sawing off his arm in a "fit of temporary insanity."

Hastings Saw Mill of Burrard Inlet became the dominant logging company in the Thurlows. Each of its camps was assigned a letter of the alphabet, attached to a specific foreman. Nova Scotia-born Solomon (Sol) Ramey carried the designation Camp O. One of his earliest shows was on a bay on the northwest point of East Thurlow Island[153] in the 1880s. By 1901 he was the company's top foreman, and as such he earned the princely sum of eleven hundred dollars a year, compared to an average annual income of three hundred to six hundred dollars. Like most other loggers of his day, he remained single. When he got too old to work in the bush the company made him a recruiter in the Vancouver office. "A foreman could send down the information of what types of jobs he needed to fill," recalled Ed DesBrisay, whose father was a superintendent for Hastings, "and Ramey would find the men. Ramey knew all the men and their haunts in Vancouver and he was familiar with the

Johnny Mahk-moo-iss and his wife Jenny in front of their home at Phillips Arm, photographed by Francis Barrow in 1935. "Mahk-moo-iss has spent [time] in jail and is a bit of a bad actor," wrote Barrow in his cruising log. "A trader a good many years ago went missing. The authorities were pretty certain Mahk-moo-iss did the trader in, but they could not prove it." PHOTO COURTESY OF MCR 20110-78.

An ox logging team hauling logs on a corduroy road at Shoal Bay on Thurlow Island in about 1890.
IMAGE A-05534 COURTESY OF ROYAL BC MUSEUM, BC ARCHIVES.

various camps upcoast. He became known as their 'man catcher.'"

In the 1880s Hastings made Bickley Bay on East Thurlow their regional headquarters and built a store and a hotel. "This is the most important establishment on the coast," said the *Daily Colonist* in 1889, "it being the point of supply for all the company's camps, timber cruisers, and also for the numerous handloggers working in that neighbourhood."

Two young Norwegians bought a boat in Vancouver in the late 1880s and sailed up the coast in search of new opportunities as traders. Nils Hjorth and (Sven) Hans Hansen liked the countryside around Bickley Bay. Its mountains and deep fjords reminded them of home, and the place was a busy hub of activity. They set up a trading depot to exchange furs with the Native people and likely also sold basic supplies to the loggers.

Large potlatches held by the Lekwiltok people at Matlaten formed an important part of the traders' business. The *Nanaimo Free Press* reported a grand two-week potlatch in 1891. "On Monday afternoon the Indians were already commencing to pour in. [They] say this is going to be a potlatch of the biggest kind and will exceed anything of this nature ever held on the coast." A year later Matlaten was destroyed by fire but quickly replaced with big houses made from lumber. When Indian Agent Pidcock visited in 1894, the row of houses that straddled the beach was fronted by a deep platform.

In 1891 Nils Hjorth and Hans Hansen pre-empted land in the region. Nils staked a quarter section at Shoal Bay, around the corner from Bickley Bay, and Hans sailed farther upcoast to settle near the mouth of Port Neville.

Nils Hjorth's chosen site and his timing were fortuitous. He opened a small store at Shoal Bay in 1891,[154] just before a gold rush transformed the place into a boom town.

The first gold claim in the area, the White Pine, is said to have been staked by Joseph Costello in 1884.[155] J.J. Chambers, "head chopper" for a

The *Camosun* at P.B. Anderson's logging camp dock at Knox Bay, West Thurlow Island. The Union Steamship Company sent weekly freight boats upcoast as far as Port Neville from 1892. They stopped to drop off mail, freight and passengers at every little settlement and logging camp.
PHOTO BY HENRY TWIDLE, COURTESY OF MARION ADAMS COLLECTION, MCR 5155.

logging camp on Channe Island, was also among the first miners. At the end of the logging season he explored Loughborough Inlet and Phillips Arm. Excited by what he found, he registered claims but couldn't find a financial backer. "They said he was crazy," reported the *Weekly News Advertiser* of Vancouver, "though recent events have proved that Mr. Chambers was right."

When the first big shipments of gold left the Thurlows in the mid-1890s, the rush was on. "The mines are notable for the abundance of copper galena and iron pyrites, most of them carrying gold, and many assaying high in the precious metals," said the British Columbia Directory for the region.

Mine claims repeatedly changed hands as bigger operators moved into the area. Some of the most successful were the Bully Boy and Queen Bee claims, in the hands of Joseph Costello and a man called McMoran, on the northwest shores of Sonora Island. The shaft of the Queen Bee went down ten metres (thirty-four feet), and the quality of the gold improved with every metre. The Bully Boy's tunnel was eighteen metres (sixty feet) long by 1896.[156] There were also the Blue Bells, the Athlete and Silver Granite claims in Frederick Arm. The latter, with a twenty-three-metre (seventy-five-foot) tunnel by 1897, was managed by R.C. Forsyth of Chicago. The Phillips Arm Gold Mines Limited had the Highland Laddie, Duke, Duchess, Jubilee, Emperor and Waterloo claims.

One of the largest mines, the Douglas Pine, perched on the mountainside behind Shoal Bay. Pack mules hauled the ore down the steep hillside to the wharf. Near the mine entrance were two log bunkhouses, a cookshack and a blacksmith shop,[157] and a rail line ran for about 2.4 kilometres (1.5 miles) from Shoal Bay to a mine and camp belonging to the Northern Belle Mining Company.

With all the busy activity in the region, Nils Hjorth added a post office to his store and a hotel—likely just an extension of his house—in 1896. Union Steamship boats brought freight and passengers from Vancouver four times a week, and Hjorth built a series of rental shacks along the beach for Native people in transit.

The amenities at Shoal Bay expanded when the Channe Mining Company bought property next to Nils Hjorth and opened a trading

The Cyanide Plant in Phillips Arm processed ore in the 1890s from the large Doratha Morton Mine at Fanny Bay. IMAGE D-01882 COURTESY OF THE ROYAL BC MUSEUM, BC ARCHIVES.

company store with "a full stock of everything needed by the mining camps." They also opened a hotel, managed by Mr. and Mrs. Largent. "The hotel is a surprise," reported the *Daily Colonist*, with "hospitable accommodation and excellent fare."

Settlers from as far away as Quadra and Cortes islands rowed to Shoal Bay with produce and livestock to sell in a place the provincial minister of mines of 1896 described as a booming centre:

> Shoal Bay is the only attempt at a town in the district and consists of a moderate accommodation, and a few houses, and is the centre of supply for the mining and lumber camps for a few miles around. The hotels were full to overflowing at the time of my visit, and I would have been at a loss to find accommodation, but for the kindness of Mr. E. Pooke, agent for the Gold Fields of BC, who kindly placed at my disposal an unoccupied furnished house belonging to his company.

With an estimated population of about a hundred people, Shoal Bay became the headquarters for the assay office and provincial police officer Henry Ford Morgan Jones. His beat ran from north of the Thurlows south to Campbell River and east across the Strait of Georgia to Lund.

By 1897 there were four hundred mine claims[158] in the region of Shoal Bay and Phillips Arm. The larger companies working in the area included Channe Mining, Northern Belle of Seattle and the Gold Fields of BC, financed by the Earl of Huntingdon and the Earl of Essex. In about 1896–97 the Gold Fields company bought Nils Hjorth's property in the centre of the bay. "The Thurlow townsite," said the *Weekly News Advertiser* of 1897, "which was recently purchased by the Gold Fields of BC, is undergoing a thorough change. Several new houses are being erected and the site is now cleared for the new hotel."

The Gold Fields company also bought up many of the mine claims in the region, including the Douglas Pine at Shoal Bay and the Yuclaw and the Puddle Dog on Channe Island. In Phillips Arm they held the rights to the Alexandra group, including the profitable Doratha Morton (which continues to have active claims in 2008) and a cyanide plant for processing the ore.

Hastings Logging tried to shift the focus from Shoal Bay to Channeton in Bickley Bay in 1897. "Bickley Bay, well known as an important logging centre, has been decided upon as the proper place for the coming city," said the *Weekly News Advertiser*. A Mr. Bauer was sent up from Vancouver to survey lots and to "re-erect" a hotel, presumably because the original hotel was razed. The new one was to have thirteen bedrooms and two small parlors. A post office also opened that year.

Shoal Bay, however, remained the nucleus. As in most other communities throughout the British Empire, the residents celebrated Queen Victoria's Diamond Jubilee in the summer of 1897. The Trading Company Store organized races, including hotly contested Native canoe races, and a picnic. "In the evening the hotel and stores were picturesquely illuminated with Chinese lanterns," said the *Weekly News Advertiser*, "and decorated with flags and other devices. Dancing was kept up with great spirit until midnight, when a very pleasant day was brought to a close by ringing cheers for the Queen." A few months later another party was held to close the summer season. "A dance and dinner were given by one of the Shoal Bay

A massive ventilating fan made from cedar split with an axe was installed at the adit of a mine at Phillips Arm in 1901.
IMAGE I-55241 COURTESY OF THE ROYAL BC MUSEUM, BC ARCHIVES.

mining men," said the newspaper. "Music was supplied by Mrs. Forrest, who owns and plays the first piano to arrive at the new townsite."

The one service these glowing reports neglected to mention was prostitution. "At this place," wrote Indian Agent Pidcock, "I found disreputable shacks, which are constantly occupied by white men and Indian women." Pidcock asked the resident constable to remove the shacks from the beach next to the Gold Fields Hotel and bar and prohibit Native people from stopping at Shoal Bay. His request likely fell upon deaf ears.

A notorious prostitute of the Discovery Islands named Kitty Coleman was at Matlaten in 1894. As was her custom, Kitty—who worked under the protection of her husband—hired girls of mixed ancestry for her logger and miner clientele. Sarah Cliff was a particular favourite with a logger named Hollingsworth, so when Kitty needed some whiskey she went to Hollingsworth with an offer. He could have Sarah for a bottle of whiskey and some cash. Hollingsworth passed off a bottle of bitters (a digestive aid) as alcohol and took the girl. When Kitty discovered she had been hoodwinked, she sent for Justice of the Peace Mike Manson of Cortes with a charge against Hollingsworth for illegal liquor sales to a Native.

Manson reported the case to the Attorney General. "Hollingsworth told me after the trial that he had paid Kitty Coleman $40 for the girl and that she wanted more money and he had refused to give it to her," wrote Manson. Hollingsworth also told Manson he was anxious to marry Sarah. "And she was willing to be married to him," reported Manson. "In fact they came to me and asked me to marry them, but as I did not have the power to do so they said they would wait until the boom of logs Hollingsworth is preparing for market is ready to ship and they would then go to Vancouver to get married." Nothing further is known of this couple, though a single logger named Henry Hollingsworth was listed in a logging camp at Elks Bay on Vancouver Island in 1901.

Other kinds of culture clash took place between Native and non-Native residents of the region. Loughborough Bill showed settler Thomas Maguire, with the promise of a hundred-dollar fee, where there were signs of gold at Heydon Bay. Maguire registered the claim and sold it for five hundred dollars, but neglected to pay Bill his share. "If you made such a promise to Loughboro Bill," Pidcock wrote to Maguire, "you should keep your word as a promise made to an Indian is as binding as to anyone else." Nothing further is recorded about this case to say whether or not Bill received his money.

As the Kitty Coleman case demonstrates, there was a strict law against selling liquor to Native people. Indian Agent Pidcock gave Native constables the authority to make arrests. One of these constables was known to whites as Indian Jim. In the late fall of 1899, Bob Iyaklan and Jim tied up a boom of logs at Yuculta Rapids and went to Shoal Bay to send a letter to their financier, Brown Brothers of Vancouver, to say their logs were ready to tow. When they got to Shoal Bay they happened upon Robert Carlson and Charles Strom selling liquor to some Fort Rupert Natives. Indian Jim went to the resident Justice of the Peace to get a warrant for the men's arrest, and an altercation and threats ensued.

When Bob Iyaklan and Jim left Shoal Bay the next morning, they found Thomas Backus towing their boom of logs. Backus said it got loose and he wanted $120 for his expenses, plus salvage rights. The Native men called upon Indian Agent Pidcock to intercede and a slightly better salvage rate was agreed upon. As for Carlson and Strom, both were convicted of the liquor offence and fined fifty dollars each plus court costs.

To the northeast of Shoal Bay, in Loughborough Inlet, another small townsite called Roy was spawned by the mining and logging activity in the region. One of the more promising mines there was at Hayden Bay, no doubt the claim Loughborough Bill discovered.

"Loughborough Inlet, a place which only a few weeks ago was merely a calling place for a few ranchers and a logging camp," said the *Weekly News Advertiser* of October 6, 1897, "now boasts of a store and large hotel. Messrs. Smith Brothers, lately of Shoal Bay, have an eye to business, and like many others have great hope of the future for our northern country. The steamer *Maude* unloaded her first consignment of lumber at Ellis's ranch on Sunday last, and the carpenters are now hard at work erecting the new hotel." A few weeks later the hotel and store were complete, and a trail was being cut to Fanny Bay in Phillips Arm. In its heyday the Roy townsite may have had as many as thirteen houses.[159]

David S. Gray, who opened a post office at Roy in 1896, lived with his wife Annie and their sons and daughter on a homestead on Gray Creek. Annie probably looked after the post office, because David and their sons also had a logging operation. "D. Gray and Sons" may have been the first outfit in the Discovery Islands to use steam donkeys, since the Grays listed themselves as "steam loggers" in the 1897 provincial directory.

The Grays' ranch, on fertile delta land, seemed the perfect location until a mudslide in 1898 undid all their hard work. It swept down from high up in the mountain behind them just after the family bedded down for the night. As it gained momentum the slide carried mud, trees, rocks and roots in its path. The Grays knew nothing of it until they were awakened by the loud crashing of timber, rushing water and wind. "On jumping out of bed," reported the *Weekly News Advertiser*, "they heard a rush of water against the back of the house. In a minute's time it was rushing all through the house, and was more like liquid mud than water. It was rising every minute."

The Grays got set to flee their house, but the waters began to subside before they could do so. The next day they found the slide had ripped open a swath that ran 2.4 kilometres (1.5 miles) down the mountainside. No one, said the newspaper, not even the oldest among the Native people, could remember a slide of this magnitude. A year later David resigned his position as postmaster at Roy, and the family moved to Vancouver.

Reverend Dugald and Kathlene McGregor had a sixty-five-hectare (160-acre) property to the south of the Grays. Dugald, who came to Canada from Scotland as a lad in 1857, married Kathlene in Ontario. They pre-empted land in Loughborough Inlet in 1894. A young friend at Shoal Bay described Dugald as "an old Scotchman" who travelled about the region to preach his "strong Free Church sermons."[160]

Nova Scotia-born William Ellis had a ranch bordering Roy on George Creek. Like so many coast dwellers of his time, Willis kept himself by a variety of means. He served as a Justice of the Peace, a trader, a fisherman and a logger. At the time of the 1901 census, he had a logging camp in the inlet with a four-man crew that included cook Ping Lee. While most of Ellis's men had an annual income of five hundred dollars, thirty-six-year-old Ping Lee earned just $150.

Ellis's nearest neighbours in the late 1890s were the lively William and Anne Christmas family. William Christmas, a logger and farmer, had married a widow with three children, and the couple had a child of their own as well.

An interesting resident of the inlet was James King, who came to BC in the 1870s with his brother Mike. While Mike was perhaps better known, Jim also left his mark. The brothers, who generally worked independently, were timber cruisers and miners. A later cruiser, Eustace Smith, idolized Jim King. He described Jim as a tall, handsome man, "a quiet chap, an expert woodsman who always travelled light. I was constantly asking myself when some problem arose, 'How would Jim King act?'"

Jim was involved in ten mine claims in Loughborough Inlet in 1897, when he was interviewed by the *Daily Colonist*. The Victoria Mine, he said, was progressing favourably. "This is the mine the ore of which, five feet below the surface, assayed at $112 in gold." Jim didn't get to see any of these mines come to fruition. He died a painful death from appendicitis at fifty in 1902 at Heriot Bay on Quadra Island.

Logging Camps and Shingle Mills

Hans Hansen's homestead at Port Neville was the last port of call for the Union Steamship boat from Vancouver, which brought mail, freight and passengers starting in 1892. Hans's home became a gathering place for people and freight in transit for the camps and homesteads to the north. In 1895 he opened a post office and built a few cabins to rent at twenty-five cents per night to people waiting for the boat. The first mail bag arrived at Hans's post office on November 20 with thirty-three letters and nine papers for the surrounding district. Two months later he received his first pay cheque of $3.33 for two months' work.

Hans's diary and his daughter Edith (Hansen) Bendickson's articles about her family provide a interesting portrait of coastal pioneer life. Hans left Tonsberg, Norway, at the age of fourteen with his father and his friend Nils Hjorth.[161] They took jobs on a ship bound for Australia, where Hans's father died. The boys worked for a time in a coal mine until they shipped out for China. From there they got jobs on the *Esmeralda*, bound for Vancouver, where they jumped ship and swam to shore near present-day White Rock in 1877. Hans worked at the Hastings Saw Mill in Burrard Inlet at a dollar a day, saving up for his return to Norway, until an accident befell him one snowy day in False Creek.

Hans was duck hunting with a muzzle-loading rifle when it exploded and shattered his left hand. He tied a tourniquet around his mangled wrist and walked many kilometres through the snow back to Gastown, where Dr. Walkem offered him an anesthetic before he started work. "But Dad refused," wrote his daughter Edith. He wanted to see what was going on as the doctor cut off his hand at the wrist.

When Hans's wrist healed, he got a blacksmith to make him an iron hook specially designed to allow him to row a boat. He soon became so adept with his iron clamp that he competed in a regatta on a winning team.

"Hans the boatman," as he became known, kept himself by various means. He shot and sold deer for fifty cents a hindquarter until he got a job in a store, hotel and post office at Hastings. Later he worked as a caretaker for an estate at Belcarra until the late 1880s, when he bought a sloop and travelled up the coast with his friend Nils Hjorth.

Hans Hansen got a land grant at Port Neville in 1891. Though he had lost one hand in a hunting accident, he cleared his homestead, built several log houses and earned his living as a rancher, fisherman and Port Neville postmaster. The house he built in the early 1920s, right centre, still stands.
PHOTO COURTESY OF BARB GILROY COLLECTION, MCR.

Hans's chosen homestead near the mouth of Port Neville was on a thickly wooded peninsula that formed a slough in back. The task of clearing first-growth trees to build a log house in the wilderness was a daunting task for any man, let alone one with only one good hand. Hans was determined not to let his handicap hinder his life, though, and exchanged work with a few neighbours. Alexander Burchett from Arkansas had an ox logging camp at the head of the inlet the year Hans arrived, and the pair became friends.

When Hans had about 1.5 hectares (four acres) cleared for a garden, large orchard and field, he ordered some cows from a ranch in Kingcome Inlet. Fencing was critical in a place overrun with deer and grizzlies, so he meticulously calculated the exact number of pickets, posts and rails he needed, along with 28,606 nails in three sizes.

Hans earned an income by handlogging and fishing for cod to sell to the logging camps. He also shipped produce and meat from his ranch to Vancouver or to nearby logging settlements.

On November 15, 1898, Hans brushed up his town suit and went to Vancouver on the Union Steamship boat to marry Elizabeth (Lizzie) Flintham, an English widow with a two-year-old son. She was thirty-one, and Hans was thirty-eight.[162] The story of how the pair came to meet has been lost over time. Lizzie lived for a few years in the mid-1890s in Detroit, where her son Billy was born and her first husband died. It's possible Hans and Lizzie met through ads in a journal or magazine. (A few years later Hans's friend Nils Hjorth also married a widow with a young son in Vancouver, perhaps through a similar avenue.)

Lizzie fit in well in her new home. Hans noted in his diary that she baked bread, canned and helped with the farm and post office, but within months of her arrival Lizzie began to ail. Hans took her to Dr. Kingston at Shoal Bay, who said there wasn't anything he could do. She had heart disease, and within eighteen months of their marriage she was dead. Hans buried Lizzie beneath a grove of fir trees near the end of the sandy spit on the farm and started a new life as a single parent to his four-year-old stepson Billy. When Hans went handlogging Billy went to work with him. Some of the more distant sites required long boat trips. "Billy

Hans Hansen married widow Lizzie Flintham in Vancouver in 1898. She died over a year later from a heart attack, leaving Hans to raise his stepson Billy on his own.
PHOTO COURTESY OF BARB GILROY COLLECTION, MCR.

After Hans's first wife died at Port Neville he went home to Norway, where he married eighteen-year-old Kathinka and brought her back to his remote homestead at Port Neville. She took over the care of his young stepson, Billy.
PHOTO COURTESY OF BARB GILROY COLLECTION, MCR.

would go to sleep in the cabin," wrote Hans's second wife Kathinka, "and when he woke up, Mr. Hansen would say, 'Where are we now, bosun?' A sleepy reply would be, 'We are right here, daddy.'"

"Our Billy," as Port Neville people affectionately called the boy, also spent time with the large Burchett family. Alex Burchett was the first to come to the area. His parents Charlotta and Captain Elisha Clark Burchett—who had served under General Lee in the American Civil War—followed with Alex's sisters, a brother and a nephew. They pre-empted land across the channel from Port Neville on Vancouver Island, and Captain and Charlotta Burchett became surrogate grandparents to Billy.

Also in the neighbourhood in the late 1890s were Hans's friends Martin and Havelock Fyfe and George Waldi, who had a small store at Robber's Nob. The Hansens' nearest neighbour was Ebenezer "The Professor" Doig, a well-educated Glaswegian with a "delightful Scottish accent."

Port Neville got its first listing as a community in the British Columbia Directory of 1899 with forty-five people, including Laura J. Smith. Laura had left her home on Read Island a few years earlier, after her husband's notorious trial for the murder of Laura's lover (see chapter 1). Though the evidence was stacked against her husband, an expensive lawyer got him off. Laura moved in with a logger at Port Neville, taking her youngest child, to serve as a "housekeeper."

In 1903 Hans arranged for old Saltern (Sam) Givins, a well-educated and kindly old man—a carpenter by trade—to look after his farm, post office and stepson while he went to Norway in search of a wife. Hans may have already come to an understanding with Kathinka before he went overseas. Kathinka was a slim-waisted beauty of only eighteen when she married forty-four-year-old Hans Hansen. "Mom was a city girl," wrote their daughter Edith years later, "a sewing and kindergarten teacher. What a drastic change to come to an isolated spot like Port Neville!"

Kathinka loved young Billy at first sight. "I can still see Billy on the beach when the old *Cassiar* finally came to a stop outside our place," wrote Kathinka years later. "Billy, then almost eight years old, was dressed in a brown velvet corduroy sport suit." With him on the shore was Givins. "He had promised not to touch liquor while looking after Billy, and I don't think he did." The house was clean and tidy, continued Kathinka, and Sam had a dinner of curried rice and homemade bread ready for them.

Kathinka, who knew only the rudiments of English, learned the language by teaching Billy to read and write. He in turn became more fluent in Norwegian than any of her own five children who followed.

Hans continued to log and fish to earn the money needed to pay for staples, leaving Kathinka and Billy on their own for long stretches. When Reverend Antle of the Columbia Coast Mission visited in 1906, Kathinka was alone with Billy and her firstborn child Karen. "Mr. Hansen, who keeps the post office, was absent, but [we] paid a visit to his home where we found his wife and two children lonely but contented," wrote Antle in his mission magazine.

Like most folks in the region, the Hansens also supported themselves by selling surplus produce at Shoal Bay. By the time Kathinka arrived, however, the Thurlows gold rush was over.[163] The big companies had abandoned their workings, leaving them in the care of watchmen. Only the most determined of prospectors remained. The rush had come and gone in less than five years.

While the big companies may have profited from their diggings, some of the men who got in at the outset, like Nils Hjorth and Joseph Costello, had little to show for their early good fortune. After Nils sold his bustling store and hotel at Shoal Bay to the Gold Fields of BC, he worked as a labourer in Vancouver, where he married widow Alma Oberg in 1900. Even that didn't last. When he moved back to the Discovery Islands, to a homestead on Read Island in 1905, he was on his own again. Joseph Costello, the first to take out a mine claim near Shoal Bay, was back logging in the Thurlows by 1901, making $350 a year.

Shoal Bay's rival townsite, Channeton at Bickley Bay, never amounted to much more than a logging centre. In 1899 the post office closed, and shortly thereafter Hastings Saw Mill moved its headquarters to Rock Bay on Vancouver Island.

Most of the people who stuck around after the collapse of the mines worked in a combination of logging, fishing and farming. Logging maintained slow but steady growth in the region, providing enough

Shoal Bay on East Thurlow Island leapt into being as a gold rush town in the 1890s. One of three hotels is seen on the right in this 1901 photo, by which time the dozens of gold mines in the region had begun to peter out. Shoal Bay, with its stores, barber shops, brothels and bath houses, remained the principle town for the Discovery Islands for another decade and then faded into obscurity. IMAGE G-07225 COURTESY OF THE ROYAL BC MUSEUM, BC ARCHIVES.

business to keep the store, two hotels and post office at Shoal Bay in operation. In 1900 eight logging camps on East Thurlow Island alone each employed between fifty and a hundred men, according to a new resident at Shoal Bay, James Forrest.

James, a Scottish immigrant, took over management of most of the Gold Fields of BC assets at Shoal Bay in 1899. Under his purview were the company's store and rental cottages and the Waverley Hotel. His letters to his fiancée Ann "Tootie,"[164] who shortly thereafter joined him at Shoal Bay as his wife, provide a snapshot view of Shoal Bay in 1900:

> We have a large store, the only one within 25 miles of this, the whole town belongs to this company. Our houses are nearly all let and those that are not let just now will be let to the summer visitors during July, August and September. Everything is under my charge, all the rents to collect, store to look after and order all that is required in the Waverly Hotel and check the money every night. I have been in charge of the store for a year and last April was given charge of all the company's

business here. It is a very pretty place on an island about 250 miles north of Vancouver. We have no road but travel everywhere in boats and canoes. The steamer from Vancouver calls three times a week but mails only arrive once a week. As well as all my other work, I am postmaster for the district and the post office being my own brings me in an extra $125 a year.

James had rooms over the store and board at the hotel, but he grew a large garden and kept a milk cow and chickens to augment his caretaker income. He also catered to tourists. The Dunsmuirs, who owned the Nanaimo and Cumberland mines, and the Rogerses, who owned sugar refineries, fished in the area from their yachts. Others rented cabins on the beach. In the fall he shipped deer hides to Vancouver and traded for furs with the Native people.

The social life at the bay was quiet. "I have got five of the cottages let for the winter and there are some very nice people staying at the hotel,"

James and Ann Forrest, with their upper-class education and upbringing, were cultured folks among rough-cut miners and loggers. They made their home at Shoal Bay for many years on the hope that their mine claims would prosper.
PHOTO COURTESY OF FOREST FAMILY COLLECTION, MCR 20346-6.

wrote James in November 1900, "so we will have a lively time of it here this Christmas. Six of us are formed into what we call the Christmas committee and they visit every house in the place on Christmas eve, even the smallest shack is not passed. Presents are given and they are invited to Christmas dinner at the hotel and a dance in the evening."

James was thrilled when provincial police constable Henry Jones, an "Edinburgh boy," brought his bride to Shoal Bay. "His wife is an awfully nice girl," wrote James. "I have a standing invitation to dine with them every Sunday at 6:30 and I have afternoon tea with them every day. You must think I am getting to be a regular old wife going to such things but I do look forward to the tea and often have two cups."

A new region called Thurlow Island was created for the 1901 census. It included the general vicinity of Shoal Bay, Loughborough Inlet, Phillips Arm and Frederick Arm. Of the 137 people listed, twenty-five were miners and ninety-one—including cooks, blacksmiths, a railway engineer and an electrical engineer—worked for logging companies. There were two hotel keepers, a store manager, two ranchers, a fisherman, a trapper, a boat builder and a police constable. Only nine of the 137 were women, including thirty-seven-year-old Maggie Campbell, who lived on her own as a single woman cooking for a logging camp.

Most of the Lekwiltok people left the area after the mines failed, relocating to the Campbell River Reserve. In the 1901 census more than half of the people there said they were born at Matlaten. By 1902 there was only one house left at Matlaten, the winter home of Loughborough Bill and his family. Bill was a self-determined man of some rank. In his autobiography Harry Assu, a LeKwiltok of Quadra Island, recalled an encounter with Bill. "There's this ba-aad Indian up there at Phillips Arm and Loughborough Inlet," Harry Assu's white skipper told him. "We're going in! You talk to him in your language." When Loughborough Bill found out Harry was Billy Assu's son, the old man let them fish in the inlet.

Loughborough Bill wasn't the only man among the Thurlows with a reputation. In September 1905 "a bad French-Canadian" named Joe Demar carried out what the *Daily Colonist* described as "a bold a piece of villainy" at Shoal Bay. The logger had been out in the woods for so long that a few drinks at the Waverley Hotel made him lose control. "Without reason," wrote John Antle in his memoirs, "Demar pulled his gun and shot the bartender in the back."

Miraculously the mission doctor was able to save bartender Dunbar's life, and in the course of his recovery, Antle learned the real culprit was the virulent whiskey served in coastal hotels like the Waverley. "They bought one barrel of the cheapest quality of whiskey," Antle wrote in his memoirs. "They then added another barrel of water, the juice of a keg of chewing tobacco (after being soaked and strained), followed then by cayenne pepper and other ingredients calculated to give the liquor a real bite. It was this vile mixture, said Dunbar, that was the cause of the shooting, and it was the same stuff traders sold to the Native people to such bad effect.

The unpretentious little settlement of Roy in Loughborough Inlet continued to operate after the gold rush. In 1900–01 the hotel was under the direction of Mrs. V.L. Ogeson, whose husband ran a sawmill in the inlet. There were twelve men listed in the provincial directory for Loughborough Inlet that year. Among them were Reverend Dugald McGregor and his wife Kathlene, prospector George "By-God" Stafford, a teller of tall tales famous throughout the Discovery Islands, and prospector Ed Dalby, a mimic who could imitate all manner of voices and accents.

Ogeson's mill may have been a fairly small operation, but J.M. Davidson and a man called Ward opened a large shingle mill at the head of the inlet in 1908. Reverend Antle of the Columbia Coast Mission met Davidson and his wife and child that year. When Antle returned in 1909 the camp was expanding to include new cottages, a club room and an emergency hospital. Davidson's crew was up to ninety men at the time of the 1911 census. Their diverse ethnic mix included fourteen Japanese, forty-three men from Hong Kong and three men from China. Over half the Asian men were married, but none had their wives with them.

The Columbia Coast Mission's medical service was a boon to remote places like Loughborough Inlet. The Mission, founded by Reverend John Antle of the Anglican Church in 1905, provided medical and religious services aboard its boats and at a choice of hospitals. The nearest one to the Thurlows was at Rock Bay, north of Campbell River on Vancouver Island.

In 1908 William and Elizabeth Vincent of Loughborough Inlet rushed their son to Rock Bay hospital. The boy was struck by a log that smashed his right leg below the knee. Dr. Hannington thought he'd have to amputate the leg, but he wanted to consult with his colleague aboard the *Columbia*, then at Lund. He sent the boy's father William off to find the *Columbia*. He got only as far as Quathiaski Cove, Quadra Island when his motor failed, so he hired another boat and carried on to Lund. Nearly twenty-four hours had passed before the doctors could confer. They decided the boy's leg could be saved, and the *Columbia* raced back to Lund to help a fourteen-year-old boy suffering from peritonitis.

The Columbia Coast Mission also came to the rescue at Ambrose Allison's camp at Green Point Rapids in October 1909. "Just before we pulled out in the a.m.," wrote Reverend Antle in the mission magazine, "word came down from the woods that Paul Fuller had been knocked out. He was standing on a log when a tree that had been cut fell across it, tossing him in the air. He fell among the stumps and debris and considering the circumstances, came off very well."

Allison, an ambitious young Englishman, was raised in Chemainus by his single mother. He worked in a sawmill as a tallyman from an early

St. Michael's Hospital at Rock Bay, north of Campbell River, was managed by the Columbia Coast Mission. Rock Bay, with its headquarters logging camp for the Hastings Company, was the main centre for the region. PHOTO COURTESY OF SISTERS OF ST. ANN COLLECTION, MCR 7276.

age and started logging in 1905. By 1908, when he was twenty-five, Allison was running his own railway show at Green Point, where his wife Jennie May was the only woman among a crew of forty-four men. Allison, who later also erected a sawmill at Green Point, became a major figure among BC's independent loggers.

Hastings Logging was a leader in the switch to railway logging, starting at Knox Bay and Bear River in about 1905, where it used Old Curly, a locomotive now on display at the Burnaby Village Museum. Its Bear River camp was considered a model for its time. In 1907 it had a row of five bunkhouses along the railway tracks and a spacious cookhouse and mess room. There were also numerous little private shacks. "There is no camp on the coast which keeps its men better than this camp," said Reverend Antle in his 1907 mission log.

One of the first among the many sawmills to operate in the area was the Thurlow Island Lumber Company, managed by R. Robertson, with backing from a partner named Little.

Reverend John Antle, photographed with his crew aboard the *Columbia II*, initiated the Columbia Coast Mission. The mission provided vital religious and medical care by boat and at several hospitals it built on the Inside Passage between Powell River and Alert Bay.
PHOTO COURTESY OF VANCOUVER THEOLOGY SCHOOL COLLECTION, MCR 17,885.

Allison's Shingle Mill in Frederick Arm. Small mills and logging camps had spread throughout the region by the early 1920s. IMAGE NA-03813 COURTESY OF THE ROYAL BC MUSEUM, BC ARCHIVES.

The mill's profits fluctuated with the vagaries of the pre–World War I lumber market, but it remained viable for many decades by cutting "first class cedar."

When the census was taken for the Thurlows in 1911, most of the two hundred people in the general region worked in logging. Their service hub continued to be Shoal Bay, where thirty-two residents were listed in the 1910 provincial directory. James Forrest and his wife Tootie owned much of Shoal Bay by this time, having bought the place from the Gold Fields of BC in 1901. Their holdings included the Waverley Hotel, a store, fourteen houses and all the company's mining properties.

Peter and Rose (Ward) McDonald and their children were also well-established residents at Shoal Bay. Rose grew up on a homestead in Knight Inlet and moved to Shoal Bay as a young adult with her parents and a sister. All four family members got jobs in the Thurlow Hotel in 1899[165] and in about 1900 they bought the hotel in equal shares. When Rose married Vancouver hotelier Peter McDonald in 1902, the couple bought out the rest of the family. Their staff listed in the 1911 census included clerk William Vincent, bartender Aralias Smith Jr., twenty-one-year-old domestic Lilly Duthie, cook Quan Foon and dishwasher Jan Hung.

When the Union Steamship boat was expected in foggy weather, someone went down to the little floating dock to clank boom chains together to guide the boat in. Hauling freight and passengers ashore became much easier in 1913 when a government wharf was built. That same year a school opened and a government trail was cut through to Bickley Bay so kids there could attend the Shoal Bay School. Miss Lillian Hood, who grew up on a homestead on Quadra Island, was the first teacher.

In 1916 the Thurlow Islands, Loughborough Inlet and Rock Bay were connected to the outside world by telephone. Provincial timber inspector George McKay, who arranged for the telephone service, reported on "the remarkable activity" among the islands. "According to Mr. McKay," said the *Daily Colonist*, "the shortage of men [during the war years] caused an era of high wages which, while it has not helped hand logging or the larger logging operations, has greatly stimulated the operations of smaller loggers, the one or two donkey engine concerns who are at work in pre-emptions or small timber leases."

Fishing was a minor enterprise on the Thurlows until W.E. Anderson, who owned a cannery on Quadra Island, built a cannery in 1916[166] at Blind Channel on the southern tip of West Thurlow Island. As cannery operators got exclusive net-fishing rights in an eighty-kilometre (fifty-mile) radius around their canneries, Anderson gained rich new fishing grounds.

The new cannery was fully modern, powered by electricity generated from a Pelton wheel (a device still available today to generate electricity from a small amount of running water). The complex included butchering machines like the Iron Chink and a cutting line where nimble-fingered women trimmed fish to fit cans. It also had four retort machines for the canning process. The cannery had a "China house" for the crew who ran the canning machines, shacks down the beach for the Native people who worked on the cutting line and fished for the cannery from small boats, and separate quarters for the seine crew. A store and a government wharf were connected to the cannery by a plank walkway.

Directly to the east was the old sawmill that Anderson purchased with the site.

The cannery was a relatively short-lived operation. When government regulations changed in 1922, individuals were allowed to hold net-fishing licences and fish where they chose. In 1925–26 Anderson closed the Blind Channel Cannery.[167] It was more cost-effective to run his fleet to and from the cannery at Quathiaski Cove on Quadra Island.

In about 1925 Anderson converted the old sawmill at Blind Channel into a shingle mill and kept it running for a number of years, using steam from the cannery boilers. His crews towed shingle bolts to the mill from his camps in Cordero Channel, Frederick Arm and Loughborough Inlet.

The independent life of the Thurlows region, and the opportunities for work in the many logging camps and mills, brought Hans and Kathinka Hansen back to Port Neville in 1916. They'd been gone for nearly a decade, living in New Westminster, where Hans worked as circulation manager for the *World*. They moved to the city in 1909 because of Kathinka's difficult second pregnancy and a need to send the two oldest children to school. When the newspaper folded, Hans and Kathinka tried commercial fishing for a while but gave that up to return to Port Neville.

Blind Channel Cannery, photographed by Henry Twidle, with stores and private residences at the left.
PHOTO COURTESY OF JESSIE LUCAS COLLECTION, MCR 10,322.

It was hard work for the couple to bring their neglected homestead, now a tangle of weeds, back into order. Hans was still a strong man, but he was past his prime, and Kathinka was pregnant with Arthur. The hard work brought on a premature delivery of the only one of her five children to be born at Port Neville.

In 1920, when Hans was sixty-one and starting to go blind, he began to build a large new log home for his growing family, using a winch, block and tackle to lift the logs into place. The two-storey house still stands. "The outside was finished by 1923," wrote their daughter Edith, "and though there was still much to be done inside, we moved in on Christmas Eve. What a thrill for us children to hang our stockings by the fireplace. Though I was just five years old, I remember it very clearly."

The kitchen, with its massive table, was the heart of the Hansens' new home. The large double windows in the kitchen overlooked the orchard, field and gardens. "The stove was a huge black monster with nickel trim and 'Albion' printed across the oven door in nickel letters," wrote Edith. "The warming oven was huge, and full of all manner of things, from dripping pot [for cooking grease] to 'sad' irons. We took

The Hansens' home and post office in Port Neville (background). The large log house, built by the Hansen family in the early 1920s, is now a museum and gift shop run by the Hansens' descendant Lorna Chesluk. PHOTO COURTESY OF BARB GILROY COLLECTION, MCR.

great pride in keeping our 'Albion' as clean as possible, and bear grease was rubbed into it vigorously to keep it shining. The only drawback to this was the odor that wafted through the air for a few minutes until it burned off." There were a couch and easy chairs in the kitchen, too, for times when the house was packed with guests. Sometimes friends brought their violins, accordions or guitars, and the table and chairs were pushed aside for a dance to old Swedish waltzes and polkas.

After Hans Hansen completely lost his eyesight, family members read to him in the evenings. "While listening to the stories," wrote Edith, "Mom would be mending or sewing and the rest of the family would be doing handwork of some kind too. Olaf once skinned a mink (he was trapping) in the kitchen, so he could hear the end of an interesting story."

In 1924 the post office was relocated back to Hansens',[168] and their eldest daughter Karen became postmistress. Shortly thereafter Karen expanded this to include a full-scale store in a room in the new house.

Life among the Thurlow Islands was on a perpetual boom and bust cycle, but it was possible for families like the Hansens to make a living until the 1950s. Then the world of conglomerate corporations and the demise of the venerable Union Steamship Company changed everything.

Big Time Operators

Hardwicke Island, near Kelsey Bay on Vancouver Island, had an exceptional stand of timber. Loggers worked on the island as early as the 1890s, but it wasn't until 1911 that William and Imogene Kelsey—for whom Kelsey Bay was named—became the first permanent non-Native settlers. The two large logging camps on the island that year had a total of fifty-one people, including a few wives and families.

In 1918 Hans and Gertrude Bendickson joined the Kelseys on Hardwicke. The Bendicksons, who were to become leaders among independent loggers on this part of the coast, had been on the move for nearly a decade, towing their floating camp from site to site.

Gertrude Bendickson, who came to BC from Norway in 1906, was among the vanguard of women who insisted upon staying with their husbands in camp. It was a lonely life. There was one time in those early years when she didn't see another woman's face for a year.

Their move to Hardwicke from south of Powell River took eight days, towing all their buildings and machinery on floats. The tugboat skipper was skeptical about such a large tow with seven children. He took the job only when the children's teacher promised to keep them inside at their lessons. Arthur Bendickson was one of those kids. "I have such a picture in my memory of all those places we passed," he wrote in his memoirs. "I was fascinated watching the plumes of steam rising above the trees from the locomotives as they travelled back and forth from the woods to the log dumps, and the steam plumes rising straight up in the air from the donkey engines here and there in the woods." The Bendickson boys, aged eleven, ten and nine, slipped out from the watchful eye of their teacher on at least one occasion. "As we were passing Myrtle Point, Barney, George and I took a couple of trolling lines and sneaked around our house onto the small floats to drop the lines," recalled Arthur. "And, by golly, we caught a good salmon."

When they reached the treacherous rapids off Stuart Island at the mouth of Bute Inlet, the skipper ordered everyone aboard his tug. The mate stood holding an axe over the towline that held their raft, ready to chop the floats adrift, but they passed through the rapids without incident.

The family's move to Hardwicke, where they pulled their floathouse ashore, allowed Gertrude the luxury of a garden. With the arrival of the Bendickson family, a school opened in 1919, and fifteen children attended.

Another school opened in 1921 on the mainland at Topaze Harbour, at a place residents called Jackson Bay (though the actual bay of that name was on the opposite shore). Henry Wright, who taught there in 1923, reported there were seven families in the area and about a hundred men engaged in logging.

Non-Native settlement in the Topaze Harbour-Jackson Bay area started in the 1890s, when a few settlers sold their produce and meat to distant logging camps. Philip Wilson of Wilson and Brady opened a railway logging camp there during World War I. He was an experienced hand, and many of his key men stayed with him for years. "Whenever

The Bendicksons of Hardwicke Island established themselves as independent loggers in the early 1900s. Various family members are seen here with a 3.35-metre (eleven-foot) cedar log they hauled over 1.6 kilometres (one mile) on a wooden fore-and-aft road.
PHOTO COURTESY OF ARTHUR BENDICKSON COLLECTION, MCR 12,447.

one of his men or their families were in difficulties, Phil Wilson was mightly generous to them," wrote Reverend Greene of the Columbia Coast Mission. "For slackers and no-goods, he had no time whatever and if they let him down, out they went in quick order and with a flow of English directing and following them."

With Wilson's large camp in the district, W.R. Kelsall opened a store and post office in 1914 at the little settlement of Jackson Bay.

Katharine and Bill Fearing moved their family of five from Vancouver to a homestead in east Jackson Bay to get away from the evils of city life, but by that time the school and store attached to the logging camp at Read Bay were closed. "The Fearings have a nice place," wrote coastal cruiser Francis Barrow in his 1938 log. One of the young men of the family came down to meet Francis and Amy at the Jackson Bay float. Amy went to the house to buy fresh milk and eggs and meet the boy's mother. "Fearing has a lot of bees, and we bought a tin of the clearest honey I have ever seen, from clover and fireweed. Mrs. Fearing insisted on us coming to dinner with them. Just before we sat down her husband and other son came in, having then returned from towing a float house from Port Neville. The son who arrived with his father played to us on his piano-accordion. The house seemed full of musical instruments of one sort or another."

Most of the single men who worked in the logging camps of the Thurlows looked forward to a break in Vancouver. When Buck Lewthwaite left camp in Jackson Bay for a short stay "in town," he fell in love with Freda Westblom, who was staying with mutual friends. Freda, with her toddler Lillian, was just getting her life back together after a string of disasters.

Freda gave birth to Lillian just before the devastating Halifax explosion of 1917, when two ships loaded with explosives collided in the harbour and destroyed a huge part of the city. Freda was at home in bed with her infant at the time. Her midwife, who stood near the window, was killed by a shower of imploding glass, but Freda yanked the blankets over herself and Lillian. Freda was badly cut and needed to be hospitalized, but Lillian was unhurt.

Scores of injured people crowded into the hospital, and in the general pandemonium all the babies were removed from their mothers. "Actually, if the truth be known, nobody knew for sure who got whose child back," said Lillian in a taped interview, "but they hoped they got the right ones."

With Halifax in ruin, Freda's husband urged her to take Lillian to BC to stay with relatives while he worked on the reconstruction of Halifax. That was the last Freda saw of him. He died in the influenza epidemic of the late war years. Freda worked as a farmhand until she met and married Buck Lewthwaite in 1921. The couple's first home was in Wellbore Channel, where they lived in camp housing until they bought a floathouse that allowed them to move to various logging shows.

Floating camps were common in the steep terrain of the Thurlows. Sometimes a few handloggers worked together and tied their houses to shore by logs they called "stiff legs," but some camps were big enough to include twenty or more buildings, from a cookshack and houses to a school and store. Where possible the floathouses were pulled ashore, where the back ends of the buildings could lodge above high tide and the fronts were propped on pilings.

There were so many floathouse dwellers in the Blind Channel area in 1919 that the provincial directory classified the estimated two hundred people living there as "floating."

The Lewthwaites' floathouse was considered quite comfortable. It had two small bedrooms and a central room that served as both sitting room and kitchen with a little pantry attached. The furniture included a round dining table and Freda's prized treadle sewing machine, where she transformed Five Roses flour sacks into curtains, tea cloths and table linen with crocheted borders. The house was small, but the walls were so thin they had two stoves, a big cookstove in the central room and a small heater in the pantry. The

"Upon a gathering of enormous rafts of cedar logs, a cluster of houses lay," wrote Francis Dickie of a float camp he visited in the early twentieth century. "Though made up of sections, the whole was held together by boom chains and cables, presenting to the viewer an air of compactness, a community stability, that certain something one senses only in established places. Ridiculous as this impression seemed regarding a so obviously transient arrangement, the feeling grew stronger upon me as I stepped upon the planking of the City. I started along the main street of this...aggregation of one-storey buildings. All were of frames, from one to five rooms in size. Several were of tarpaper covering, others of cedar shakes, others of neat boards. In little yards at the front and back of these, flowers and vegetables flourished in earth held in old dugout canoes, long boxes, barrels and tins. From the nearby shore pipelines, tapping mountain springs, had been carried to supply the householders with running water." PHOTO COURTESY OF MCR 20110-54.

walls had bare studs covered in thick paper attached with flour-and-water paste. You could see the light of day through the shake roof and the sea beneath the scrubbed floorboards, recalls Lillian. The outhouse, on the deck, was a safe place for kids to fish through the toilet hole into the sea.

Some of the houses were primitive by comparison. Rose Smith of Hardwicke called her first floathouse "a damned old shack—you could see to heaven and you could see to hell!" Em Carmichael's first home near Rock Bay was built entirely from split cedar, including the furniture. "Even the baby's crib was made from shakes," said Em in a taped interview. "When we first went up there we didn't have the price of a chair. We sat on boxes, orange boxes and we had butter boxes nailed together up the wall for cupboards. I put curtains in front." Eventually they built a trim floathouse, and when Em's husband left to tow it to the new location, Em put a match to the cabin. "What happened to the shack?" asked her husband when he returned. "I burned it," she replied, "because I don't want anybody to go through what I went through in that shack!"

When it was time for Lillian to go to school, her stepfather Buck Lewthwaite towed their floathouse to Roy at Loughborough Inlet, where many families congregated for schooling. Living in one place meant Lillian's father had to work away from home. He'd cut a big stack of firewood, recalls Lillian, and take off for a month or more at a stretch. The pleasure of having other women and children for company, with fourteen kids at the Roy School, still stands out in Lillian's memory.

When enrollment dropped at the Roy School in the late 1920s, the Lewthwaites moved their house to Blind Channel, where a school had been open since1921. The cannery was no longer in operation, but the sawmill was a going concern and there were about fifty people living in the little community. Sid Boardman had a store and post office where Union Steamship boats stopped at the dock with freight, passengers and mail. An additional luxury at Blind Channel was a dance hall, converted from the cannery's Chinese bunkhouse.

Swedish logger P.B. Anderson was a prominent lumberman in the Thurlows area, starting in 1917 when he bought a camp on West

Thurlow Island. With him were his grown sons Clay and Dewey, until they joined up for the war. I now had a good railroad outfit," wrote Anderson in his memoirs, "twelve miles of rails, twelve new logging cars, six donkeys and rigging to run two sides, a 52-ton locomotive and money in the bank to move and open up the new camp."

Anderson made and lost several fortunes in his lifetime. He got his start in logging with money he made in the Klondike gold rush. He was a risk taker, a quality that brought him both gains and problems in a volatile market. When he bought the Knox Bay camp he was just resurfacing from a near bankruptcy, but this camp proved a shrewd investment:

> This tract of timber on Thurlow Island was one of the finest quality of old growth fir and cedar on the Pacific coast. We had to build camps in the woods as well as at the beach. There was also a long wharf from the shore to deep water for steamboats to land, and there was a big booming ground to drive. Got this all completed and started to log about the first of October 1917. Finally the boys came back from the army. While they were away I had bought twelve timber claims, twelve square miles adjoining my original holdings so now I had timber to last me eight years. My oldest son was superintendent and Clay was foreman.

A few years later, around 1920, Anderson overextended himself again with a gamble on a sawmill. He lost everything but his home and about twenty thousand dollars in cash. "Such is life in the lumber game," wrote Anderson. "I had to start over again but I was now a little over 60 years old so I had to be more careful from now on. My credit had not been hampered so if I could get a piece of timber I could start again. I had a small piece of timber, only eight million board feet (about 743,000 square metres), near Greene Point Rapids on Cordero Channel. It was handy to the water and it would give me a start."

Fire was a constant threat in the forests. In one of Anderson's camps he had to divert his 160-man crew to fire fighting for two months to save his stand of timber. He lost bridging and structures but saved enough timber to turn a profit. Camp operators in Port Neville in 1925 weren't so lucky. A fire broke out in one of their camps at Robber's Nob, a favourite picnic place for inlet residents, and moved so fast there was barely time for the

Henry Twidle photographed P.B. Anderson's logging camp in Knox Bay on Thurlow Island.
PHOTO COURTESY OF MARION ADAMS COLLECTION, MCR 5142.

men and their families to escape. "The fire came up very suddenly during the intense heat of last week and many people were trapped," reported the *Comox Argus*. "It jumped three miles across an inlet in one place."

Oliver Gosfold Clark, the assistant fire ranger at Port Neville, helped get everyone safely to the beach and went back through the flames to make sure no one had been missed. He didn't make it out. His body was later found just 1.8 metres (six feet) from the beach. Clark, who became a hero among his workmates, was the only one to perish. He was awarded a posthumous citation for bravery, and the forestry service named a boat for him.

Buck and Freda Lewthwaite's daughter Lillian finished school in Blind Channel when she was about thirteen. She got a job with her mother, running the cookshack for a horse-logging outfit in Loughborough Inlet. Freda cooked and Lillian was the flunky, setting and waiting tables and peeling vegetables. To vary her day in a place where you couldn't walk on shore alone for fear of bears, to get exercise she helped the teamster curry the horses.

Lillian's next job was as a home helper for the Clay and Doris Anderson family (one of P.B. Anderson's sons) at their Granite Bay logging camp during the Depression. She earned the luxurious amount of thirty dollars per month.

Lillian married her first husband at nineteen, after a three-month courtship. Her husband got a job in Victoria, where they lived in a one-room apartment until she got pregnant and went home to Blind Channel. There she rented a room from the storekeeper for three dollars a month. For her final month, Lillian stayed at the Rock Bay hospital. "See you had to go there and stay a whole month before you had the baby," recalled Lillian in a taped interview. "But you didn't just wait around. You were helpful in the running of the hospital, though you paid a dollar a day. You made bandages, you made the beds, filled water for other patients and served them tea."

When war broke out in Europe in 1939, upcoast people with radios followed the news from overseas, but most carried on as before, buffered from the outside world by their isolation. The only visible difference was the emplacement on York Island at the entrance to Johnstone Straits.

A fire at Robber's Nob in Port Neville in 1925 engulfed several logging camps and took the life of fire warden Oliver Clark, who went back into the blazing camp to be sure no one was left behind.
IMAGE NA-04976 COURTESY OF ROYAL BRITISH COLUMBIA MUSEUM, BC ARCHIVES.

One hundred soldiers were reputedly stationed there, at the ready to defend the inner coast. Boats going through Johnstone Straits had to stop for inspection or risk being fired at.

Life in Victoria wasn't a good fit for Lillian. "It was like taking a wild animal and putting it in the zoo," said Lillian. When her husband enlisted for war service in 1939 and went overseas, she took her two children and headed back to Blind Channel. Her brother bought her a small float-house for $125, and she got a job as a cook in a logging camp. Settled back into a lifestyle she loved, Lillian realized she had to end her marriage. Her old school chum Cecil Carroll proposed to her, paid for her divorce and became the stepfather of Lillian's children.

Lillian and Cecil were married in Campbell River, on the understanding their wedding must be timed by the tide so they could get back home. "He bought me a very pretty dress to be married in," reminisced Lillian. "It was all flowered and pretty. I thought it was so nice."

The Carrolls lived and worked side by side for the remainder of their married lives. When provincial regulations shifted in favour of larger companies in the 1950s, many small operators like the Carrolls were squeezed out. Cecil took over the old store at Shoal Bay for a year. Then he and Lillian got contracts to tow logs for Crown Zellerbach, which owned a big new pulp mill in Campbell River. Crown Zellerbach and its partner Comox Logging Company were granted thousands of hectares of land for their exclusive use in a new system of large-scale forest management licences to encourage them to open the Elk Falls pulp mill. Their licence covered a big part of the Discovery Islands.

The Bendickson family of Hardwicke Island had the foresight and means to secure one of these large licences in 1952. "At least one small logging outfit thinks the forest management licence system is not designed solely for the big interest," said the *Campbell River Courier*. When the Bendickson brothers were awarded 6,500 hectares (sixteen thousand acres) on Hardwicke Island, it allowed them to make long-term plans.

Also in the 1950s, the Union Steamship Company went out of business due to competition from seaplanes. Job loss and the lack of affordable and convenient transport led to a mass exodus from the Discovery Islands. Where hundreds of people had lived and worked throughout the Thurlows area in the 1920s, by the late 1960s the region was a graveyard of abandoned homesteads and settlements. It became a great recreational pursuit for city boaters to cruise the islands scavenging fruit and building materials.

A few people stayed. Two of the Bendicksons' children married into the Hansen family of Port Neville. Hans Hansen died at his homestead in 1939 and was buried under the fir trees near the point on his beautiful farm. Karen, the postmistress, and her mother were hospitalized in Nanaimo in 1964. Karen died that year, and Kathinka passed away in 1965. When the two women left Port Neville, Edith (Hansen) Bendickson remarked to an old family friend that Port Neville didn't seem the same without her mother. "Port Neville IS your mother," the man replied. Kathinka's and Hans's son Olaf and his family continued to live at Port Neville. The post office and store is now in the hands of their daughter, Lorna Chesluk. Lorna has turned the old family home into a gallery and museum frequented by cruisers.

Ada Carroll's floathouse at Blind Channel around 1950. Her daughter-in-law Lillian Carroll and her grandchildren Doris, Glee, Winston and Connie are on the porch.
PHOTO COURTESY OF LILLIAN CARROLL COLLECTION, MCR 20281-9.

In the late 1960s and 1970s a new generation of pioneers discovered the Thurlow Islands area. While some of the remaining long-time residents took a dim view of the long-haired newcomers, with their fancy education and naive ideas about going back to the land, Lillian and Cecil Carroll welcomed them. Numerous hippies learned how to navigate the tides, set a prawn trap and fish for salmon from the Carrolls. Cecil hired some of these long-haired youths to work on his tow boats. Some took to the life and stayed; others quickly gave up on a place where earning a living meant endless hard work.

Helen Piddington and Dane Campbell were part of this new wave. Helen was raised in BC but spent years in France studying art before she married Dane, a son of the groundbreaking BC publisher Gray Campbell of Sidney. The twosome worked along the coast of BC in Dane's boat for a few years before they bought land in Loughborough Inlet across from the now deserted townsite of Roy in the early 1970s. Helen describes their life in her lyrical autobiography, *The Inlet*.

Loughborough Inlet was full of remnants of its busy past: slumped homestead shacks, logging camp buildings, machines and even the odd cemetery. Helen and Dane cleaned up their long-neglected 1930s logging camp house and cleared the scrub alder away from an orchard, where they planted dozens more trees.

Other newcomers discovered the inlet too. Helen lists five families who moved onto leased land, barges, boats and floathouses. "Gradually all of them drifted away: some to different jobs," wrote Helen, "others to different partners." But, the Piddington-Campbell family stuck it out to become the old-timers of the inlet. The freedom and autonomy of their lifestyle made all the hard work worthwhile. They've made a living in a variety of ways over the years. Helen has an international following for her artwork, and the couple also fish for prawns and manage a woodlot across the inlet from their home.

The Richters of Vancouver also discovered the Thurlows while on a cruising trip and bought the cannery site almost on a whim in 1969. They moved their family upcoast to take over the old store, post office and gas station at the dock, where they refuelled boats from a barrel with a hand pump. "Signs of the area's recent history [lay] rusted along the shore and rotted in the encroaching brush and forest," say the Richters on their Blind Channel Resort website. "Still, there was a secluded peacefulness, the ever-changing rapids flowing past, the mountains reflecting the afternoon sun."

The Richters transformed the derelict site at Blind Channel—with its old cannery and sawmill buildings in various stages of decrepitude— into a resort with wharves, a fuel dock, a store and cabins. Their resort has a personalized feel, with old bottles embedded into the walls of some of the buildings and the late Annemarie Richter's mosaics made from shards of china, glass and metal she found on the beach.

The Sonora Island Lodge, owned by London Drugs, is hardly competition for the homey operations at Blind Channel and nearby Cordero Lodge fishing resort. Sonora Island Lodge is a world unto itself, a major international resort on a massive scale that would leave Thurlow folk of prior generations speechless. But even this resort, with all its luxury and finery, has had its troubles. A fire in January 2005 destroyed a new 1,200-square-metre (12,500-square-foot) lodge being added to the complex. The forty-member construction crew, joined by firefighters from Quadra Island, managed to keep the fire from spreading to nearby structures by bulldozing an adjacent building, later replaced on a grand scale.

Shoal Bay village has suffered numerous fires over the years. By the time Seattle investors bought the property in the 1960s, all that remained of the once populous townsite were a store and the wharf, built in 1959. The owners built a new lodge that was never completely successful. In the 1990s Mark McDonald of California leased the lodge. It had become a frumpy old place full of ghosts, but it had rustic charm.

As Mark says in his website journal, Shoal Bay captured his heart. His periods of work—buying horses in Europe for California clients— became intrusive. "I have just now returned after spending about a month out in fantasyland," wrote Mark in one of his last journal entries. "It is an odd, difficult to describe feeling when you step off the boat onto the Shoal Bay dock after being away for any length of time . . . I resisted the temptation to kneel down and kiss the planking and instead started carrying boxes up to the upper dock."

Mark was in the process of negotiating the purchase of Shoal Bay Lodge when cousins came up for a summer visit in 2000. They were heading back from checking crab traps in his little runabout when Mark spotted smoke coming from the direction of the lodge. By the time they rounded the corner into Shoal Bay, the lodge was in flames. "We could hear the crackling before we could see it," wrote Mark. "When we did round the corner the entire lodge was engulfed in flames. Every upstairs window was a fireball, smoke was pouring out of every downstairs window and door. By the time I first saw the fire, the lodge and everything in it was a total loss." Fortunately no one was hurt.

Undeterred, Mark bought the property and built a couple of cottages on the old townsite, renting them out to summer guests. His plan was to rebuild the lodge and make Shoal Bay his permanent residence, but that was not to be.

As of the summer of 2008 Shoal Bay Lodge was back in the real estate listings. Mark will carry away grand memories of his dreams for Shoal Bay and the steely characters who make their permanent homes among the northern Discovery Islands.

The former gold rush townsite of Shoal Bay will enter the next phase of its history, as will the Thurlows area in general. Corporate logging tenures in the inlets will send non-resident crews to work in the rich stands of timber for decades to come. And perhaps the urban-style houses that have popped up in Shoal Bay and elsewhere in the Thurlows signify a future of part-time residents who value the area's wild nature.

Suggested Reading

Andersen, Doris. *The Columbia is Coming!* Sidney, BC: Gray's Publishing, 1982.

Andersen, Doris. *Evergreen Islands, The Islands of the Inside Passage: Quadra to Malcolm.* Sidney, BC: Gray's Publishing, 1979.

Barnett, Homer G. *The Coast Salish of British Columbia.* Eugene, OR: University of Oregon, 1955.

Blanchet, M. Wylie. *The Curve of Time.* Vancouver, BC: Whitecap Books, 1968.

Cox, Harold R.W. *Greenhorns in Blue Pastures.* New York, NY: Smith and Durrell, 1945.

Douglas, Gilean. *The Protected Place.* Whaletown, BC: Battle Maid Press, 2001.

Drushka, Ken. *Working in the Woods, A History of Logging on the West Coast.* Madeira Park, BC: Harbour Publishing, 1992.

Emery, Maud. *A Seagull's Cry.* Surrey, BC: Nunaga Publishing, 1975.

Harbord, Heather. *Desolation Sound, A History.* Madeira Park, BC: Harbour Publishing, 2007.

Henry, John Frazier. *Early Maritime Artists of the Pacific Northwest Coast, 1741–1841.* Vancouver, BC: Douglas & McIntyre, 1984.

Hill, Beth. *Upcoast Summers.* Ganges, BC: Horsdal & Schubart, 1985.

Kendrick, John, ed. and trans. *The Voyage of Sutil and Mexicana 1792, The last Spanish exploration of the Northwest Coast of America.* Spokane, WA: The Arthur H. Clark Company, 1991.

Kennedy, Dorothy, and Randy Bouchard. *Sliammon Life, Sliammon Lands.* Vancouver, BC: Talonbooks, 1983.

Lamb, W. Kaye, ed. *The Voyage of George Vancouver, 1791–1795*, Vol. 2. London, UK: The Hakluyt Society, 1984.

Lambert, Barbara Ann. *Chalkdust & Outhouses, West Coast Schools, 1893–1950*. Powell River, BC: Barbara Ann Lambert, 2000.

Newcombe, M.D., ed. *Menzies' Journal of Vancouver's Voyage, April to October, 1792*. Victoria, BC: Province of BC, 1923.

Piddington, Helen. *The Inlet: Memoirs of a Modern Pioneer*, Madeira Park, BC: Harbour Pubishing, 2001.

Taylor, Jeanette. *River City, A History of Campbell River and the Discovery Islands*. Madeira Park, BC: Harbour Publishing, 1999.

White, Howard, and Jim Spilsbury. *Spilsbury's Coast: Pioneer Years in the Wet West*. Madeira park, BC: Harbour Publishig, 1987.

Williams, Judith. *High Slack, Waddington's Gold Road and the Bute Inlet Massacre of 1864*. Vancouver, BC: New Star Books, 1996.

Williams, Judith. *Dynamite Stories*. Vancouver, BC: New Star Books, 2003.

Williams, Judith. *Clam Gardens, Aboriginal Mariculture on Canada's West Coast*. Vancouver, BC: New Star Books, 2006.

Notes

Chapter One: Read Island

1   For a fuller decription of the village in Whiterock Passage, see chapter 4.

2   Robert Galois, *Kwakwaka'wakw Settlements, 1775–1920, A Geographical Analysis and Gazetteer* (Vancouver: UBC Press, 1994), p. 262. Tatapowis was designated as a reserve of the Klahoose of Cortes Island in 1900 (see chapter 5), but the Xwemalhkwu dispute their ownership.

3   *The Log of the Columbia* (Rock Bay, BC) (the magazine of the Columbia Coast Mission), "Aumoc, and the White Chief, Red Dougal," Aug. 1906, p. 1.

4   *Daily Colonist* (Victoria), Apr. 2, 1908, p. 6, "Wylie." Wylie's obituary says he claimed to be the first permanent non-Native resident.

5   *Weekly News Advertiser* (Vancouver), Nov. 13 and Nov. 20, 1895, "Vancouver Assizes." The story quotes Wylie as saying he was chief of police at Ballard City, Dakota.

6   *Weekly News Advertiser* (Vancouver), Nov. 20, 1895, "Vancouver Assizes." Smith murder trial. See also British Columbia Directory listings for Quadra Island (which included Read Island in 1892) and Read Island in 1893, BC Archives.

7   There are three reports of William Blaney's logging camp in 1889 issues of the *Nanaimo Free Press*, including mention on Sept. 3, 1889 of a boom of logs that broke up.

8   The 1891 Dominion census, BC Archives, does not mention their daughters Emma and Stella, though Stella was later listed as Estillea Anderson in the British Columbia Directory for Read Island. She was on hand, according to family legend, to nurse her father in his final days.

9   Etta Byers, family history manuscript, Cortes Island Museum Archives. Etta wrote that Wiley's daughter Stella married Anderson, and her son Norman was

the first white child born on Read Island. In vital statistics records, BC Archives, Stella married William Belding of Read Island in 1901.

10 Memories of Wally Aldrich, as related by Etta Byers, Museum at Campbell River Archives.

11 Liquor licensing records, GR 93, BC Archives.

12 Several Read Island residents are listed in the 1912 voters list, Museum at Campbell River Archives, with addresses given as the Burdwood Hotel.

13 For more on Moses Ireland, see chapter 2 and the forthcoming book by Jeanette Taylor, *Tidal Passages: Quadra Island* (Madeira Park: Harbour Publishing, 2009).

14 *Daily Colonist* (Victoria), Nov. 20, 1903. Lilly's original name was Lilly Dale Grow. She married Daniel Wilson in Washington state. She had at least one child with Daniel Wilson, and they lived for some time in Arizona, working in a mining town. She was a widow when she met Bernard Ward in Seattle.

15 *The Log* (Jan. 1907): 11

16 *The Log* (Apr. 1906): 8.

17 For the full poem, see *The Log* (Sept. 1907): 19.

18 There is no death certificate in BC vital statistics records for Lilly Joy Ward. Roland Woolsey, a later resident at the Bold Point ranch, recalled two graves near the barns at the former Ireland-Ward ranch, one containing the remains of a Mrs. Ward and the other an unknown occupant. These graves are now unmarked.

19 Jeanne Alexander Donald, a twenty-two-year-old maid, married thirty-nine-year-old Bernard Edwin Ward on Feb. 21, 1917, marriage certificate, BC vital statistics records, BC Archives. On July 1, 1917, Alice Robertson of Cortes Island noted in her diary, copy at Museum at Campbell River Archives, that her two eldest children went to Village Bay on Quadra Island, where they saw Bernie Ward and "heard his laments about the wife who went away." In June 1920 he married again, listing himself as a widower.

20 Doris Andersen, *Evergreen Islands, The Islands of the Inside Passage: Quadra to Malcolm* (Sidney: Gray's Publishing Limited, 1979).

21 Violet (Lambert) Elmer interview, A264, Museum at Campbell River Archives.

22 Police Records, Correspondence Inward, Attorney General Records, GR429, BC Archives.

23 The *Weekly News Advertiser* (Vancouver), Nov. 15, 1893.

24 Michael Taft, *Tall Tales of British Columbia* (Victoria: Provincial Archives of British Columbia, 1983), pp. 52–53.

25 The 1911 Dominion census listed John Rosen as the head of the family. He was farming, and Charlie was logging. By 1919 only Charlie Rosen was listed in the British Columbia Directory for Read Island. There is no death certificate for John Rosen in BC.

26 For more on Lord Bacon, see Jeanette Taylor, *River City, A History of Campbell River and the Discovery Islands* (Madeira Park: Harbour Publishing, 1999), pp. 77, 76, 85–86, 92–93.

27 For more on the Fred and Ameenie Foort Family, see the forthcoming book by Jeanette Taylor, *Tidal Passages: Quadra Island* (Madeira Park: Harbour Publishing, 2009).

28 Garry Keeling recalls foundations being laid for the current store in 1935; interview with the author, Sept. 15, 2003. Tom Widdowson recalls the store was enlarged considerably in the late 1940s; email to the author 2008.

Chapter Two: Cortes Island

29 Barnett, *The Coast Salish of British Columbia* (Oregon: University of Oregon, 1955), p. 29.

30 Randy Bouchard and Dorothy Kennedy, eds. *Indian Myths and Legends from the North Pacific Coast of America: A Translation* (Vancouver: Talonbooks, 2002), 227–28. In Boas's telling, one paw of the girl's dog skin was not burned, but this significant detail does not play out again in his recounting of the tale. It may have been this bit of her remaining magic self that gave the capes she wove for her family such value that the Sun would want to trade for her cape.

31 Randy Bouchard and Dorothy Kennedy, eds. *Indian Myths and Legends from the North Pacific Coast of America: A Translation* (Vancouver: Talonbooks, 2002), 227–28. Chief Darren Blaney of the Xwemalhkwu understands from his elders that the eldest brother was the founder of his people. The younger brothers formed the various families of the other Mainland Comox groups.

32 This extensive village may still have been in use after the arrival of the first Europeans in 1792. Cortes resident Ian Disney recalls blue glass trade beads were found in the midden many years later when roads were put in.

33 Etta Byers remembers seeing this trench as a child and says it was later filled in, as communicated to author. There were other trenched and palisaded sites in the region, notably at Rebecca Spit Marine Provincial Park on Quadra Island.

34 Tom Hazlitt, "Toast to Whaletown–Paradox on Pacific," *Province* (Vancouver), June 11, 1960.

35 Rose (Manson) McKay's memoirs, Museum at Campbell River Archives. George McGee recalled three other fights with the Lekwiltok: at Hernando Island, at Smelt Bay and at Lund.

36 The Nellie Jeffery family found these bones in an unspecified site above Mansons Landing, as related to the author by Joan (Jeffery) Hewison.

37 For more on Moses Ireland, see chapter 2 and the forthcoming book by Jeanette Taylor, *Tidal Passages: Quadra Island* (Madeira Park: Harbour Publishing, 2009).

38 *Daily Colonist* (Victoria), March 6, 1889.

39 Mike Manson may have been referring to Ireland's hotel in his 1895 *Log of the Tug Stella*, Museum at Campbell River Archives, Manson vertical file, when he said he was picking up supplies at the Alhambra Hotel.

40 Library and Archives Canada website www.collectionscanada.gc.ca, Post Offices and Postmasters, Whaletown. Drinkwater gave up the position of postmaster in 1897, and William Robertson took over from 1898 to 1903. The British Columbia Directory, BC Archives, for 1899, however, lists Charles I. Allen as the postmaster for Whaletown. Robertson officially purchased the Drinkwaters' Whaletown property in 1898.

41 Samuel moved to Vancouver in about 1901. He died in 1905, still a hotel-keeper, from a hemorrhage in the stomach.

42 Frank Tooker said Bill had "picked up" Mary McLeod in San Francisco and brought her up to Whaletown "and one thing and another." See binder on Whaletown, Cortes Island Museum. In a letter Mary wrote to her former neighbours, the Marlatts, she referred to Bill as "uncle"; see Marlatt Collection, Museum at Campbell River Archives.

43 Nicholas had several other large properties in the Whaletown area at the time, which may be the reason for registering titles in the name of other family members.

44 Alice (Shaw) Jackson understands Alice Robertson's Welsh father lived in India for many years and was married a number of times. His last wife, Alice Robertson's mother, was Indian, though her Anglo-Saxon maiden name suggests she was of mixed ancestry.

45 Dorothea Robertson Carter wrote in her typed notes that Alice was a medical missionary, vertical files, Cortes Island Museum.

46 Charlie Allen's diary for 1909, typescript, Cortes Island Museum.

47 Mike Manson, "Log of the Steam Tug Stella," 1895, typescript, Museum at Campbell River Archives. Manson was based on Cortes Island when he described the effects of a particularly high tide, saying it was the highest he'd seen in eight years. In his book *British Columbia Coast Names, Their Origin and History*, Captain John T. Walbran says Mansons Bay was named for Mike Manson, who came to Cortes in 1882. Provincial Land Registry records, BC Archives, GR 2636, however, give the dates of his property purchase and pre-

emption as 1887 and 1888. The Nanaimo newspaper, *Free Press*, British Columbia Directory listings and property tax assessments for Nanaimo, website viHistory, www.vihistory.ca/, Properties, show that he still kept his residence in Nanaimo until 1892.

48 "Sketches of the Life of Michael Manson," unpublished memoir written by Michael Manson, MS-1122, BC Archives.

49 "Memories of Mr. of Mrs. Laurence Manson," written by one of their adult children. No author, no date. BC Archives, Laurence Manson vertical file.

50 Laurence Manson and his sons continued to operate this store for seventy-six years, eventually selling the contents to form the basis of a museum exhibition at Barkerville.

51 The fire was suspected arson, as noted in the Nanaimo *Free Press* May 15, 1886. A man was charged with the felony after it was revealed he knew who burned Manson's store but refused to tell. There is no further mention of charges or convictions.

52 Mike's uncle in Comox noted that he and Leask visited on Jan. 14, 1887, on their return from a search for sheep farming land "up north," William Duncan diary, Courtenay Museum Archives.

53 Mike Manson's brother Laurence said in his memoirs that Mike qualified for his captain's papers at this time and went into shipping. BC Archives, Laurence Manson vertical files.

54 Mike Manson is listed in the Nanaimo directory to 1892, with a gap in 1890. The family home was on Selby Street, the same street where one of his brothers and Jane's parents lived. In the 1891 tax rolls for Nanaimo, Mike and Jane's house was valued at $700, while his brother's home was valued at $250. See property tax assessments for Nanaimo, website viHistory, www.vihistory.ca/, Properties.

55 Rose (Manson) McKay memoirs, Museum at Campbell River Archives.

56 Mike Manson, "Log of the *Stella*," Feb. 8, 1895, typescript, Museum at Campbell River Archives.

57 In his memoirs, "Sketches from the Life of Michael Manson," typescript, BC Archives, MS-1122, Mike recalled delivering these goods to Cape Mudge in 1886, but the actual date was probably 1890, as reported in the newspapers of the day. His memory of 1886 as the potlatch date, however, suggests he was making trips to the Discovery Islands while he was still in business in Nanaimo.

58 William Blaney's 1893 obituary said he was the first settler on Hernando Island, but he didn't register for a pre-emption on Hernando until 1890. The first official registry of land for Hernando was in 1884, when R. Reid purchased 2,380 acres on the island; see Provincial Land registry records, GR-2635,

BC Archives.

59   In a letter to May Ellingsen, Cortes Island Museum, Abner Conant said his parents arrived in 1887. The Conant's great-grandson Dennis Ruhl gave the same date. The Conant's daughter Cora, however, was born in North Dakota in 1888, see BC vital statistics records, BC Archives.

60   No death certificate seems to have been registered for Forest Conant in BC's vital statistics records, BC Archives. Forest's son, Abner, later recalled that he was buried with a child on William Blaney's property on the east coast of the island; see Cortes IslandMuseum vertical file on Hernando Island.

61   Dan McDonald's grave marker in the Old Whaletown Cemetery says "Donald McDonald McArthur, 1845–1930 at rest."

62   The list of settlers of the early 1890s comes from the 1891 Dominion census, GR-0288, and land transaction records, GR 2635 and GR 0039, BC Archives.

63   For more on the Myers murder case, see chapter 1. This was one of many criminal investigations Mike Manson carried out.

64   According to the 1891 Dominion census, twenty-nine-year-old Ellen Britto lived with Mike, Jane and their eight-year-old daughter Maggie in Nanaimo. Mike's occupation was listed as seal hunter.

65   "Cortes Island Straws," *Weekly News* (Comox), March 29, 1893.

66   B.A. McKelvie, *Province* (Vancouver), May 13, 1926. This article on Mike's disastrous search for gold says that Mike was with his brother John, though an Aug. 5, 1890 report in the *Nanaimo Free Press* says Mike went off for thirty days with his brother William.

67   Richard Somerset Mackie, *The Wilderness Profound, Victorian Life on the Gulf of Georgia*, (Victoria: Sono Nis, 1995), p. 258.

68   Both the 1891 and 1901 Dominion census, BC Archives, showed that Ellen had only her two youngest Conant children living with her, though Arthur Rorison, who came to the island as a child in 1891, named all four of her children as his acquaintances. See his letter to May Ellingsen, Cortes Island Museum. Ellen may have been forced to send the two eldest out to work for their keep. Certainly in the 1901 census nineteen-year-old Della Conant was listed as a domestic at the Heriot Bay Hotel on Quadra Island.

69   It's possible they did not officially marry for several years because they didn't want to lose Ellen's homestead claim, which became their permanent residence.

70   Mabel (Hague) Christensen, taped interview, A216, Museum at Campbell River Archives.

71   Henry Hague's memoirs, Cortes Island Museum. He implies he had lived on the island prior to eventually taking out a pre-emption in 1899, and in

1895–96 four of his children's names appear in the records for the Cortes Island school; see school records compiled by May Ellingsen from BC Archives records, in Cortes Island Museum. A son of one of the Weiler brothers in Victoria later became a prominent resident on Cortes, perhaps attracted to the island by the Hagues.

72   A school opened on Read Island in 1894, followed by schools on Quadra and Cortes in 1895.

73   Mike Manson, "Log of the Steam Tug Stella, 1895," typescript, Museum at Campbell River Archives.

74   Available school records indicate that the Hernando Island school closed in 1899, but the British Columbia Directory says the school was still running until 1901. Miss Mary M. Creech, who came to teach at the school in 1896, continued on until it was closed. This was an anomaly; teachers in small rural schools rarely stayed more than a year.

75   John Manson is listed as a trader until 1899 in the British Columbia Directory, while his brother is listed as a master mariner and postmaster from 1895 on.

76   Charlie Allen diaries, typescript, Cortes Island Museum.

77   Cora Smith left Read Island after the infamy of her father's trial for murder; he was accused of killing his wife's lover. See chapter 1.

78   In the 1901 Dominion census, Tiber is listed as arriving in 1893. His first land pre-emption was also in 1893; see land records compiled by May Ellingsen at the BC Archives, in the Cortes Island Museum.

79   Henry and Rose White were married in Sapperton on Oct. 18, 1900, where Rose had relatives; vital statistics records, BC Archives.

80   Two of the Tiber girls married into the Marquette family.

81   Alice Robertson's diary for 1906, photocopy, Museum at Campbell River Archives. She notes that August was getting set to buy Alex Heay's place.

82   Mike Manson's descendants aren't sure how Mike came to have this property. Etta (McKay) Byers wonders if he fell heir to it through debts owed to him at his trading post when the 1890s settlers left the island.

83   Electoral History of British Columbia website, www.llbc.leg.bc.ca.

84   Charlie Allen diary for 1908, transcript, Cortes Island Museum.

85   Electoral History of British Columbia website provides a list of elected candidates. See also obituary for W. Manson, *Daily Colonist* (Victoria), July 26, 1953. William J. Manson and William Manson (cousins) were both elected in by-elections a few years prior to the general election of 1909.

86   Alice Robertson diary for 1908, Cortes Island Museum. She mentions the wharf at Whaletown, which may have been in existence for some time. The

Mansons and Hernando docks were built in the 1890s.

87 Charles Marlatt memoir, Museum at Campbell River Archives.

88 Charlie Allen's diaries, transcripts for 1906, Cortes Island Museum. His first mention of the Padgetts is in 1906. Their son Roy Padgett is quoted in Bill Thompson's *Boats, Bucksaws and Blisters, Pioneer Tales of the Powell River Area* (Powell River: Powell River Heritage Research Association,1990), p. 135, saying his family arrived on Cortes in 1904.

89 Dan McDonald, farmer, was still living on Twin Island at the time of the 1911 Dominion census and the 1911–12 Voters List.

90 Etta Byers's family recollections, personal conversation with author; *Daily Colonist*, "Mysteriously Wounded," Aug. 8, 1915, p. 2 and "Injured in Same Way," Sept. 5, 1915, p. 14.

91 For more on Theosophy and another adherent, Lilly Joy Ward, see chapter 1.

92 Electoral History of British Columbia website. Michael Manson lost his riding by a narrow margin in the 1916 election and didn't run again until 1924. Family history, however, has it that he was re-elected during those years in a by-election.

93 May Ellingsen, notes in a photo album of pictures of Hernando Island, Cortes Island Museum.

94 The 1919 British Columbia Directory listing of male residents includes thirty-four names under Whaletown, thirty-four at Mansons (called Cortez), seven on Mary Island, fourteen at Seaford, and eight at Squirrel Cove. Tripling these numbers to account for families gives an estimated total of 291. George Griffin, however, recalls that the population on the island was about six hundred when he first arrived in 1920; see taped interview A211, Museum at Campbell River Archives.

95 Binder on Whaletown to 1930, Cortes Island Museum. Frank Tooker gave 1921 as the year for the opening of this new store, but 1926 has been given elsewhere.

96 Eleanor Swain Smith, "The Nine Lives of Cougar Smith," unpublished manuscript, Museum at Campbell River Archives.

97 The British Columbia Directory listings for 1945 were fifty people on "Cortez," seventy-three at Mansons, forty-eight at Seaford, eighty-eight at Squirrel Cove and 139 at Whaletown, for a total of 398. This number multiplied by three, to account for the fact that children and some women were not included, gives a total of 1,194.

Chapter Three: Desolation Sound

98 Doris Andersen, *Evergreen Islands, The Islands of the Inside Passage: Quadra to Malcolm* (Sidney, BC: Gray's Publishing, 1979), 121.

99 1911 Dominion census, New Westminster district.

100 The 1901 Dominion census lists Walter Tefler Barnes as living with his mother and brother in New Westminster. His mother Annie immigrated from England to the Gaspé area in Quebec with her husband James in the 1880s. She appears to have separated from her husband and by 1901 kept herself by taking in boarders. Walter moved to Toba in 1906 or earlier. A note on his and Lucie's marriage certificate of 1918 says the couple had been living together for twelve years.

101 1911 Dominion census.

102 The 1911 Dominion census gives Andrew Shuttler's date of arrival as 1887, as does his death certificate.

103 *Evergreen Islands*, 122.

104 Library and Archives Canada's list of post offices and postmasters shows a change of postmasters, from John Ronald Tindall to Mrs. Olive Vivian Hope in 1945.

105 Tom Manson, unpublished history of Redonda Bay, manuscript, BC Archives. He suggests this railway was probably just a wooden track with a donkey pulling a wheeled vehicle by cables. Frank Millerd, unpublished memoir in the Cortes Island Museum, said the camp operated a 914-metre (three-thousand-foot) "funicular" railway in the 1890s, cabling vehicles up a ninety-one–metre (three-hundred-foot) elevation.

106 A later owner, Frank Millerd, thought the cannery may have first opened in about 1910, as he wrote in a letter to Cortes Island historian Mae Ellingsen, Cortes Island Museum. Tom Manson, who wrote a history of Redonda Bay (see note 105), in a later interview cited Millerd as saying the cannery was opened during World War I.

107 Fire insurance maps, UBC Library, Rare Books and Special Collections.

108 The 1931 British Columbia Directory listed the cannery as being in operation, with S. Vickery as manager. The population of Redonda Bay was estimated at fifty.

109 Population estimate from the 1943 British Columbia Directory.

110 Barbara Ann Lambert, *Chalkdust & Outhouses, West Coast Schools, 1893–1950* (Powell River, BC, 2000).

111 Judith Williams, *Dynamite Stories* (Vancouver: New Star Books, 2003).

Chapter Four: Sonora and Maurelle Islands

112   Remnants of these fortifications were still visible as late as 1900. See Robert Galois, *Kwakwaka'wakw Settlements, 1775–1920, A Geographical Analysis and Gazetteer* (Vancouver: UBC Press, 1994).

113   *Kwakwaka'wakw Settlements.*

114   *Kwakwaka'wakw Settlements.*

115   Wilson Duff papers, GR 2809, BC Archives.

116   Department of Indian Affairs records, Kwawkwelth Agency, GR 2043, BC Archives.

117   Ambrose Wilson interview, Museum at Campbell River Archives, First Nations–Homalco vertical file.

118   Mogg Collection, Museum at Campbell River Archives.

119   According to the Provincial Land Registry records, William Hughes owned property in 1905 on Sonora across from Chonat Bay, and David Vanstone had property at Barnes Bay on Sonora that same year. Their camp could have been at either of these locations at the time of Annie Assu's death.

120   The total population figure is approximate because Quadra, Sonora and Maurelle were still listed together as Valdez Island, and the Rendezvous Islands did not have a separate listing. Granite Bay appears to end on page 12, when compared to names given in British Columbia Directory listings. Dominion census for 1911, p. 13–20, Comox District 8 have assumed to be, Okisollo Channel, Sonora and Maurelle.

121   Logan Schibler's obituary, *Courier* (Campbell River, BC), Oct. 23, 1957. The obituary says he came to the area in 1921.

122   The Provincial Land Registry records show Henrik Williamsen sold his property to Gunhild Schibler for $1,200 in installments, with no date set for payments. There was a verbal agreement that the Schiblers were to provide a home and care for Henrik through his life.

123   Barbara Ann Lambert, *Chalkdust & Outhouses, West Coast Schools, 1893–1950* (Powell River, BC: 2000), 249. The book says the first school at Owen Bay opened in 1926. "The List of Rural and Assisted North Vancouver Island Schools," BC Archives, however, says the school opened in 1927.

Chapter Five: Bute Inlet and Stuart Island

124   Kwakwaka'wakw has been accepted by some, but not all, of the Kwakwala-speaking people as a name for their linguistic group. Bill Assu of the We-Wai-Kai Band at Cape Mudge prefers Kwakwala speakers. In years past, the name Kwakiutl was used for this group.

125 Tiedemann's journal and report to Waddington, 1862, E/B/T44A, BC Archives.

126 *British Colonist* (Victoria), April 13, 1861.

127 H. Barry Cotton, "Robert Homfray C.E.L.S.," *BC Historical News* (Spring 1998): 32.

128 Frank Leonard, "'A Closed Book': The Canadian Pacific Railway Survey and North-Central British Columbia," *Western Geography* 12 (2002): 163–84.

129 Fred J. Saunders, "Homathtcho or Story of the Bute Inlet Expedition and the Massacre by the Chicaten Indians," *The Resources of BC*, BC Archives.

130 British *Colonist* (Victoria), July 16, 1872; Aug. 3, 1872; and Aug. 18, 1872.

131 Letter from P. O'Reilly, Indian Reserve Commissioner, 1888, Department of Indian Affairs, BC Archives, GR-0934.

132 Randy Bouchard and Dorothy Kennedy, eds. *Indian Myths and Legends from the North Pacific Coast of America: A Translation* (Vancouver: Talonbooks, 2002). A photo caption says the second church was built in 1896.

133 *Daily Colonist* (Victoria), April 18, 1888, and June 27, 1888.

134 Doyle Collection, UBC Library, Rare Books and Special Collections.

135 Ambrose Wilson of the Xwemalhkwu Band recalled in an interview on Feb. 15, 1989, that when he was a child there were pilings and cannery machinery (boilers) in the shallow water at the head of Bute Inlet, between the Ka'tewk River and the mouth of the Homathko River.

136 *Comox Argus* (Comox, BC), 1895.

137 Dennis Walker said in his memoirs that the settlement at its peak comprised about sixty people. This is the number also given in a survey report of 1895 by F.A. Devereaux, GR1088, BC Archives.

138 French, Diana, *The Road Runs West: A Century Along the Bella Coola Chilcotin Road* (Madeira Park: Harbour Publishing, 1994), p. 46.

139 Martin Blanchfield referred to this Syndicate in an 1895 *Daily Colonist* article, but no other records of this alienated land are currently available.

140 *Whistle Up the Inlet*, Rushton and GR 441, 1896 correspondence on the granting of the subsidy and the fight to maintain it.

141 *The Shoulder Strap*, periodical, "The Spirit of Waddington Harbour," BC Archives, NW 905 5559 #1-7, p. 73. c. 1933.

142 T. Bernard is listed as manager of the Southgate Logging Camp in the 1918 British Columbia Directory. In 1931 he's listed as president of the Homalco Logging Company, along with Fred Bernard (manager) and Robert Bernard.

143 Beth Hill, *Upcoast Summers*, (Ganges, BC: Horsdal & Schubart, 1985). Hill quotes Bill Law's column in the periodical *The Deckhand*.

144   Marion Parker and Robert Tyrrell, *Rumrunner, The Life and Times of Johnny Schnarr* (Victoria: Orca Book Publishers, 1988).

145   Doris Andersen, *Evergreen Islands, The Islands of the Inside Passage: Quadra to Malcolm* (Sidney: Gray's Publishing Limited, 1979). Andersen recalled this incident but did not name the family who was attacked. It may have been George Bruce and his wife, who were reported in the *Comox Argus* (Comox, BC), July 20, 1922, to have been attacked by a "demented" man, Murdoch Matheson.

146   Sandra Parrish's notes on her family's Stuart Island years, personal correspondence. Jack and Margaret Parrish went to Redonda Bay in 1927 and then to Stuart Island. They are listed in the 1931 British Columbia Directory on Stuart Island.

Chapter Six: Thurlow Islands

147   There are many different anglicized spellings of the place name Matlaten. I have adopted the one preferred by Lekwala speaker George Quocksister, who had ancestors from Matlaten.

148   Robert Galois, *Kwakwaka'wakw Settlements, 1775–1920, A Geographical Analysis and Gazetteer* (Vancouver: UBC Press, 1994), 250.

149   HBC Chief Factor James Douglas, journal of 1843, A/B/40 D75.4A, BC Archives. He listed six of the Lekwiltok groups with a total of 1,060 men. If this number is multiplied by four it gives an estimated total population of just over four thousand. Anthropologist Wilson Duff, in his research papers held in the BC Archives, tabulated census records that John Work compiled 1836–41. Work also listed six Lekwiltok groups but he estimated their population at 10,060.

150   Wilson Duff papers, BC Archives. This is a shortened retelling of this legend, from an account written to Wilson Duff. Galois quotes the full legend in *Kwakwaka'wakw Settlements*, 245–49.

151   The 1881 Dominion census for Native people divides people into their sub-tribes but does not indicate where they were currently living. Most of the Kweeha were still living at Green Point Rapids, but some had begun to move to the Discovery Passage region.

152   Cameron and McCrae's camp is referred to several times in the 1887–88 trial for the murder of the *Seabird* traders at Blenkinsop Bay, as is "Kane's" (perhaps King's?) camp. The camps at Bickley Bay and on the west coast of West Thurlow were mentioned in a memoir of this period by police officer John Flewin. He told Hazel King, the daughter of Discovery Islands logger Mike King, there were only two small logging camps in the area, at Bickley Bay and Nodales Channel; see article in BC Archives vertical file on Mike King.

153 Ken Drushka, *Working in the Woods* (Madeira Park: Harbour Publishing, 1992), 50.

154 Provincial Land Registry records, BC Archives; *Weekly News* (Comox, BC), July 26, 1893.

155 *Daily Colonist*, Dec. 4, 1896.

156 *Weekly News Advertiser* (Vancouver), Dec. 16, 1896.

157 Charles Forrest, former resident of Shoal Bay, *Daily Colonist*, "Shoal Bay as a Mining Centre," Oct. 15, 1972.

158 *Weekly News Advertiser* (Vancouver), "The Coast Outlook," March 3, 1897. Other reports of these years say there were two hundred claims.

159 A.H. Beamer, unpublished history of Loughborough Inlet, manuscript, BC Archives. He was quoting Mr. Conway.

160 James M. Forrest of Shoal Bay, letter to his fiancée in Aug. 1900, Museum at Campbell River Archives, James Forrest fonds. He wrote, "We have no church but have a hall and the minister is a rancher, he is an old Scotchman, and preaches strong Free Church Sermons." Presumably this was the Reverend Dugald McGregor of Loughborough Inlet.

161 Hans's daughter Edith Bendickson, the family historian, recalled that Hans's companion was Nils Hjorth. Both the 1901 and 1911 Dominion censuses, however, said Nils arrived in Canada in 1883. Family history says that Hans arrived in 1877, on the other hand, and his census records support this. The pair certainly did have the Bickley Bay trading post together before 1891, and it's likely they rowed up the coast together from Vancouver.

162 Hans described himself as a widower on his marriage certificate with Lizzie, but a prior marriage is not known of in the Hansen family.

163 "Since about 1902 there has been no activity in the mining industry, either on Thurlow Island or in the neighbourhood," reported the Minister of Mines for 1918–19. NW 971.35 B862a, BC Archives.

164 Brooks Family Collection, 2002-1, Museum at Campbell River Archives.

165 The Wards are first listed in 1899 in the British Columbia Directory for Shoal Bay.

166 Fire insurance map, UBC Library, Rare Books and Special Collections.

167 Tommy Hall interview notes, Jan. 17, 1987, Museum at Campbell River Archives.

168 Post Offices and Postmasters list, Library and Archives Canada.

Index